THIS PLANNER BELONGS TO

_____

Copyright 2018

please smile

2019 Calendar

January

S	M	T	W	T	F	S
30	31	1	2	3	4	5
6	7	8	9	10	11	12
13	14	15	16	17	18	19
20	21	22	23	24	25	26
27	28	29	30	31	1	2
3	4	5	6	7	8	9

February

S	M	T	W	T	F	S
27	28	29	30	31	1	2
3	4	5	6	7	8	9
10	11	12	13	14	15	16
17	18	19	20	21	22	23
24	25	26	27	28	1	2
3	4	5	6	7	8	9

March

S	M	T	W	T	F	S
24	25	26	27	28	1	2
3	4	5	6	7	8	9
10	11	12	13	14	15	16
17	18	19	20	21	22	23
24	25	26	27	28	29	30
31	1	2	3	4	5	6

April

S	M	T	W	T	F	S
31	1	2	3	4	5	6
7	8	9	10	11	12	13
14	15	16	17	18	19	20
21	22	23	24	25	26	27
28	29	30	1	2	3	4
5	6	7	8	9	10	11

May

S	M	T	W	T	F	S
28	29	30	1	2	3	4
5	6	7	8	9	10	11
12	13	14	15	16	17	18
19	20	21	22	23	24	25
26	27	28	29	30	31	1
2	3	4	5	6	7	8

June

S	M	T	W	T	F	S
26	27	28	29	30	31	1
2	3	4	5	6	7	8
9	10	11	12	13	14	15
16	17	18	19	20	21	22
23	24	25	26	27	28	29
30	1	2	3	4	5	6

July

S	M	T	W	T	F	S
30	1	2	3	4	5	6
7	8	9	10	11	12	13
14	15	16	17	18	19	20
21	22	23	24	25	26	27
28	29	30	31	1	2	3
4	5	6	7	8	9	10

August

S	M	T	W	T	F	S
28	29	30	31	1	2	3
4	5	6	7	8	9	10
11	12	13	14	15	16	17
18	19	20	21	22	23	24
25	26	27	28	29	30	31
1	2	3	4	5	6	7

September

S	M	T	W	T	F	S
1	2	3	4	5	6	7
8	9	10	11	12	13	14
15	16	17	18	19	20	21
22	23	24	25	26	27	28
29	30	1	2	3	4	5
6	7	8	9	10	11	12

October

S	M	T	W	T	F	S
29	30	1	2	3	4	5
6	7	8	9	10	11	12
13	14	15	16	17	18	19
20	21	22	23	24	25	26
27	28	29	30	31	1	2
3	4	5	6	7	8	9

November

S	M	T	W	T	F	S
27	28	29	30	31	1	2
3	4	5	6	7	8	9
10	11	12	13	14	15	16
17	18	19	20	21	22	23
24	25	26	27	28	29	30
1	2	3	4	5	6	7

December

S	M	T	W	T	F	S
1	2	3	4	5	6	7
8	9	10	11	12	13	14
15	16	17	18	19	20	21
22	23	24	25	26	27	28
29	30	31	1	2	3	4
5	6	7	8	9	10	11

January 2019

Sunday	Monday	Tuesday	Wednesday
30	31	1	2
6	7	8	9
13	14	15	16
20	21	22	23
27	28	29	30

Thursday	Friday	Saturday
3	4	5
10	11	12
17	18	19
24	25	26
31	1	2

MON DECEMBER 31, 2018

TUE JANUARY 1, 2019

WED JANUARY 2, 2019

THU JANUARY 3, 2019

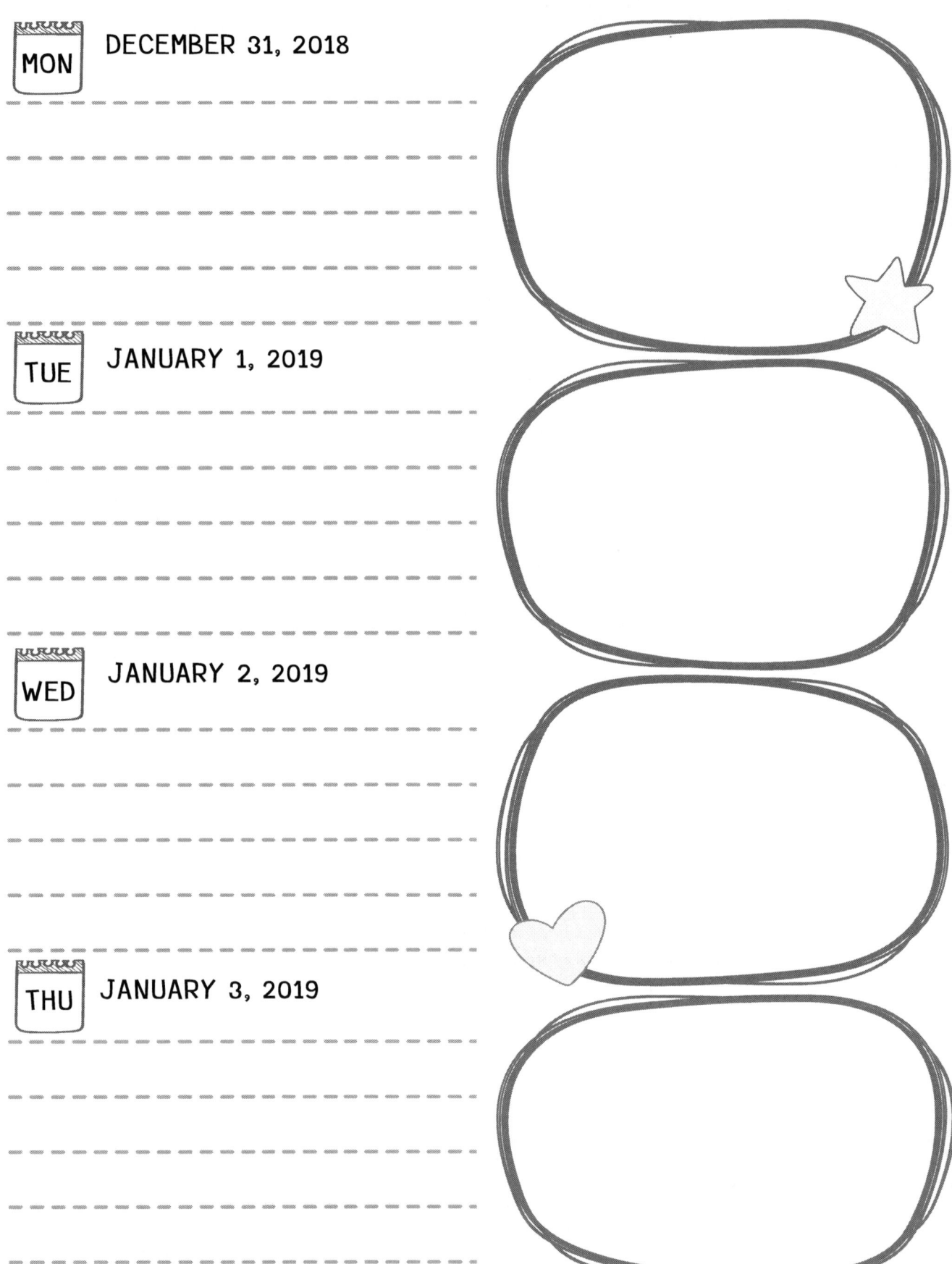

NOTES

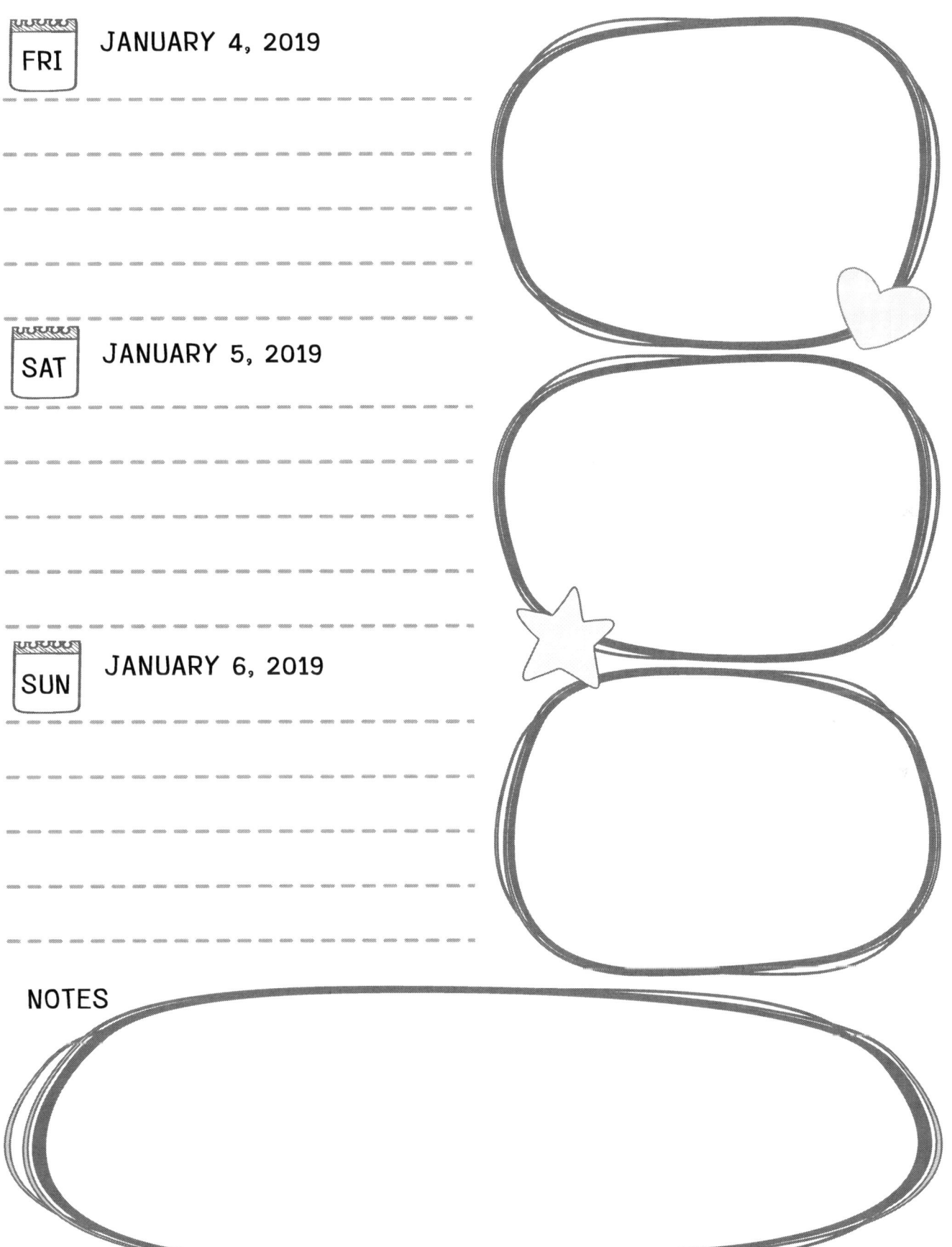

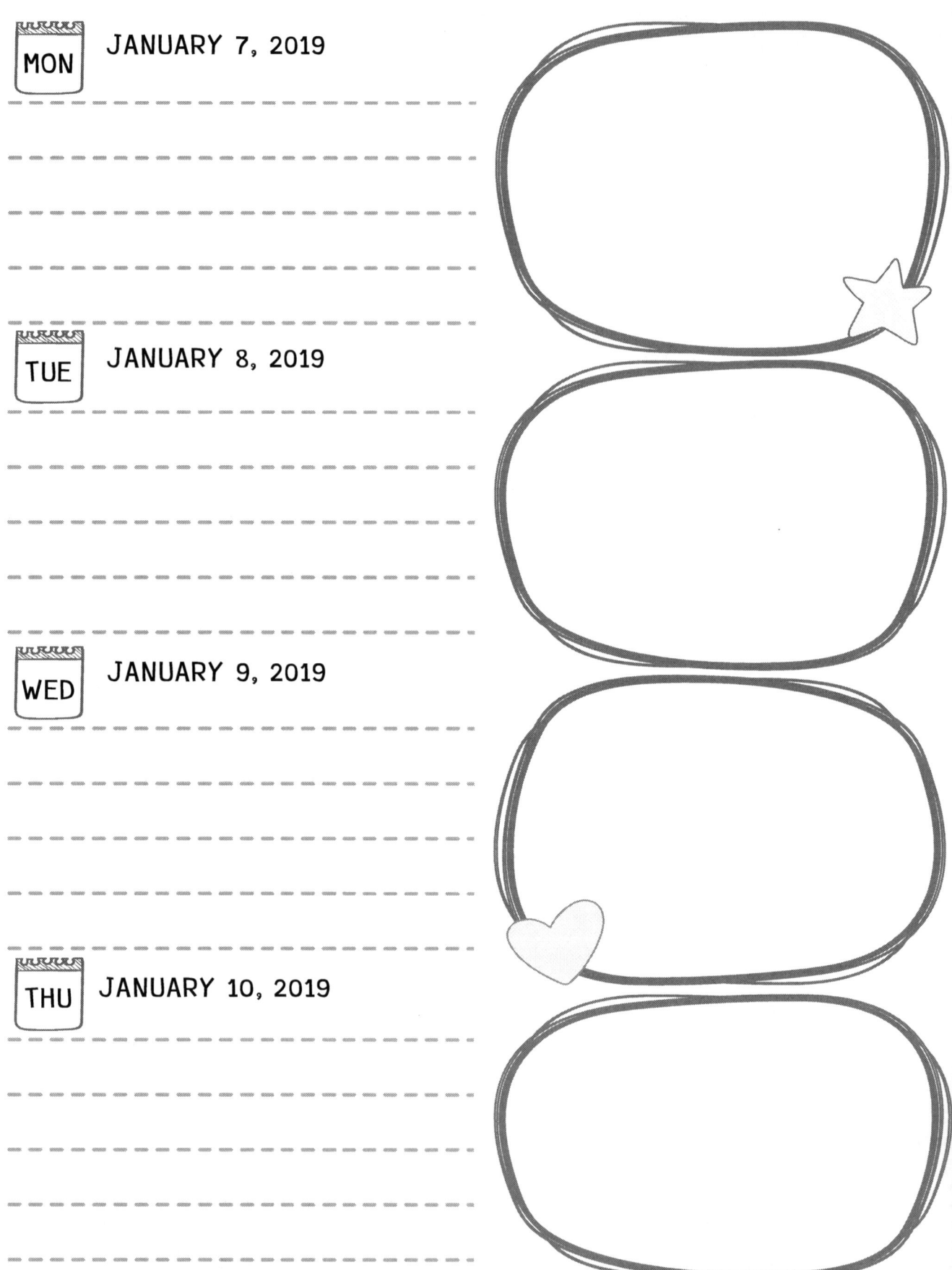

MON JANUARY 7, 2019

-------- -------- -------- --------
-------- -------- -------- --------
-------- -------- -------- --------
-------- -------- -------- --------

TUE JANUARY 8, 2019

-------- -------- -------- --------
-------- -------- -------- --------
-------- -------- -------- --------
-------- -------- -------- --------

WED JANUARY 9, 2019

-------- -------- -------- --------
-------- -------- -------- --------
-------- -------- -------- --------
-------- -------- -------- --------

THU JANUARY 10, 2019

-------- -------- -------- --------
-------- -------- -------- --------
-------- -------- -------- --------
-------- -------- -------- --------

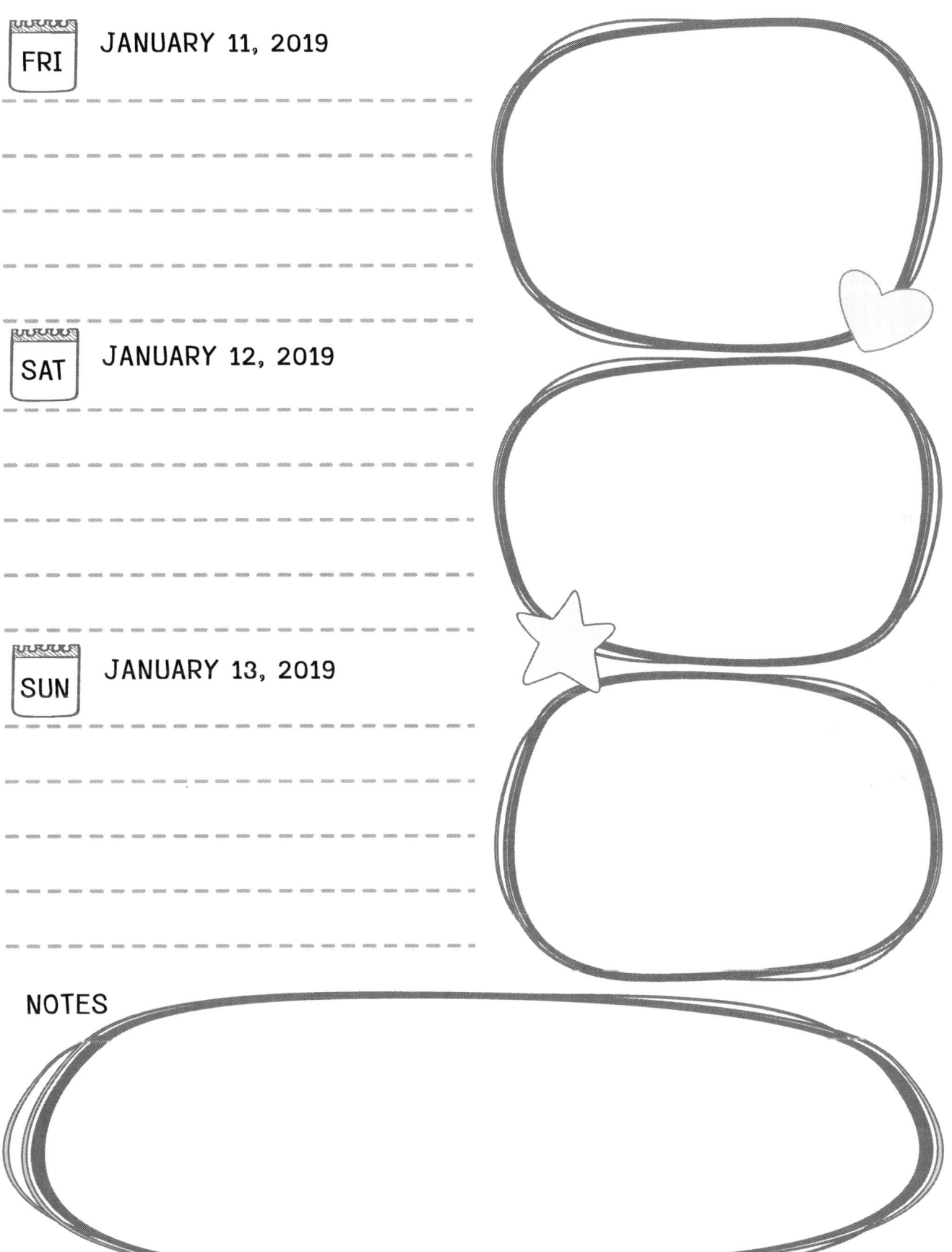

FRI JANUARY 11, 2019

SAT JANUARY 12, 2019

SUN JANUARY 13, 2019

NOTES

MON JANUARY 14, 2019

TUE JANUARY 15, 2019

WED JANUARY 16, 2019

THU JANUARY 17, 2019

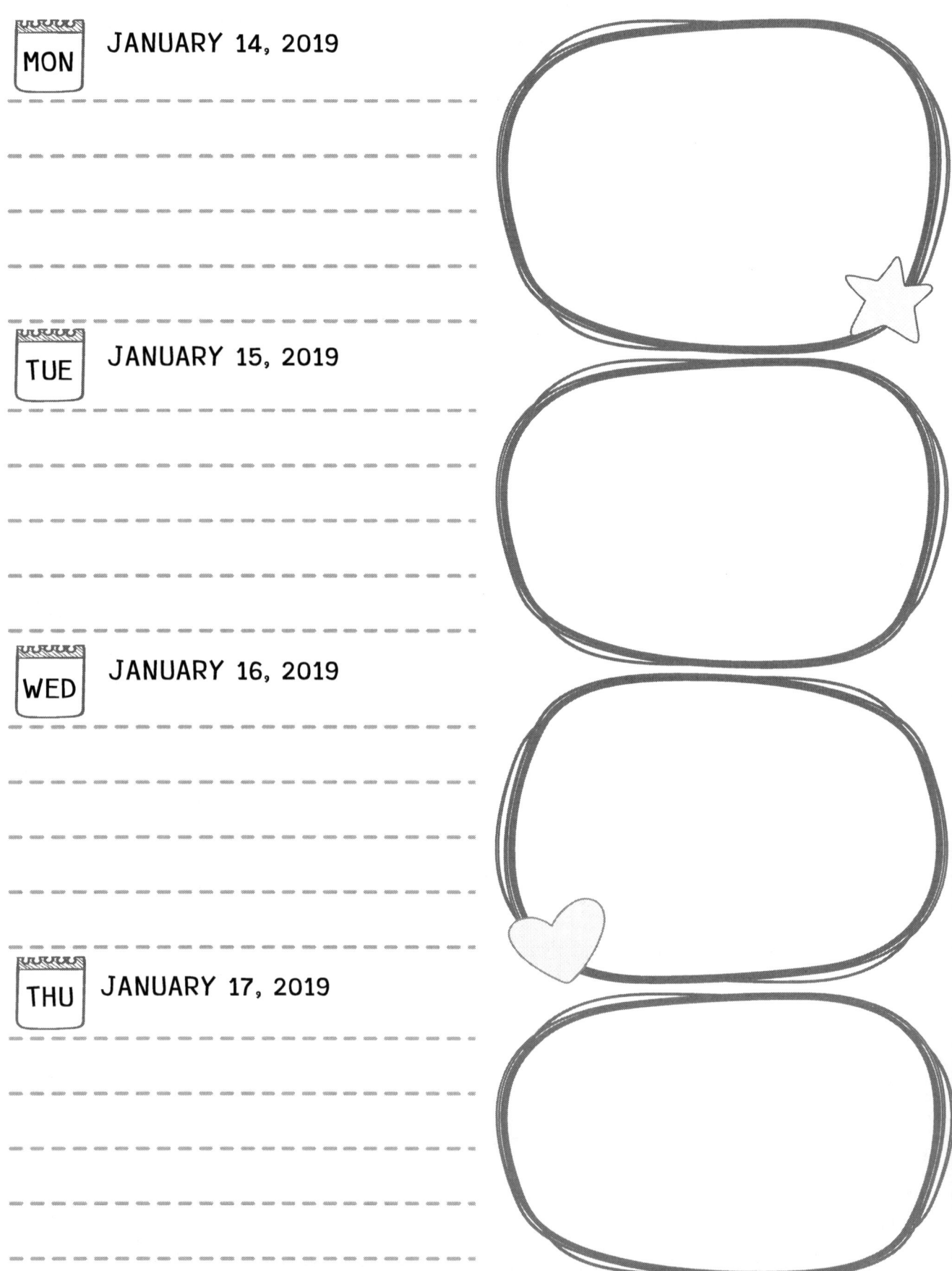

FRI **JANUARY 18, 2019**

SAT **JANUARY 19, 2019**

SUN **JANUARY 20, 2019**

NOTES

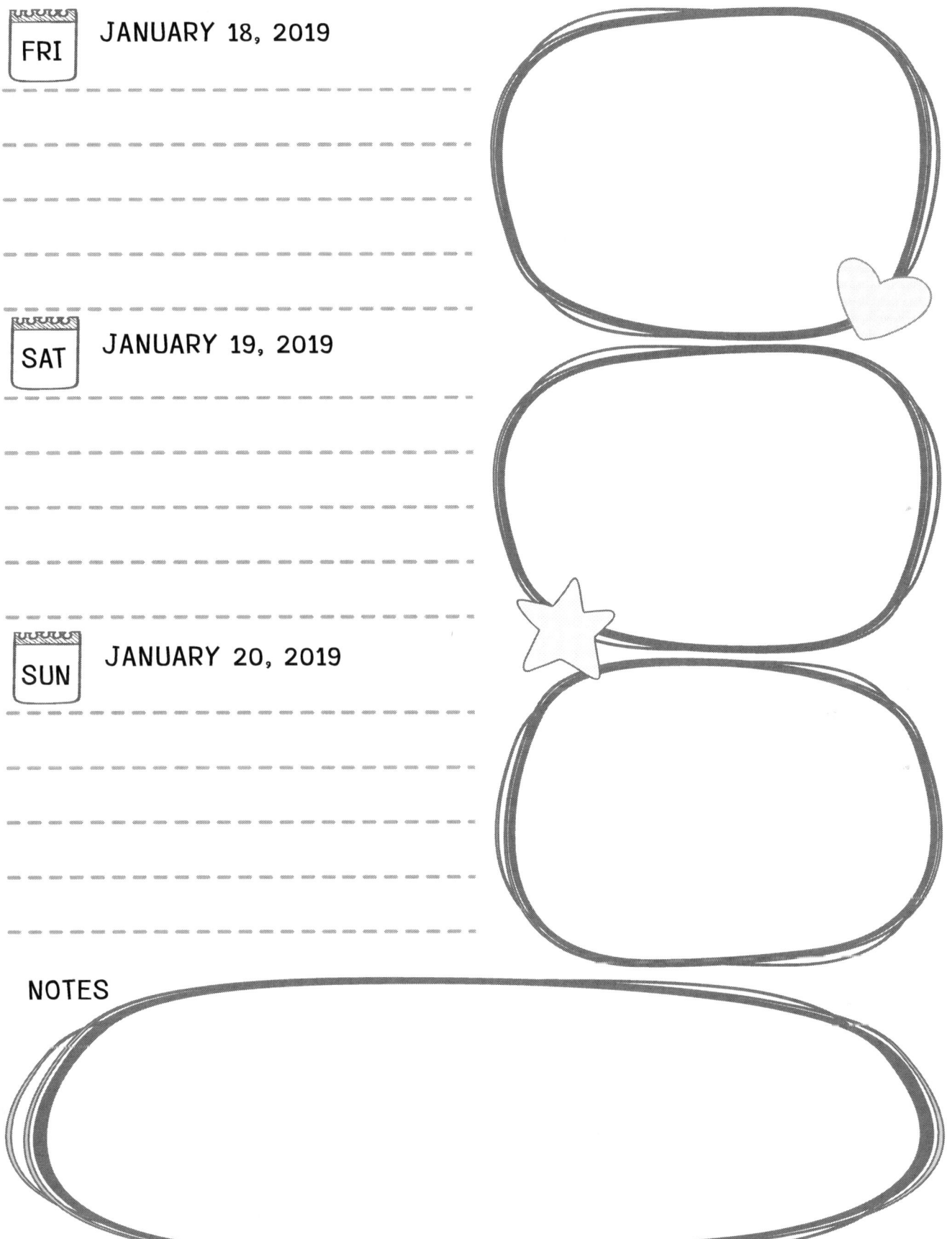

MON JANUARY 21, 2019

TUE JANUARY 22, 2019

WED JANUARY 23, 2019

THU JANUARY 24, 2019

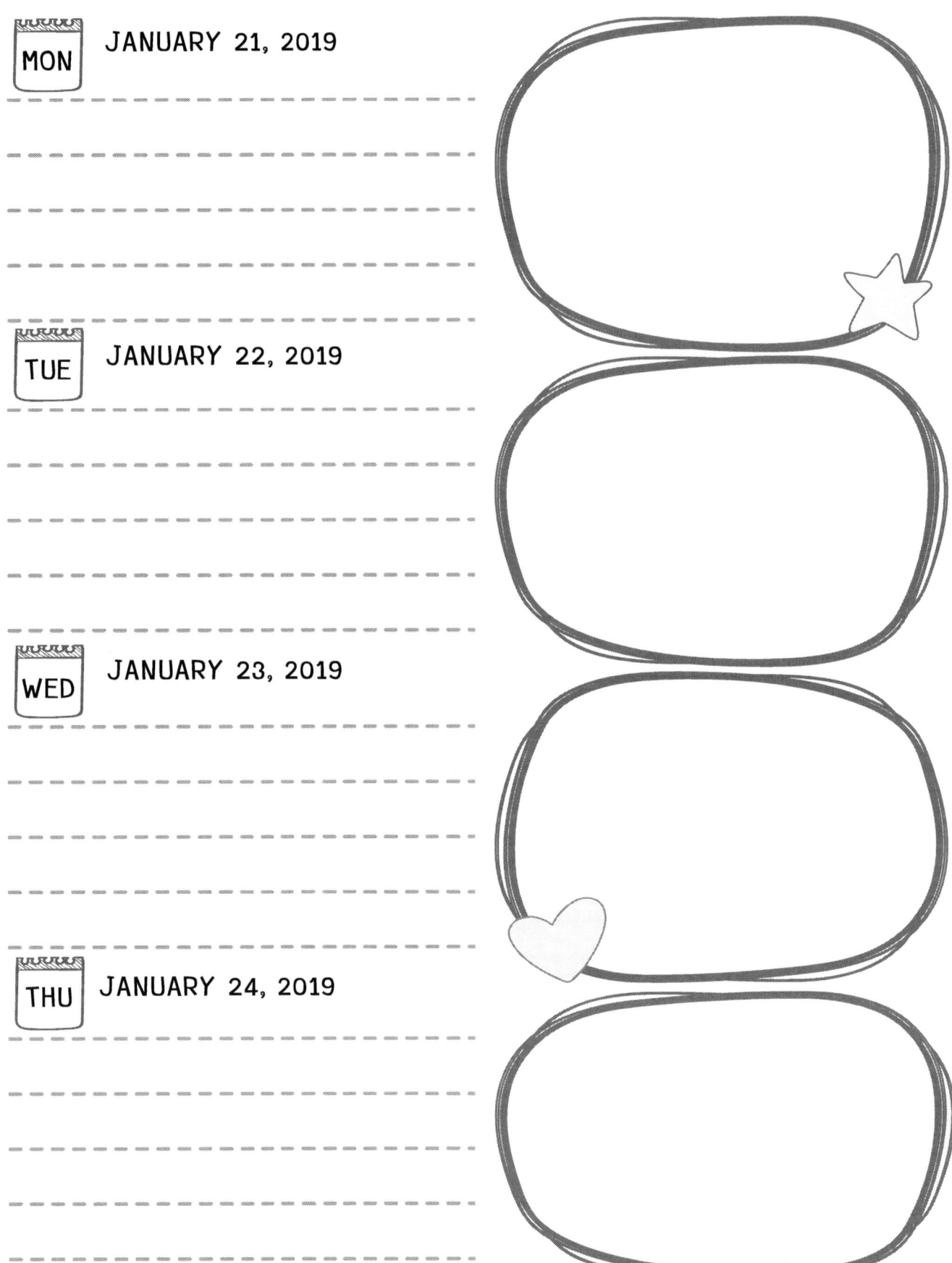

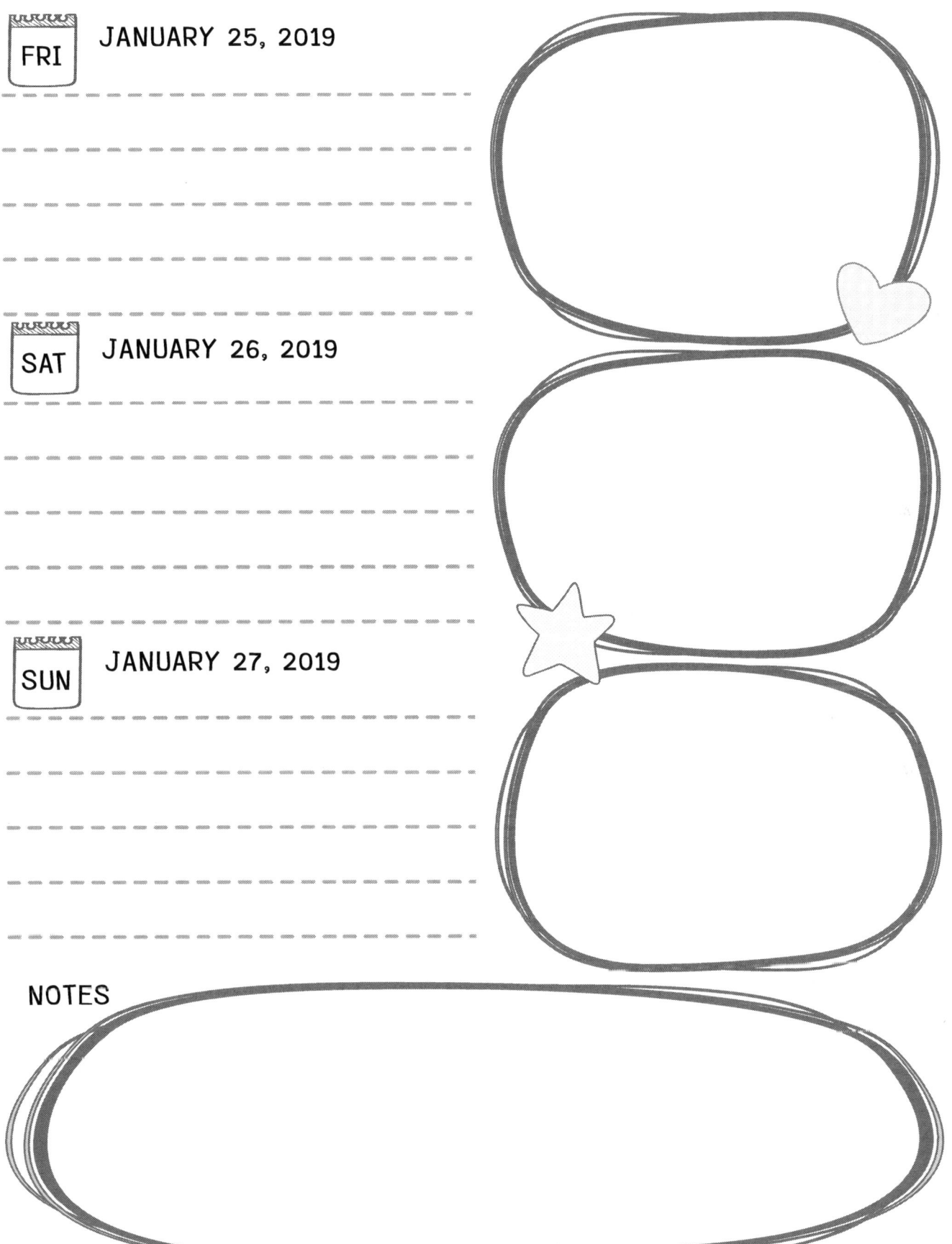

FRI JANUARY 25, 2019

SAT JANUARY 26, 2019

SUN JANUARY 27, 2019

NOTES

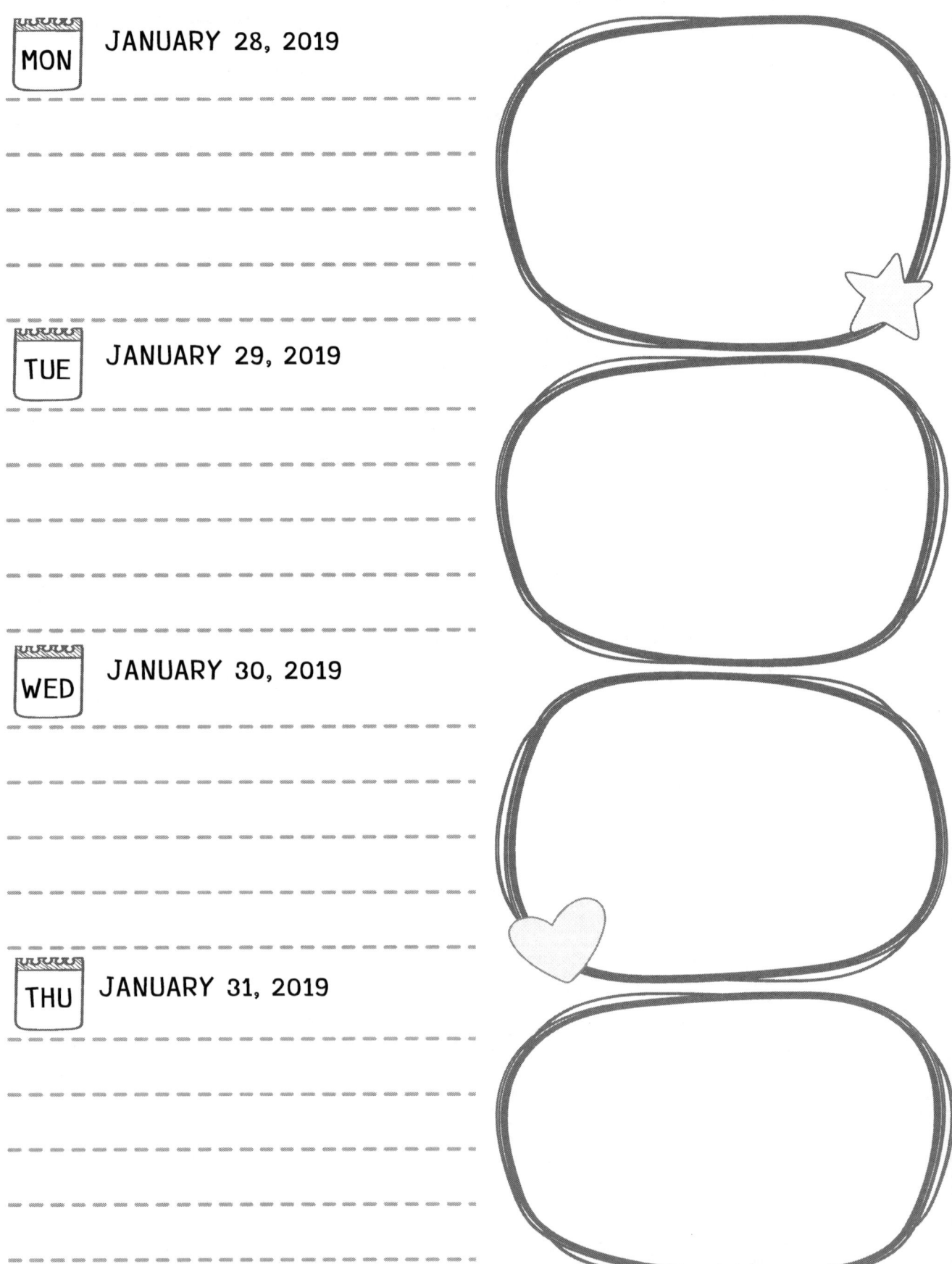

MON   JANUARY 28, 2019

TUE   JANUARY 29, 2019

WED   JANUARY 30, 2019

THU   JANUARY 31, 2019

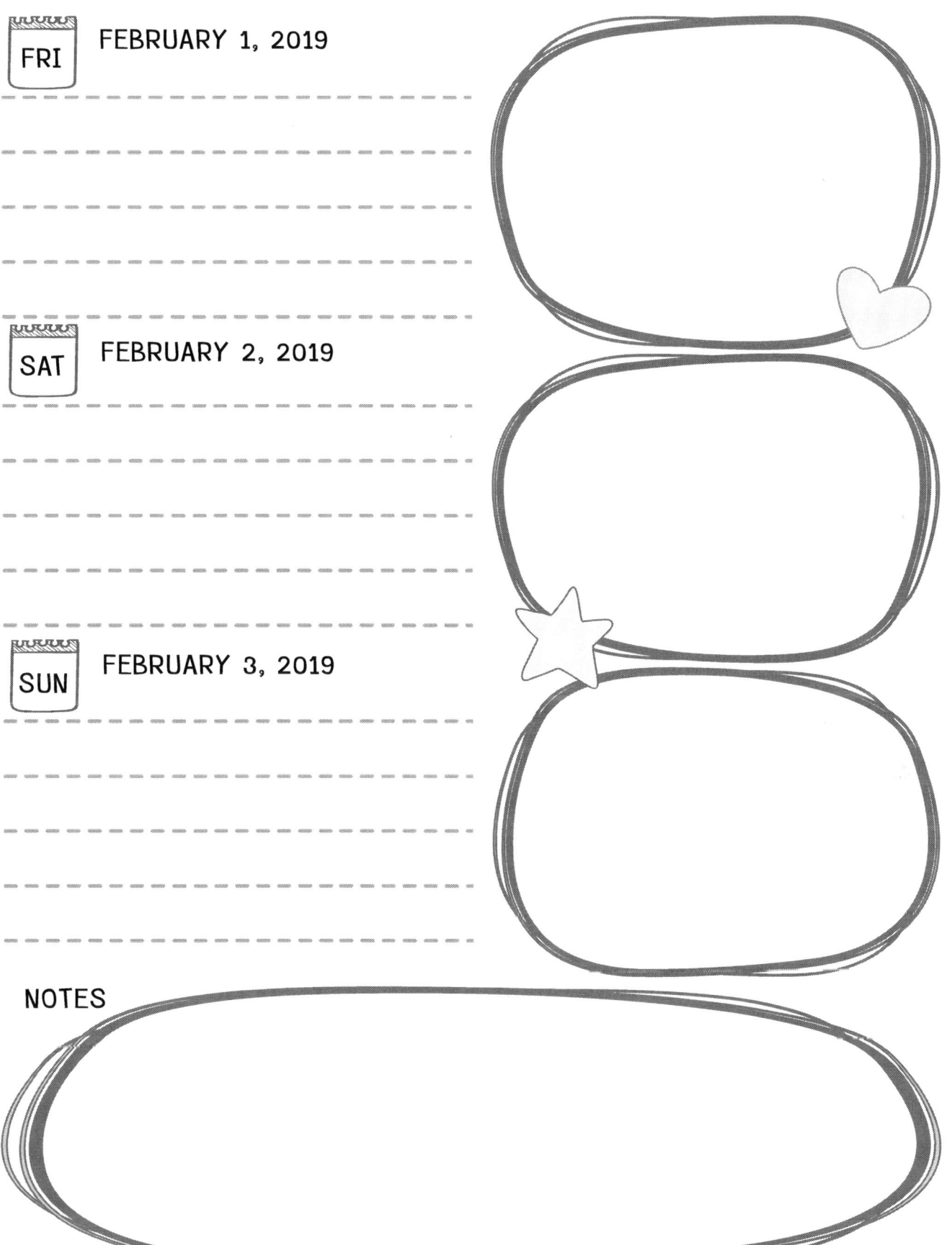

FRI FEBRUARY 1, 2019

SAT FEBRUARY 2, 2019

SUN FEBRUARY 3, 2019

NOTES

February 2019

Sunday	Monday	Tuesday	Wednesday
27	28	29	30
3	4	5	6
10	11	12	13
17	18	19	20
24	25	26	27

Thursday	Friday	Saturday	
31	1	2	_____ _____
7	8	9	_____ _____ _____
14	15	16	_____ _____ _____
21	22	23	_____ _____ _____
28	1	2	_____ _____ _____

MON FEBRUARY 4, 2019

TUE FEBRUARY 5, 2019

WED FEBRUARY 6, 2019

THU FEBRUARY 7, 2019

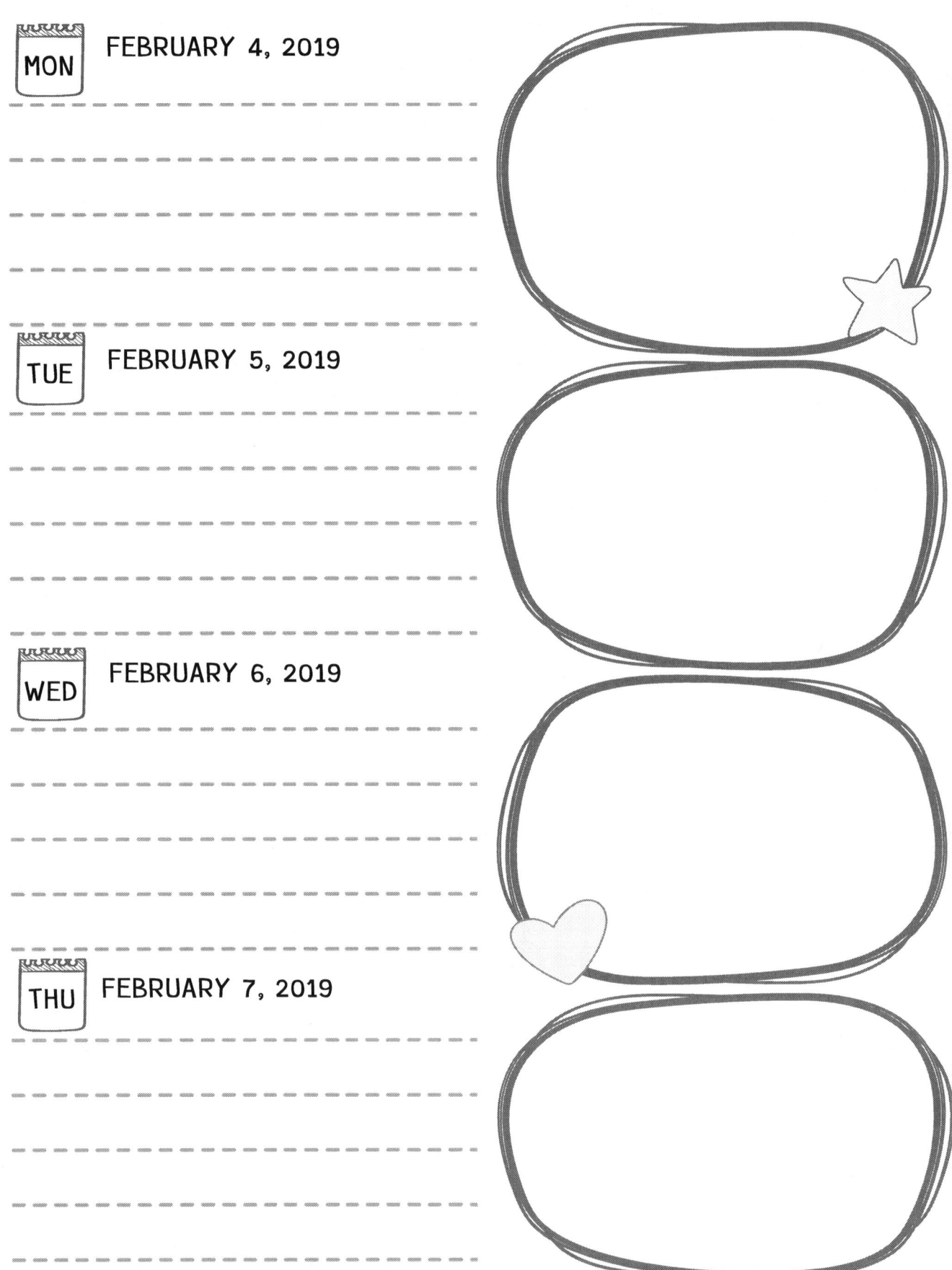

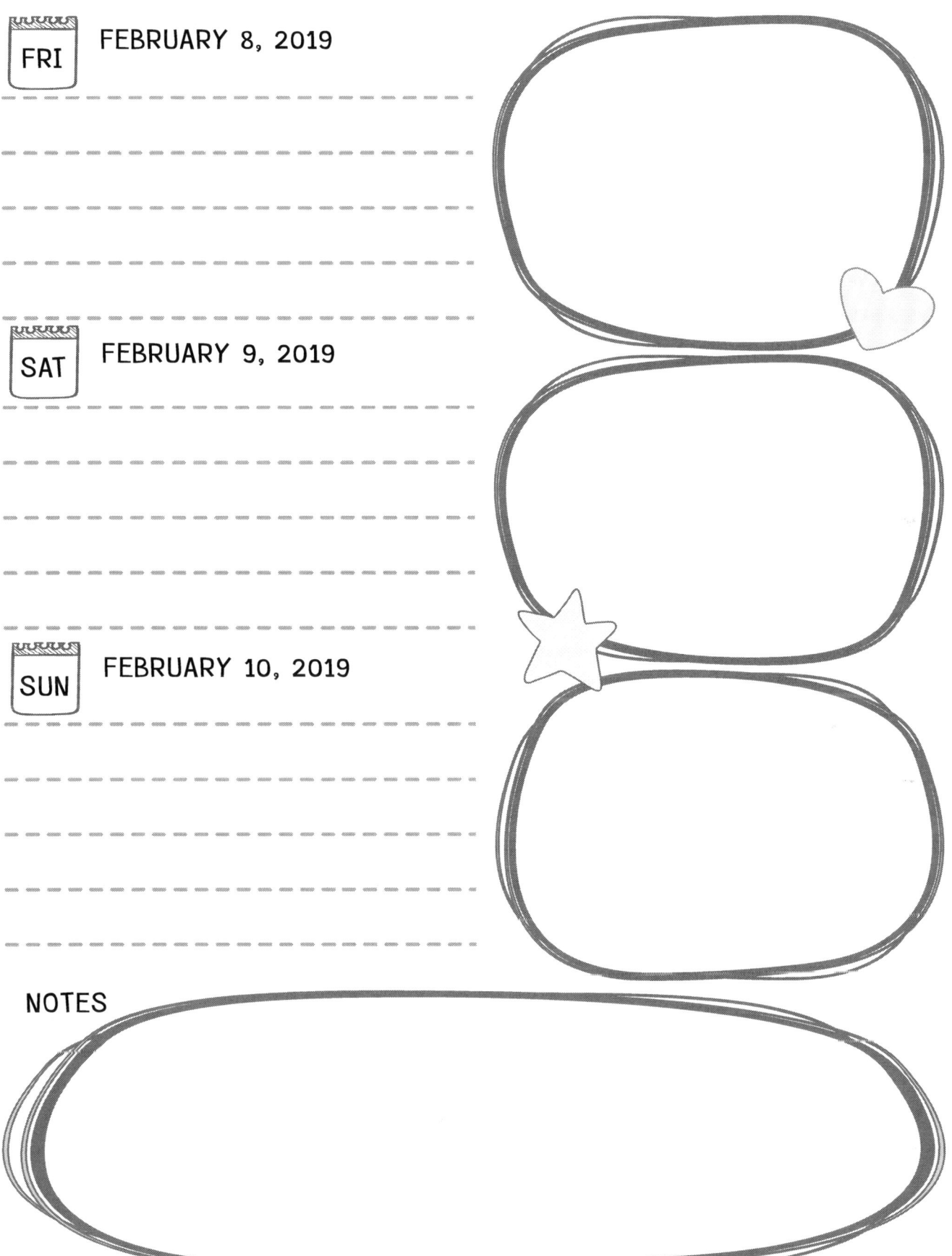

FRI | FEBRUARY 8, 2019

SAT | FEBRUARY 9, 2019

SUN | FEBRUARY 10, 2019

NOTES

MON FEBRUARY 11, 2019

TUE FEBRUARY 12, 2019

WED FEBRUARY 13, 2019

THU FEBRUARY 14, 2019

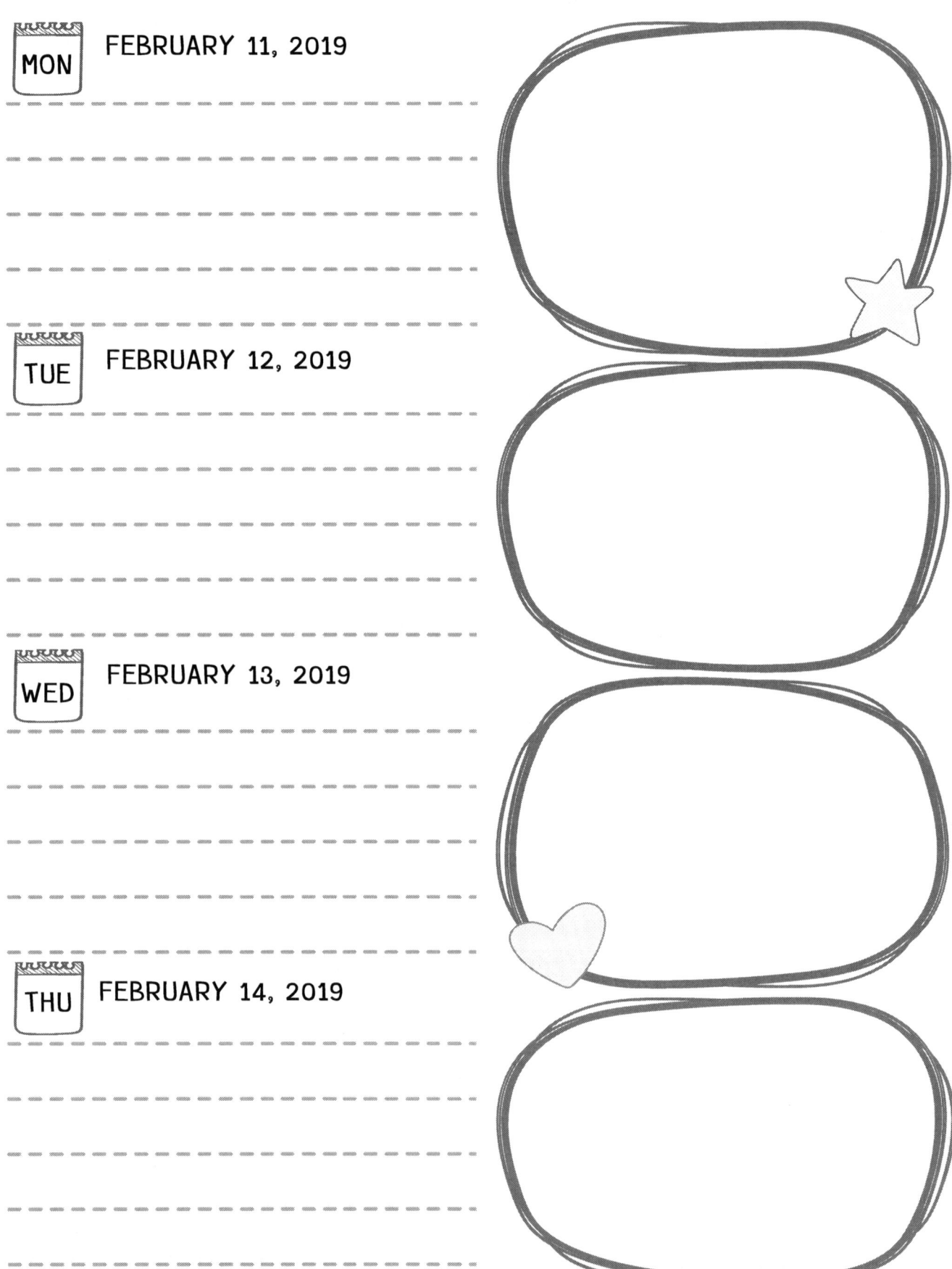

FRI FEBRUARY 15, 2019

SAT FEBRUARY 16, 2019

SUN FEBRUARY 17, 2019

NOTES

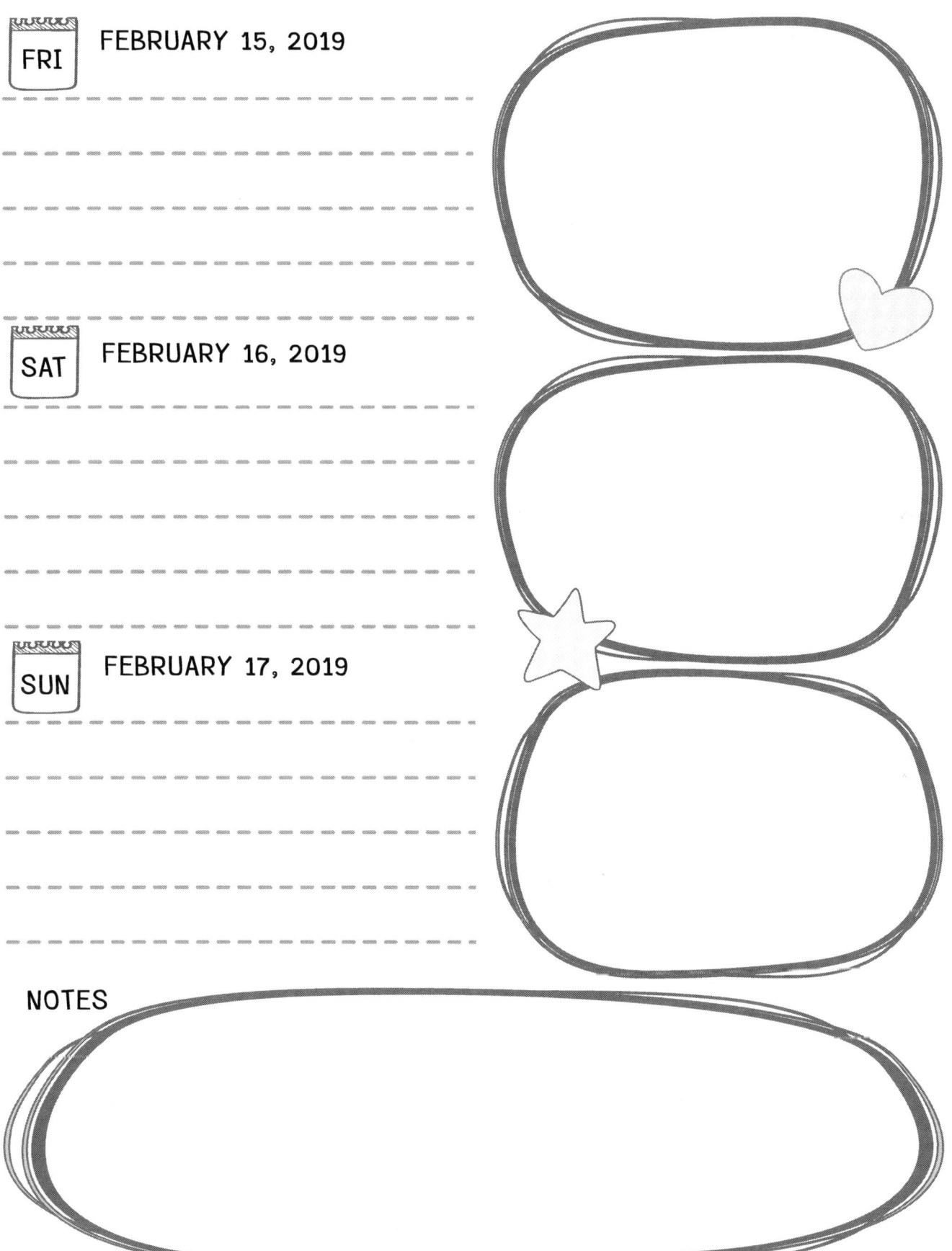

MON FEBRUARY 18, 2019

TUE FEBRUARY 19, 2019

WED FEBRUARY 20, 2019

THU FEBRUARY 21, 2019

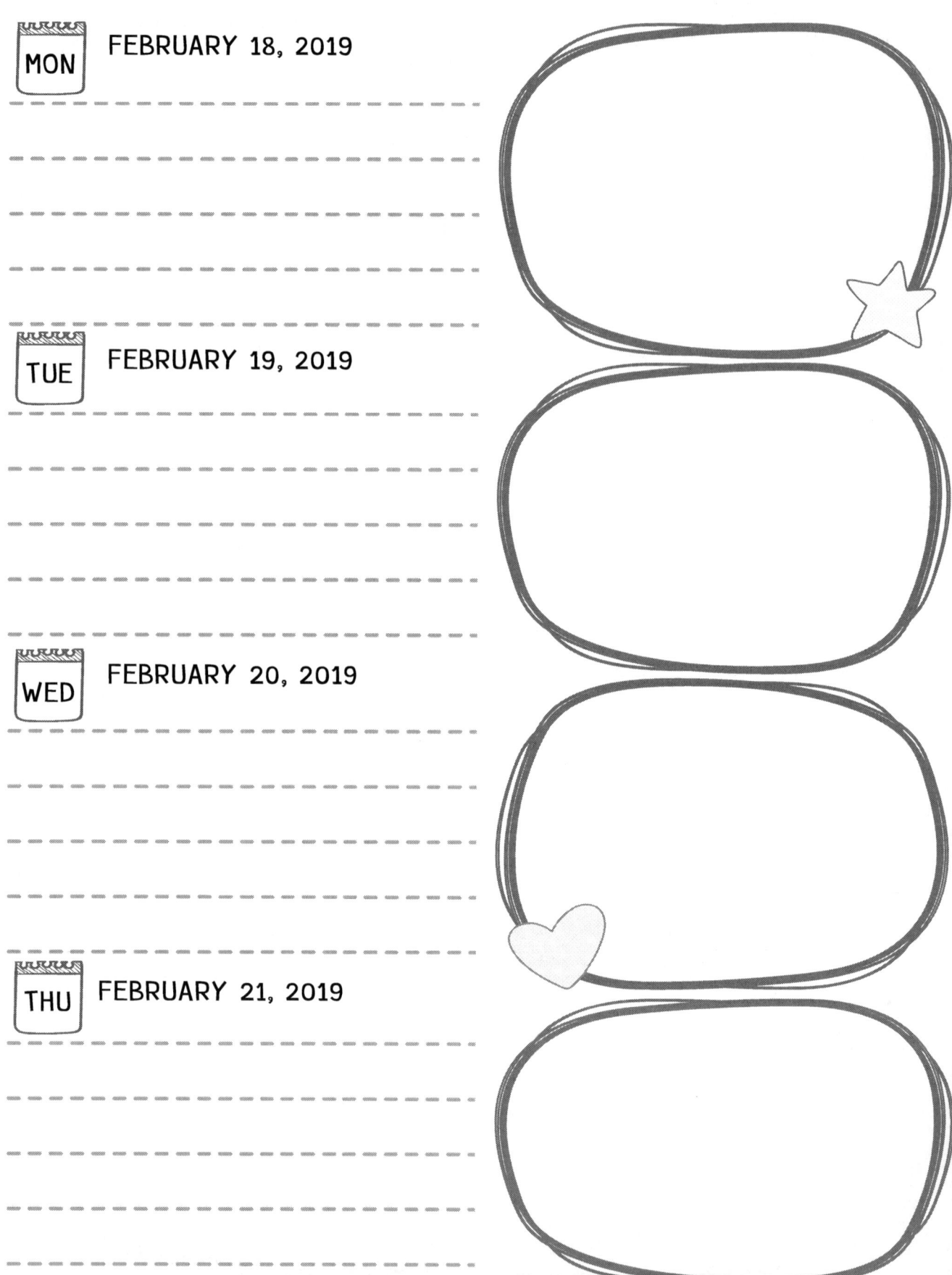

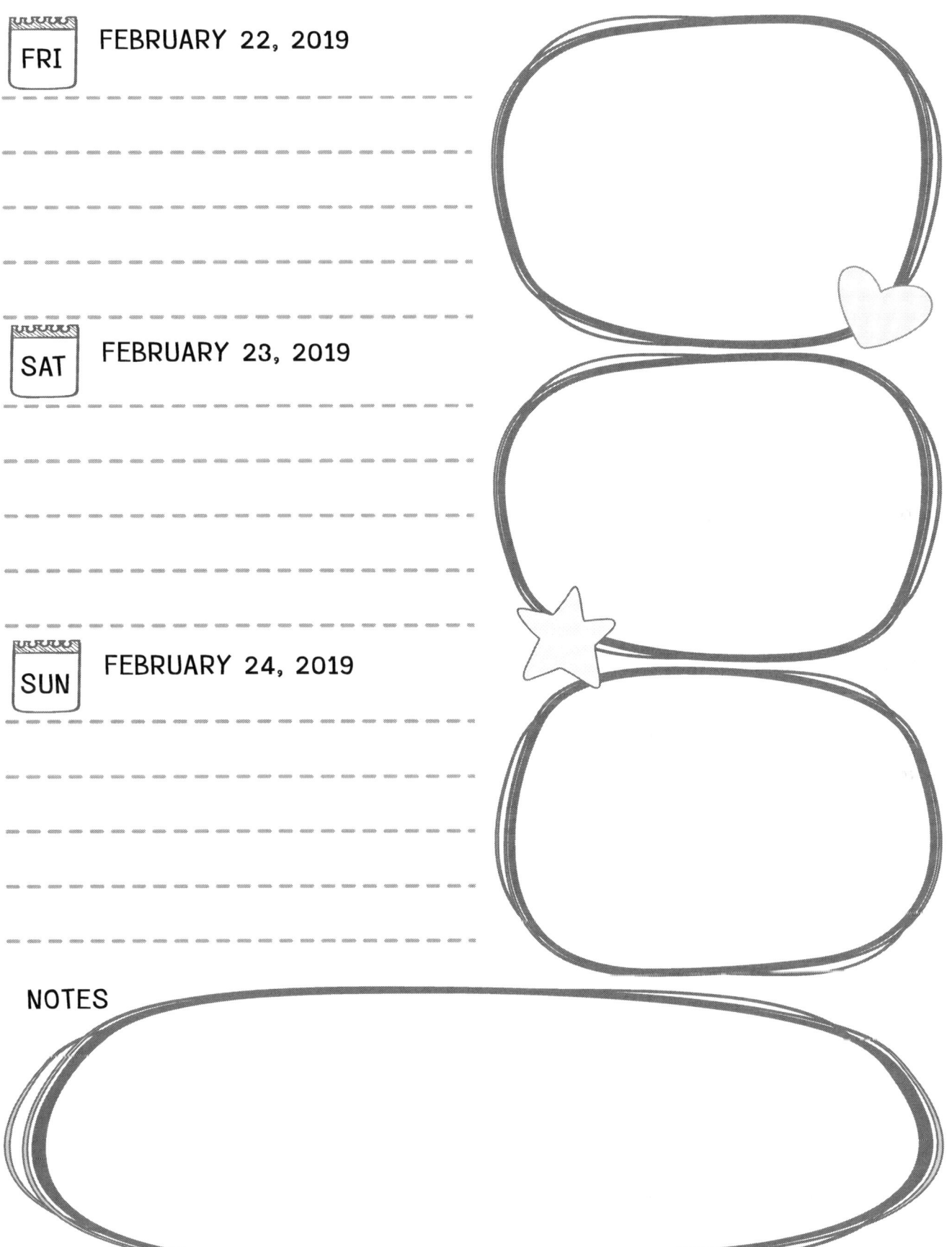

FRI FEBRUARY 22, 2019

SAT FEBRUARY 23, 2019

SUN FEBRUARY 24, 2019

NOTES

MON FEBRUARY 25, 2019

TUE FEBRUARY 26, 2019

WED FEBRUARY 27, 2019

THU FEBRUARY 28, 2019

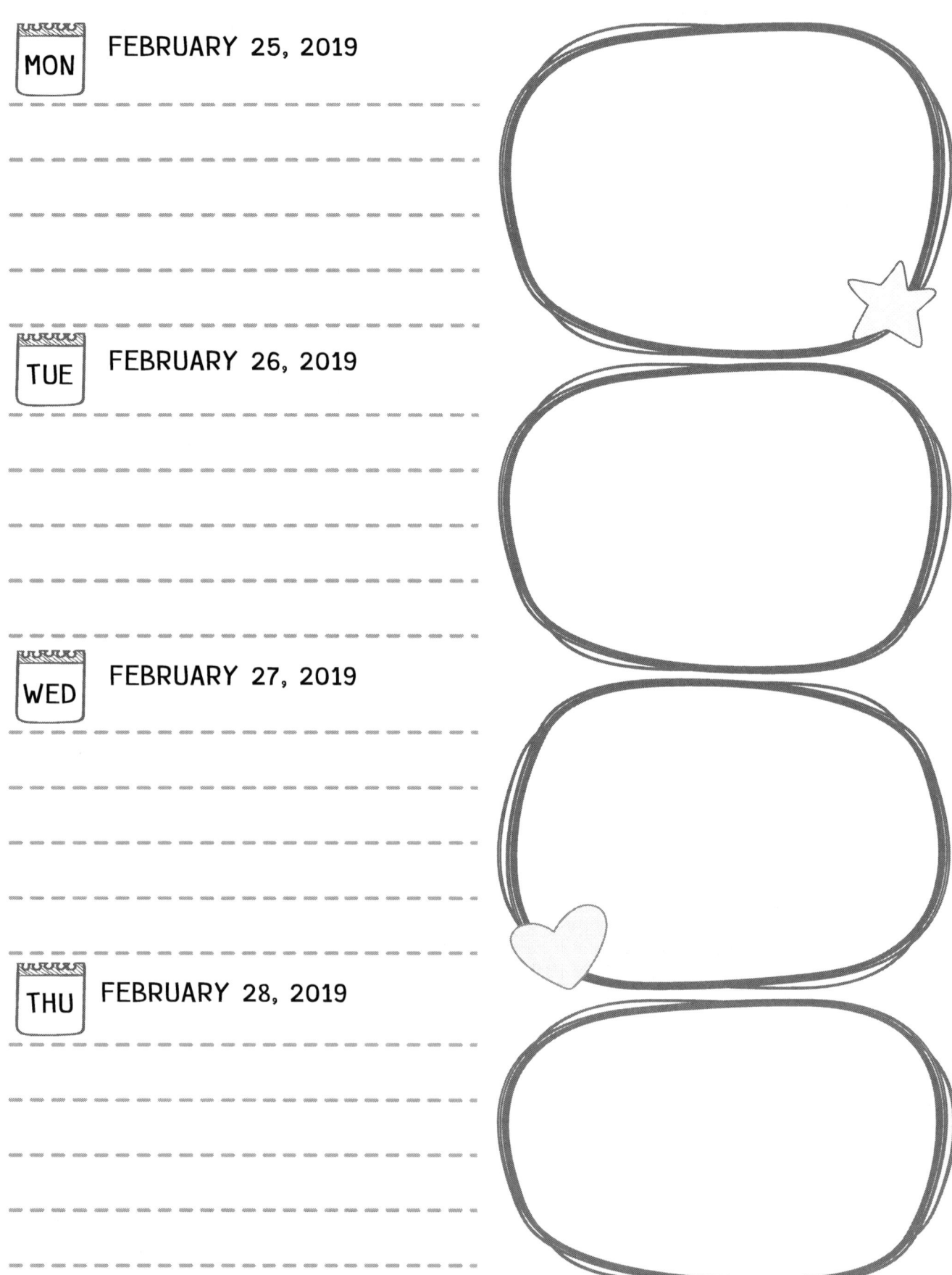

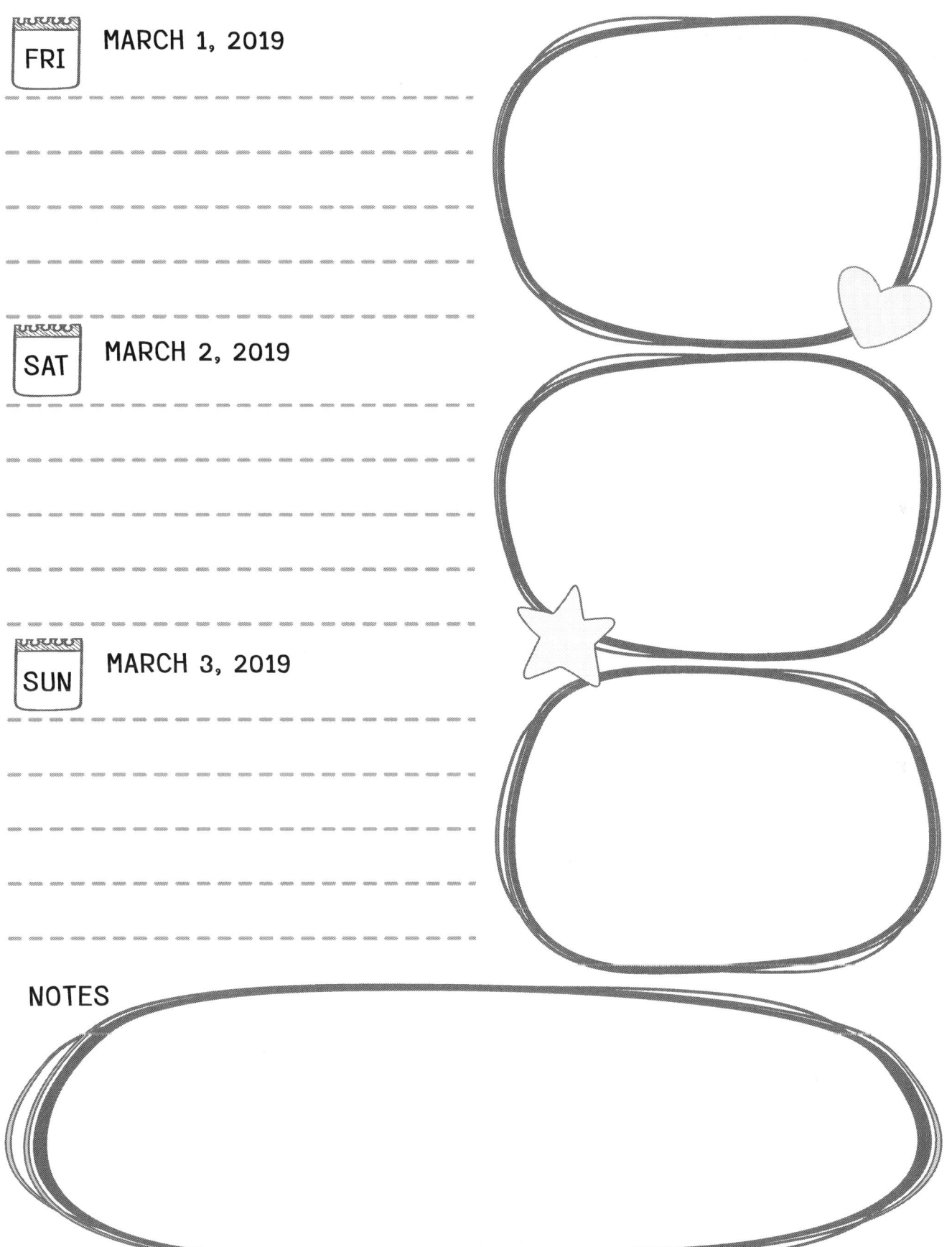

FRI MARCH 1, 2019

SAT MARCH 2, 2019

SUN MARCH 3, 2019

NOTES

March 2019

Sunday	Monday	Tuesday	Wednesday
24	25	26	27
3	4	5	6
10	11	12	13
17	18	19	20
24	25	26	27
31	1	2	3

Thursday	Friday	Saturday	
28	1	2	⭐
7	8	9	_____ _____
14	15	16	_____ _____
21	22	23	_____ _____
28	29	30	_____ _____
4	5	6	_____ _____

MON MARCH 4, 2019

TUE MARCH 5, 2019

WED MARCH 6, 2019

THU MARCH 7, 2019

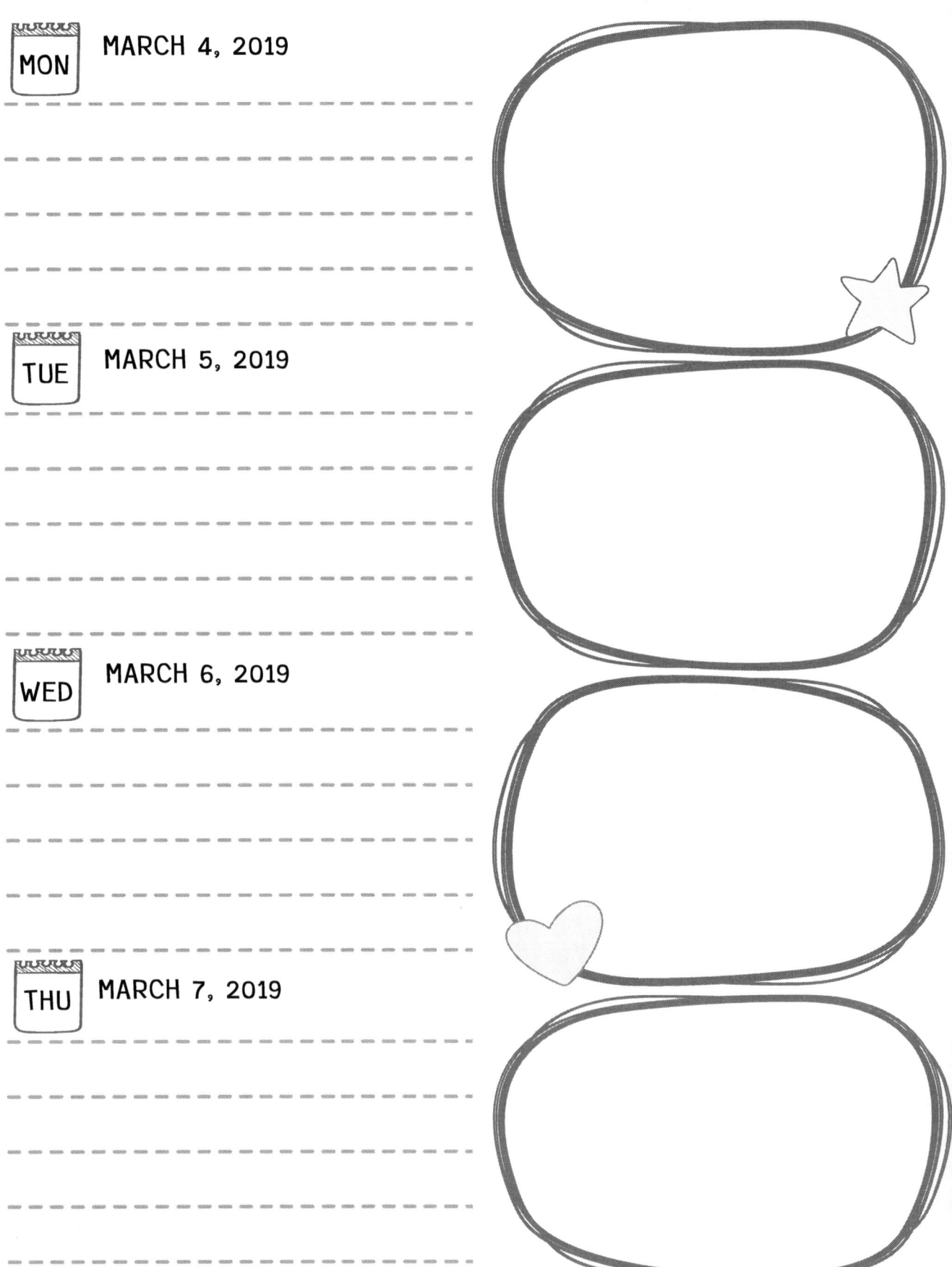

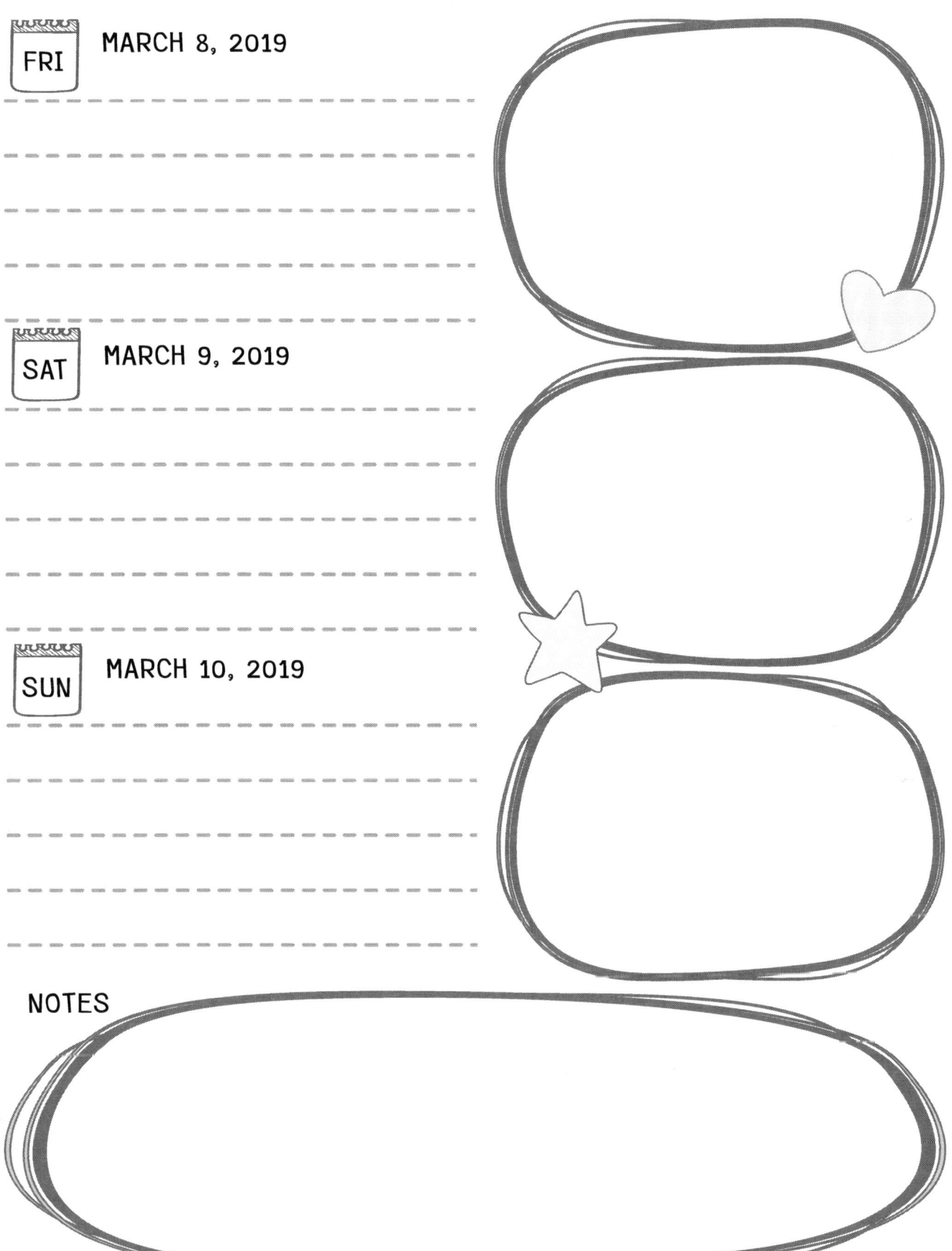

FRI MARCH 8, 2019

SAT MARCH 9, 2019

SUN MARCH 10, 2019

NOTES

MON MARCH 11, 2019

TUE MARCH 12, 2019

WED MARCH 13, 2019

THU MARCH 14, 2019

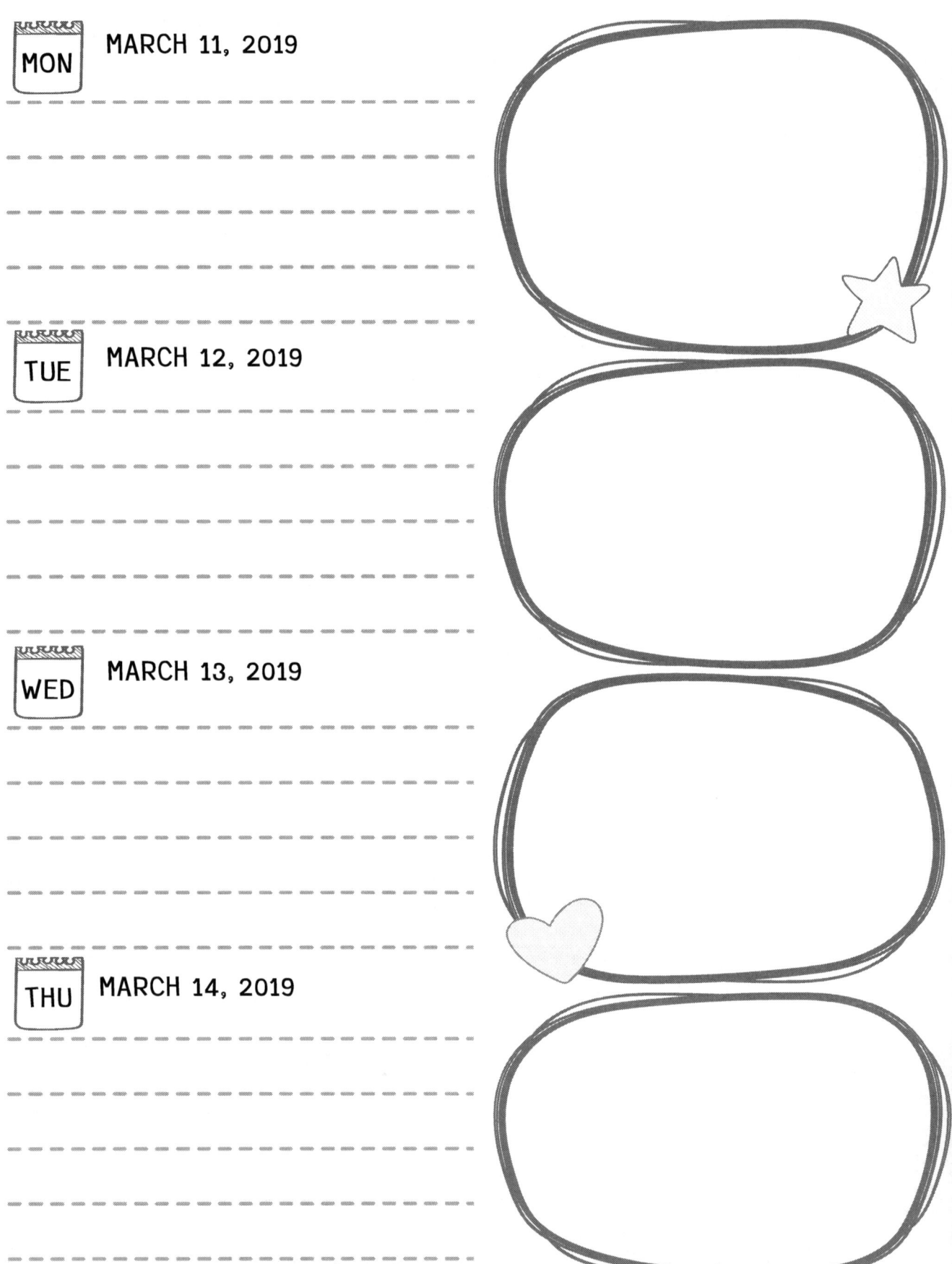

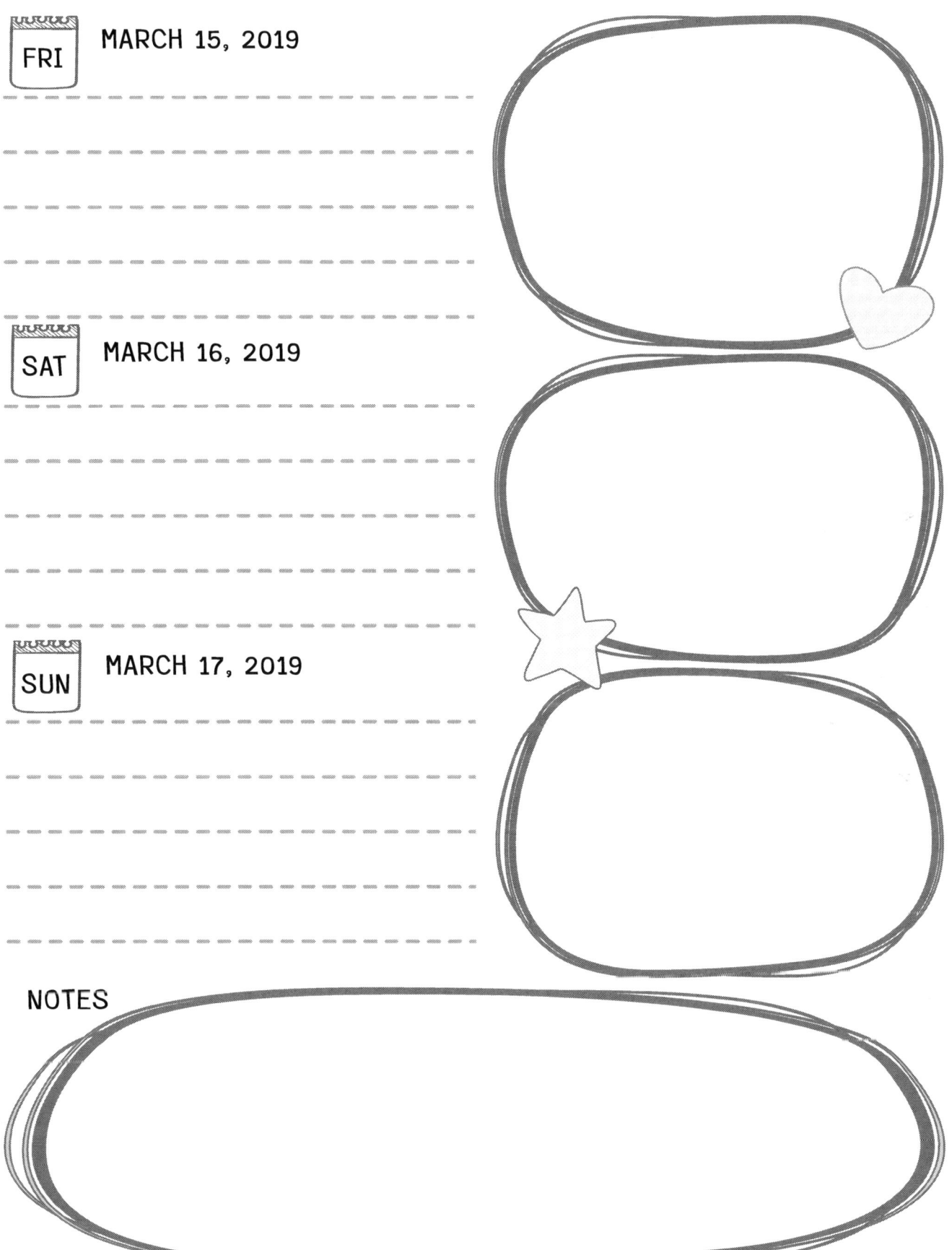

FRI MARCH 15, 2019

SAT MARCH 16, 2019

SUN MARCH 17, 2019

NOTES

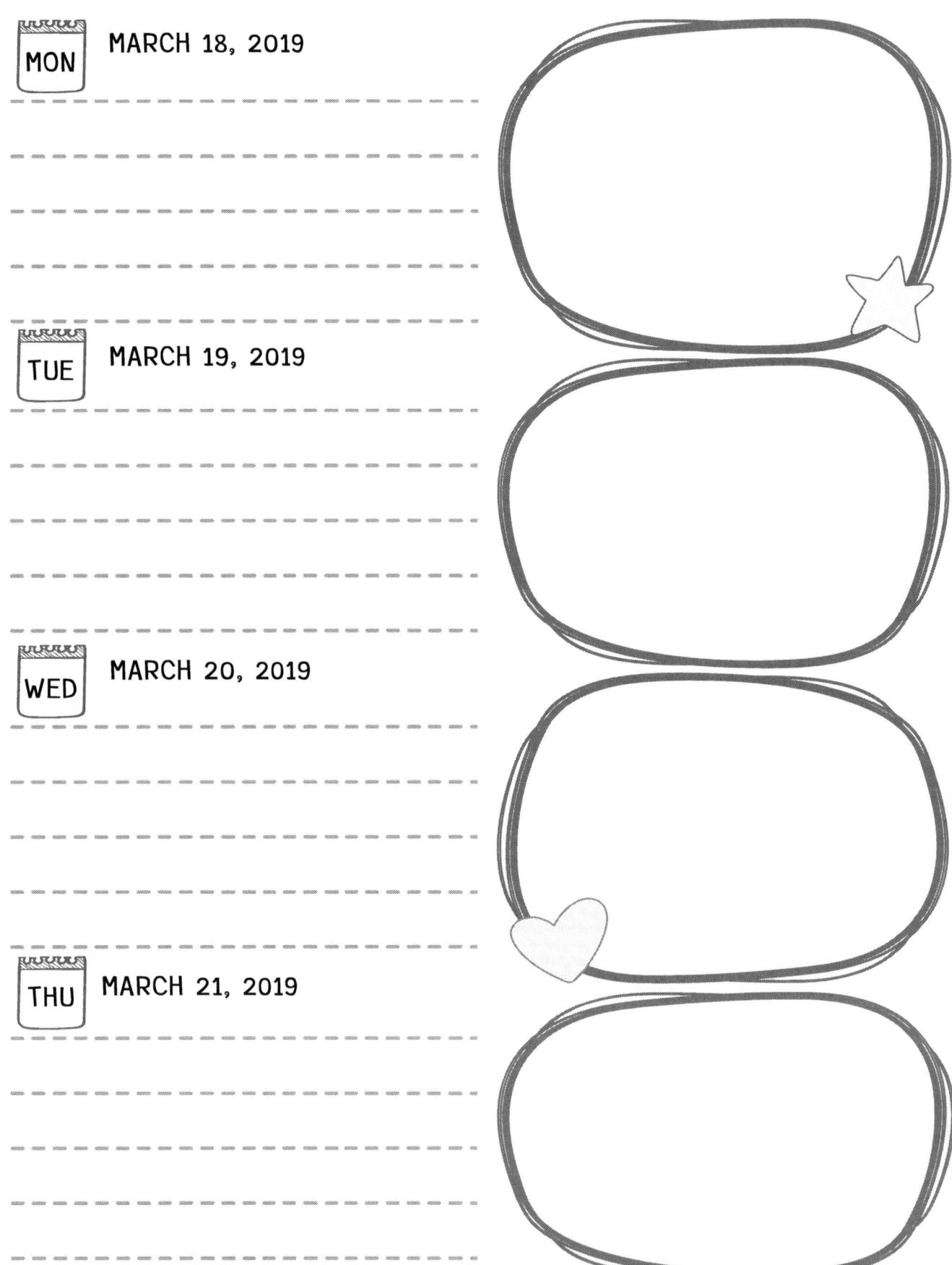

MON MARCH 18, 2019

TUE MARCH 19, 2019

WED MARCH 20, 2019

THU MARCH 21, 2019

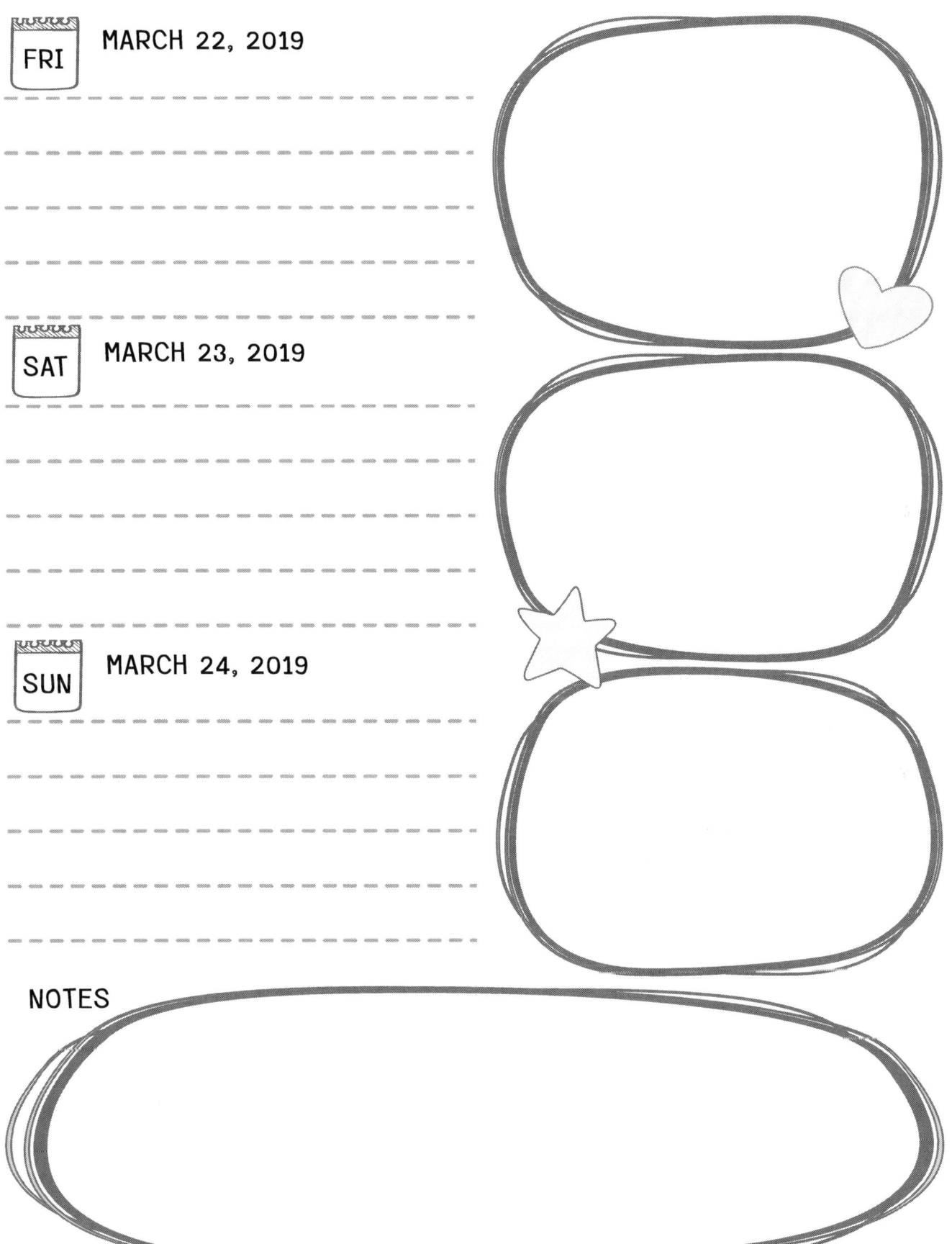

FRI   MARCH 22, 2019

SAT   MARCH 23, 2019

SUN   MARCH 24, 2019

NOTES

MON MARCH 25, 2019

TUE MARCH 26, 2019

WED MARCH 27, 2019

THU MARCH 28, 2019

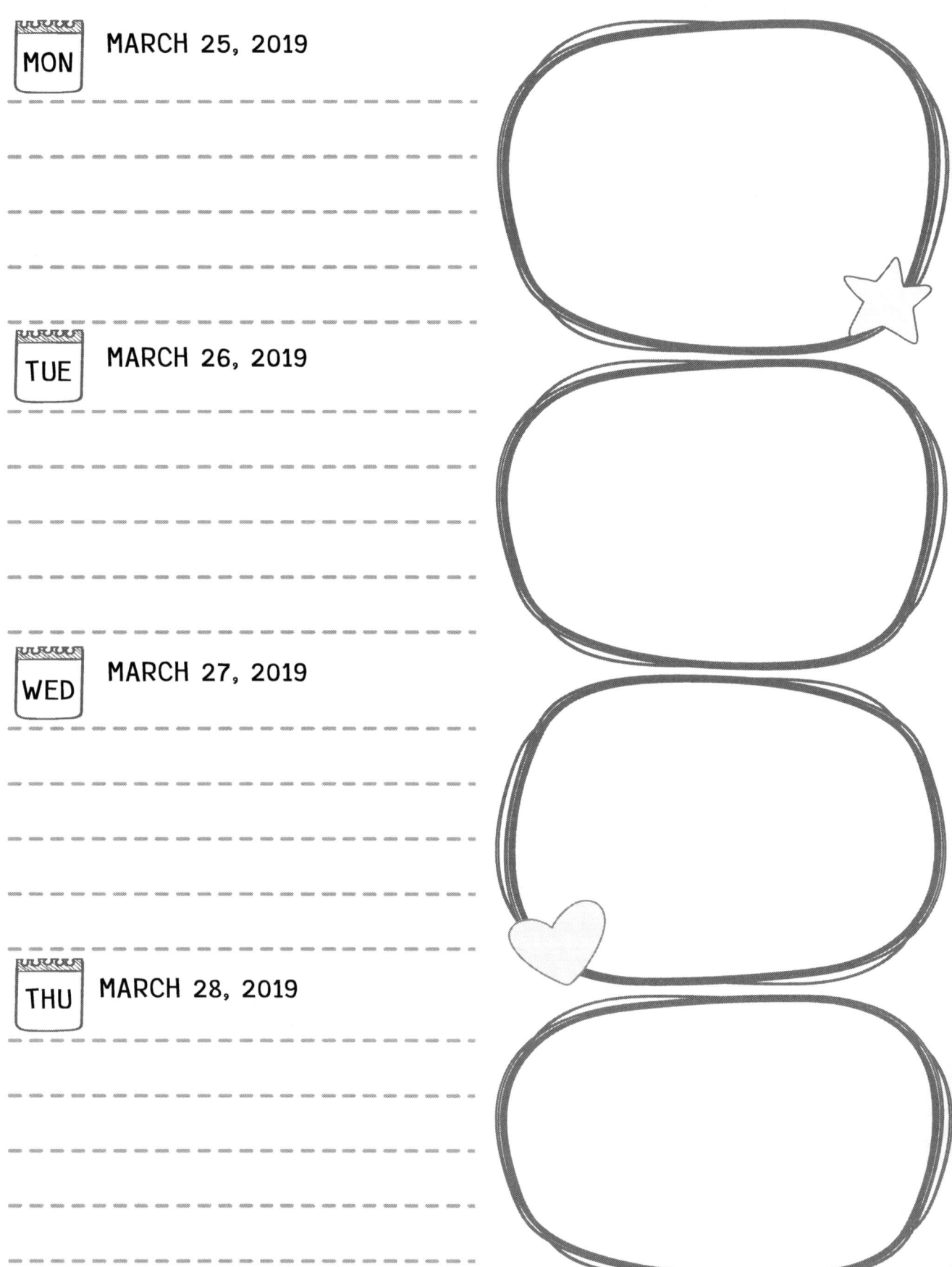

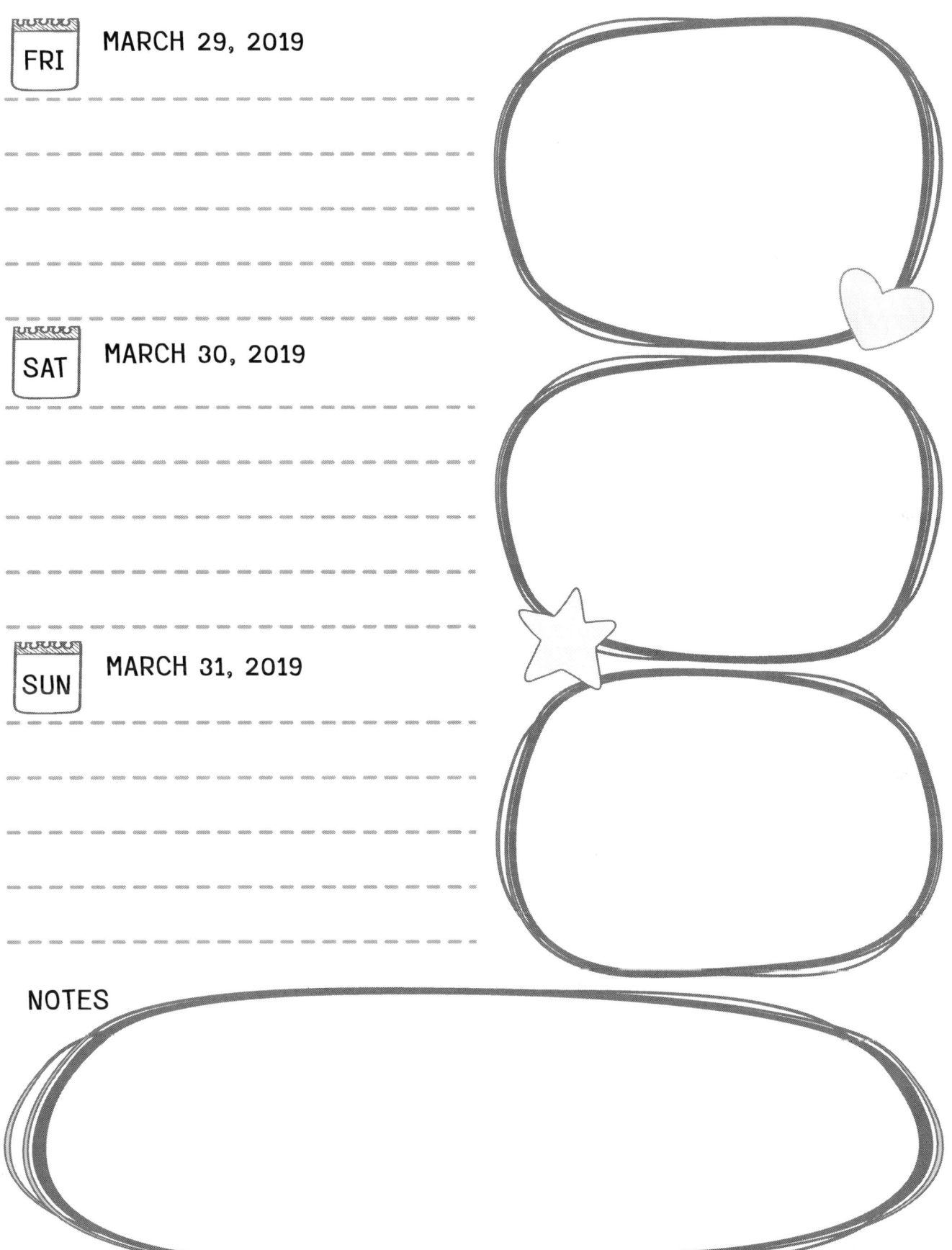

FRI | MARCH 29, 2019

SAT | MARCH 30, 2019

SUN | MARCH 31, 2019

NOTES

April 2019

Sunday	Monday	Tuesday	Wednesday
31	1	2	3
7	8	9	10
14	15	16	17
21	22	23	24
28	29	30	1

Thursday	Friday	Saturday	
4	5	6	
11	12	13	
18	19	20	
25	26	27	
2	3	4	

MON APRIL 1, 2019

TUE APRIL 2, 2019

WED APRIL 3, 2019

THU APRIL 4, 2019

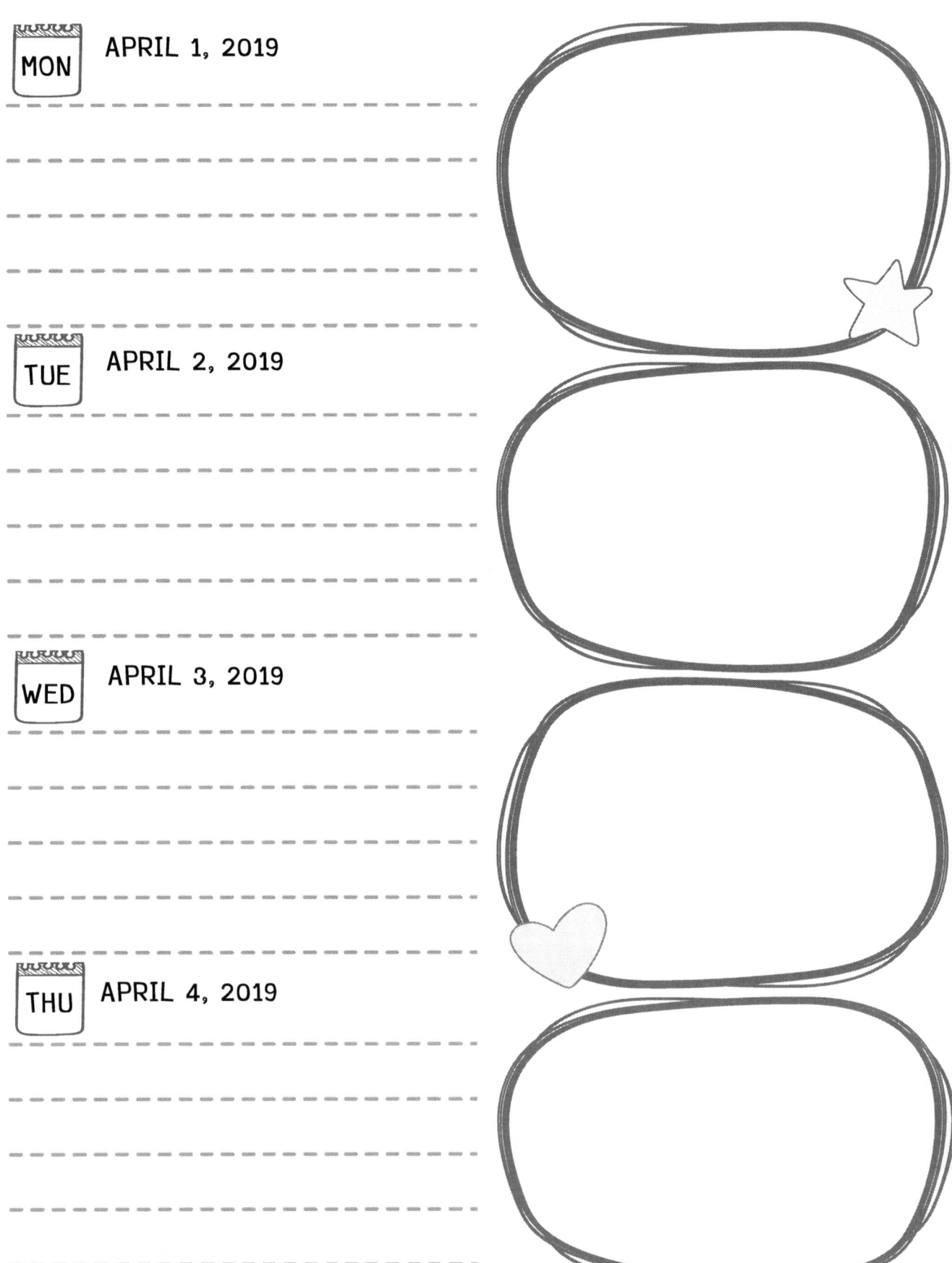

FRI APRIL 5, 2019

SAT APRIL 6, 2019

SUN APRIL 7, 2019

NOTES

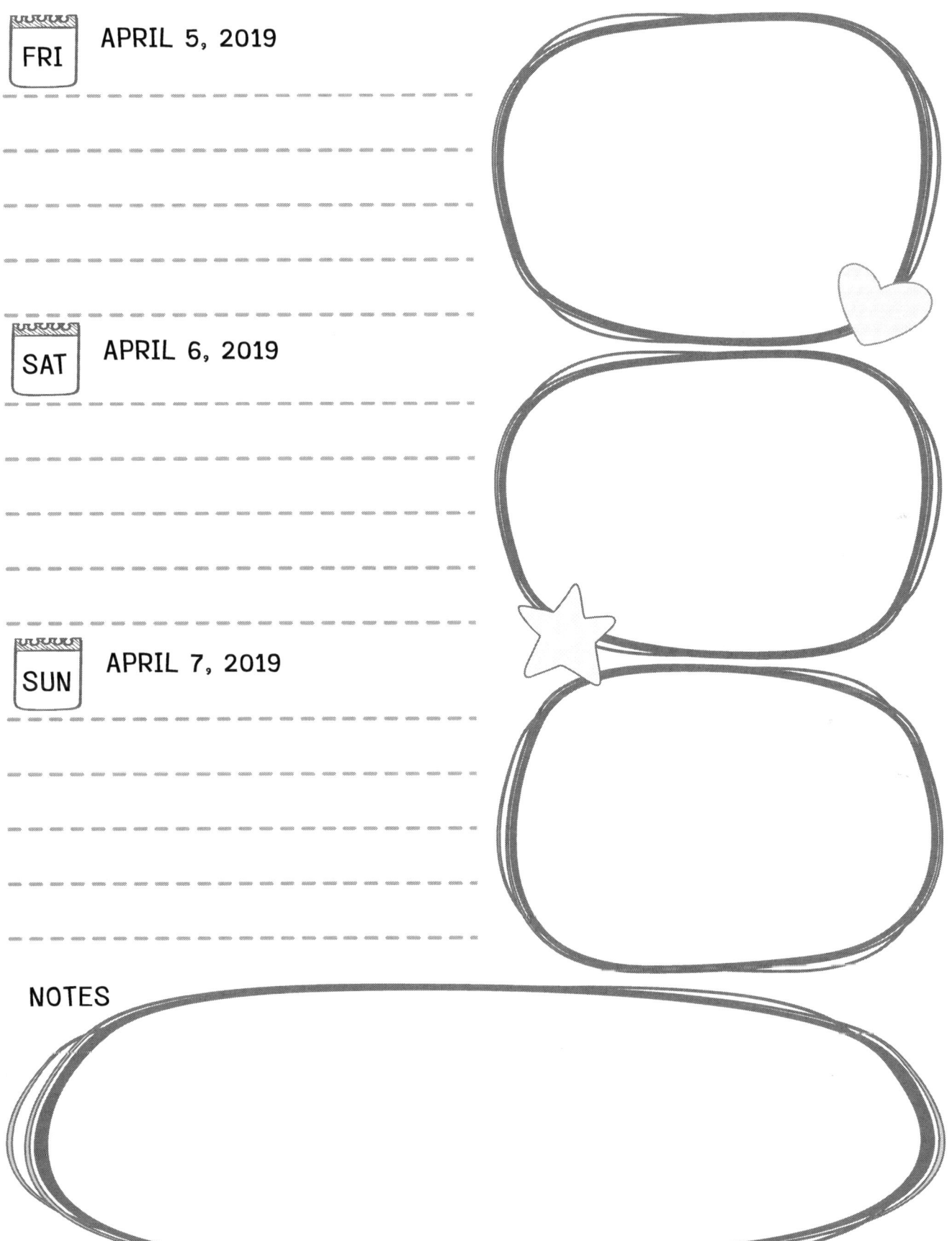

MON APRIL 8, 2019

TUE APRIL 9, 2019

WED APRIL 10, 2019

THU APRIL 11, 2019

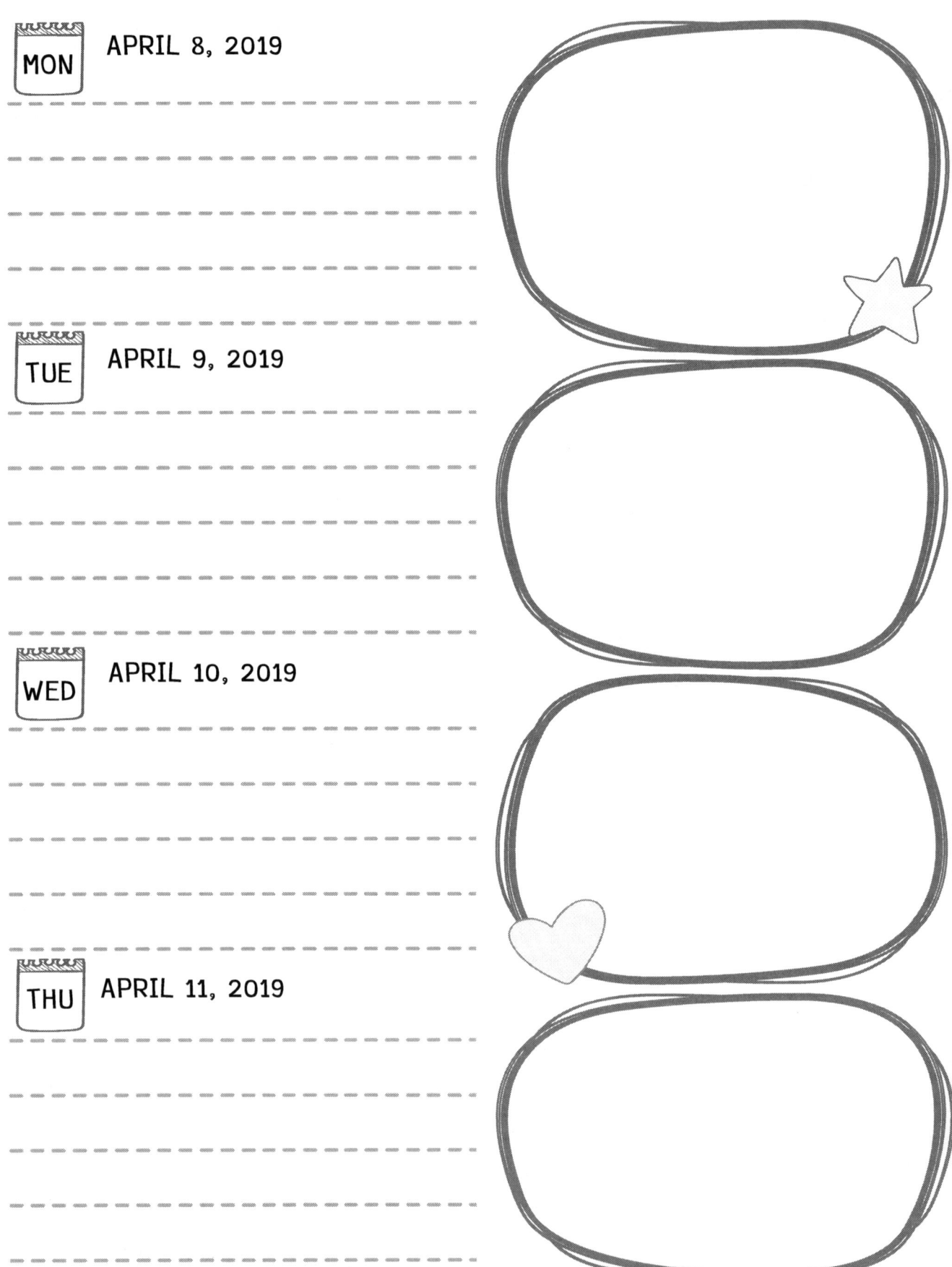

FRI | APRIL 12, 2019

SAT | APRIL 13, 2019

SUN | APRIL 14, 2019

NOTES

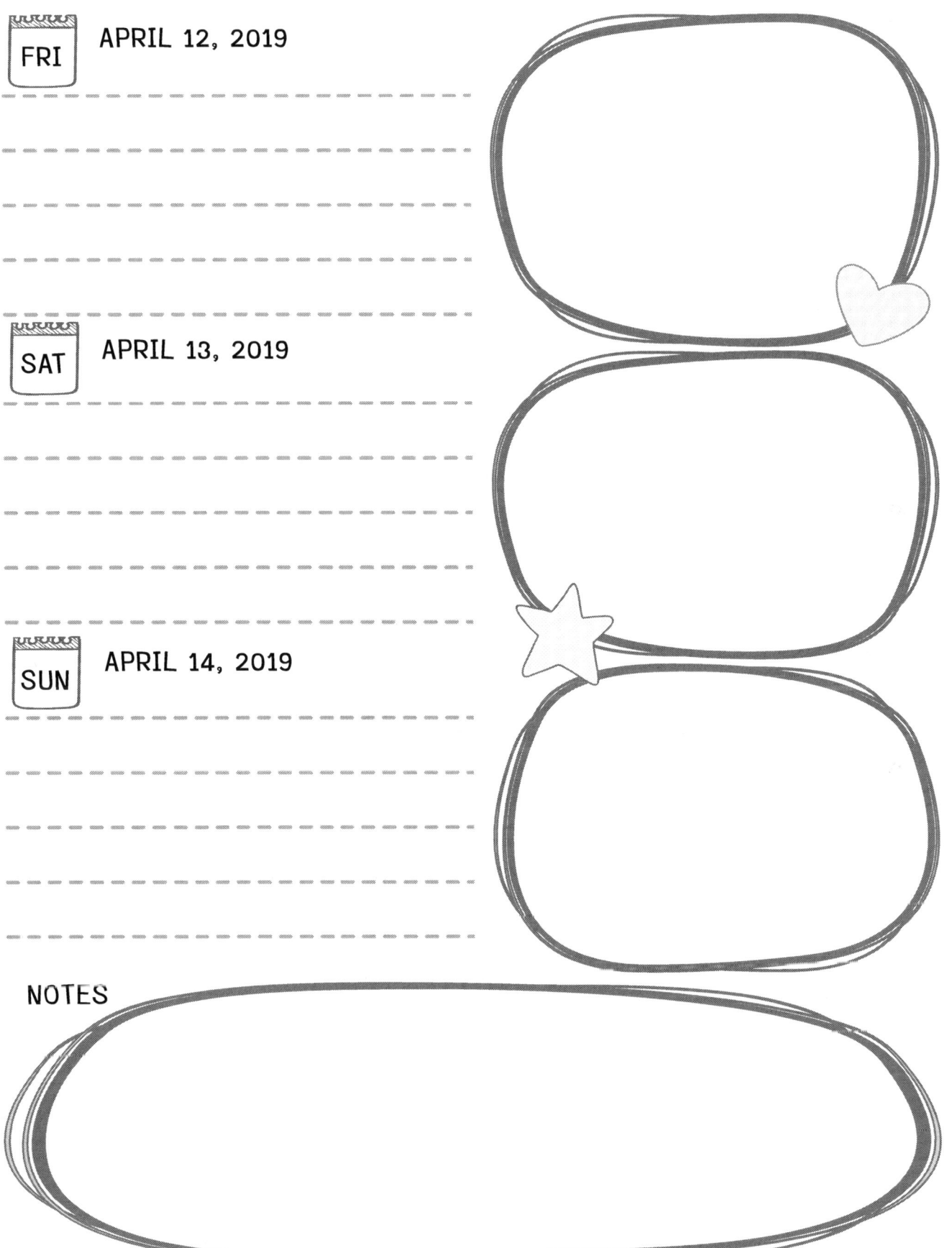

MON APRIL 15, 2019

TUE APRIL 16, 2019

WED APRIL 17, 2019

THU APRIL 18, 2019

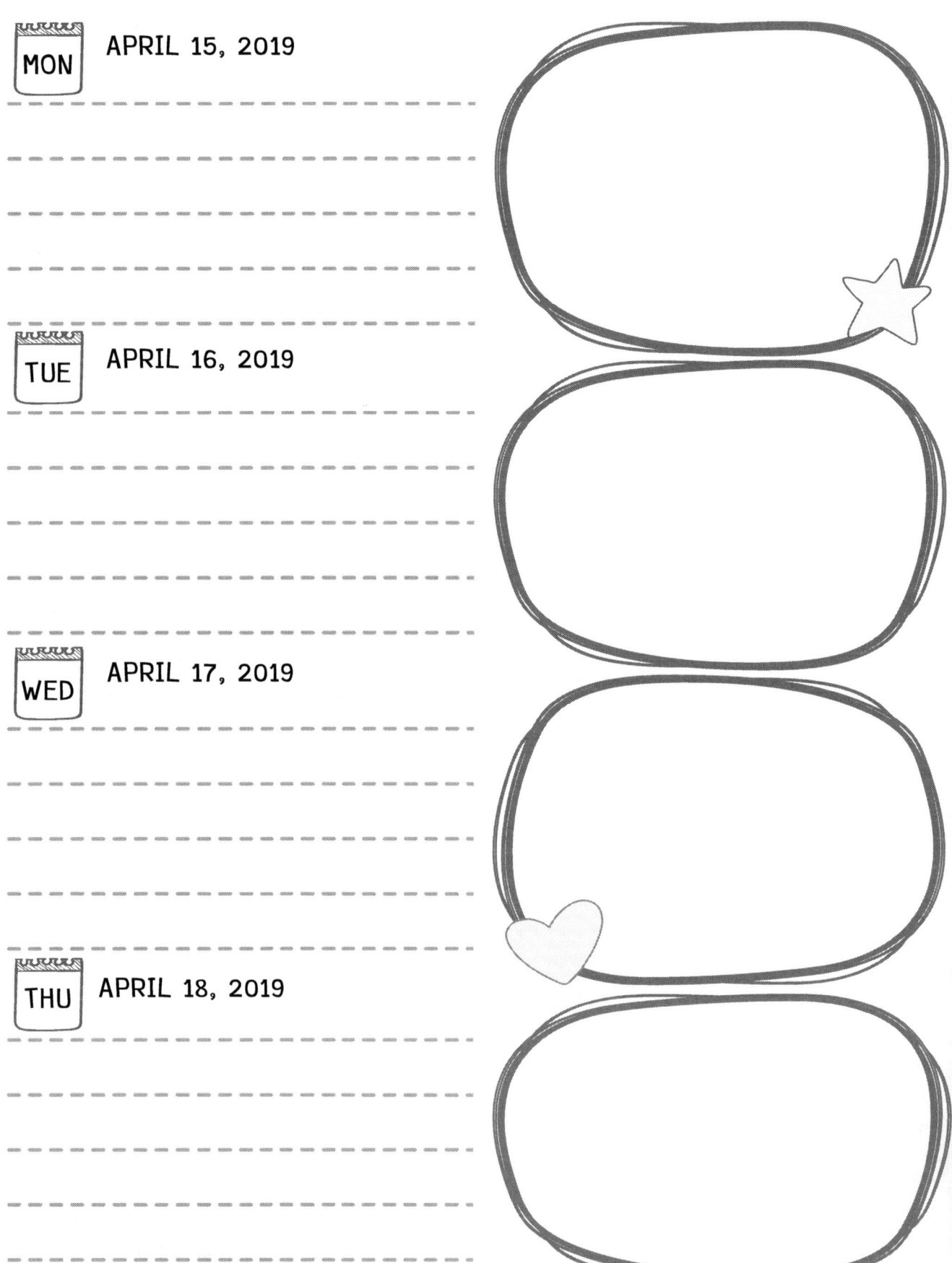

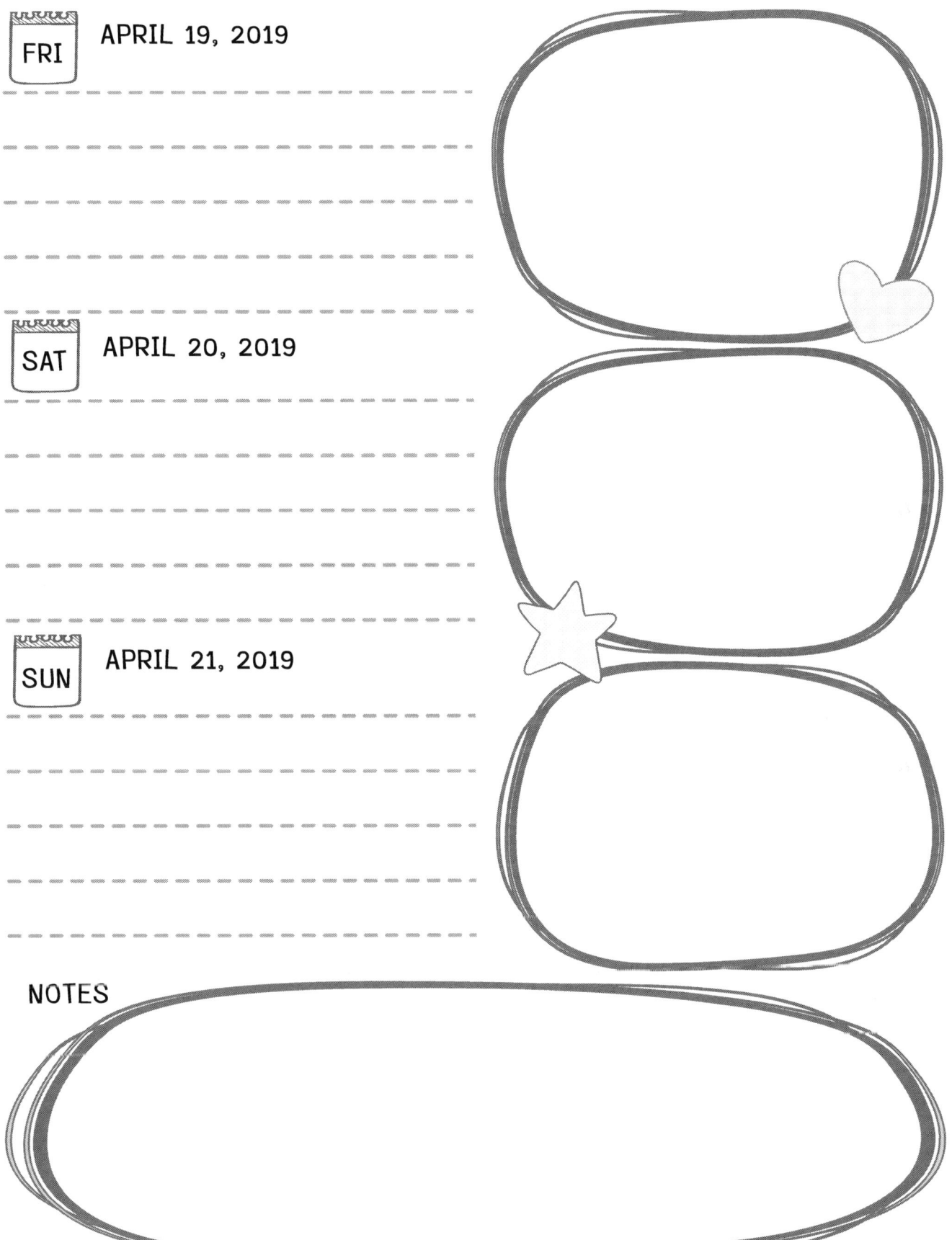

FRI APRIL 19, 2019

SAT APRIL 20, 2019

SUN APRIL 21, 2019

NOTES

MON APRIL 22, 2019

TUE APRIL 23, 2019

WED APRIL 24, 2019

THU APRIL 25, 2019

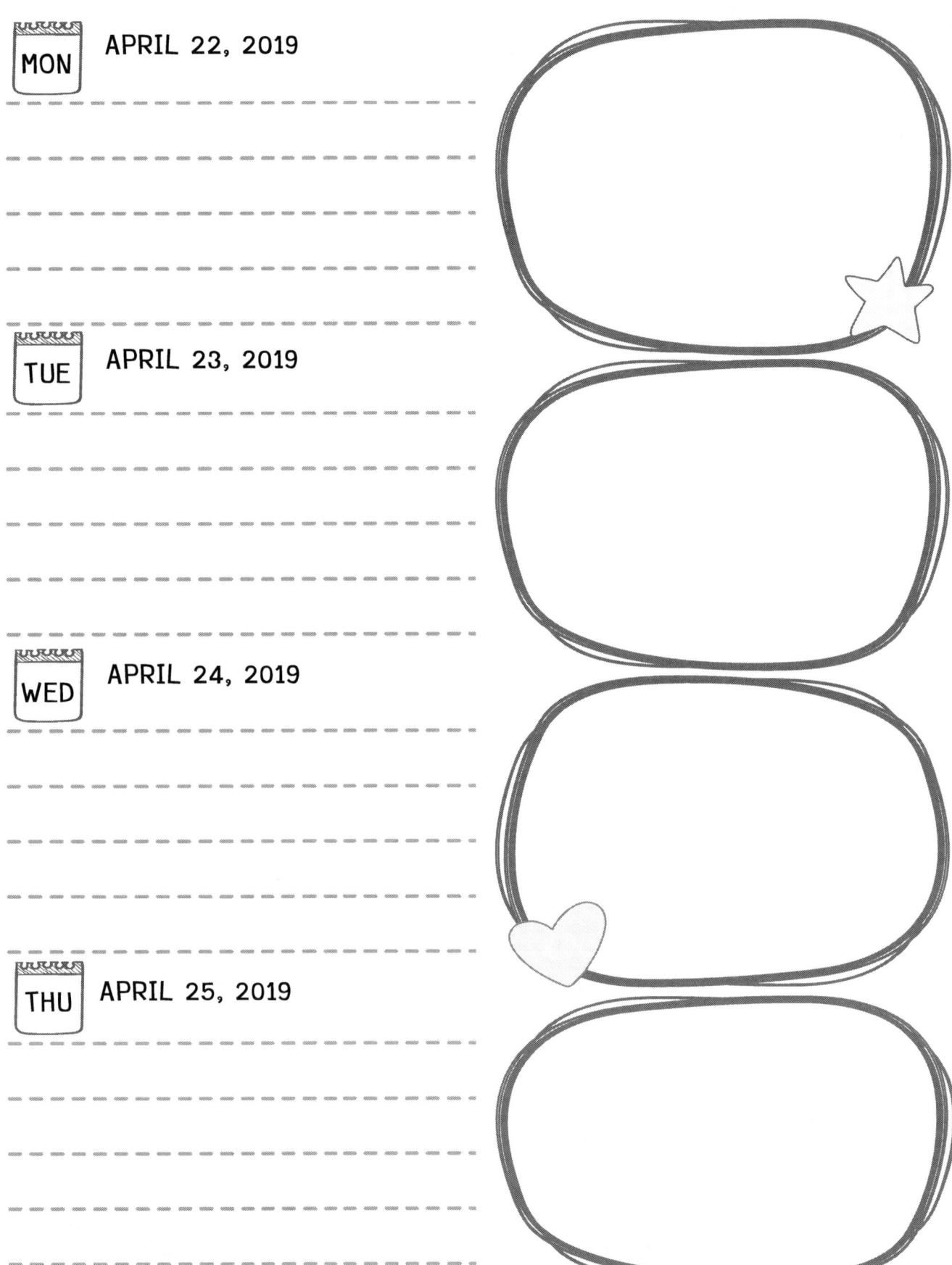

FRI APRIL 26, 2019

SAT APRIL 27, 2019

SUN APRIL 28, 2019

NOTES

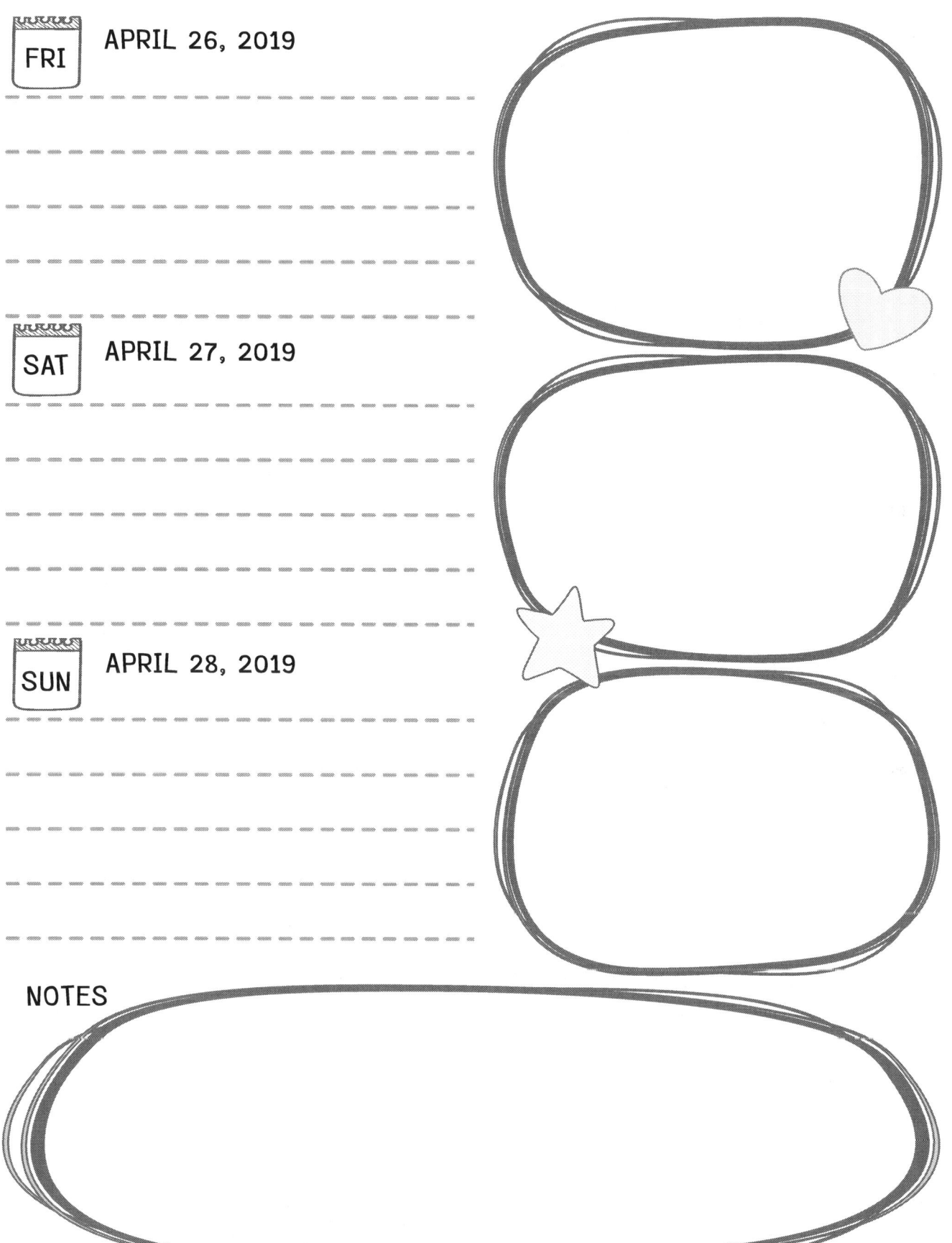

MON APRIL 29, 2019

TUE APRIL 30, 2019

WED MAY 1, 2019

THU MAY 2, 2019

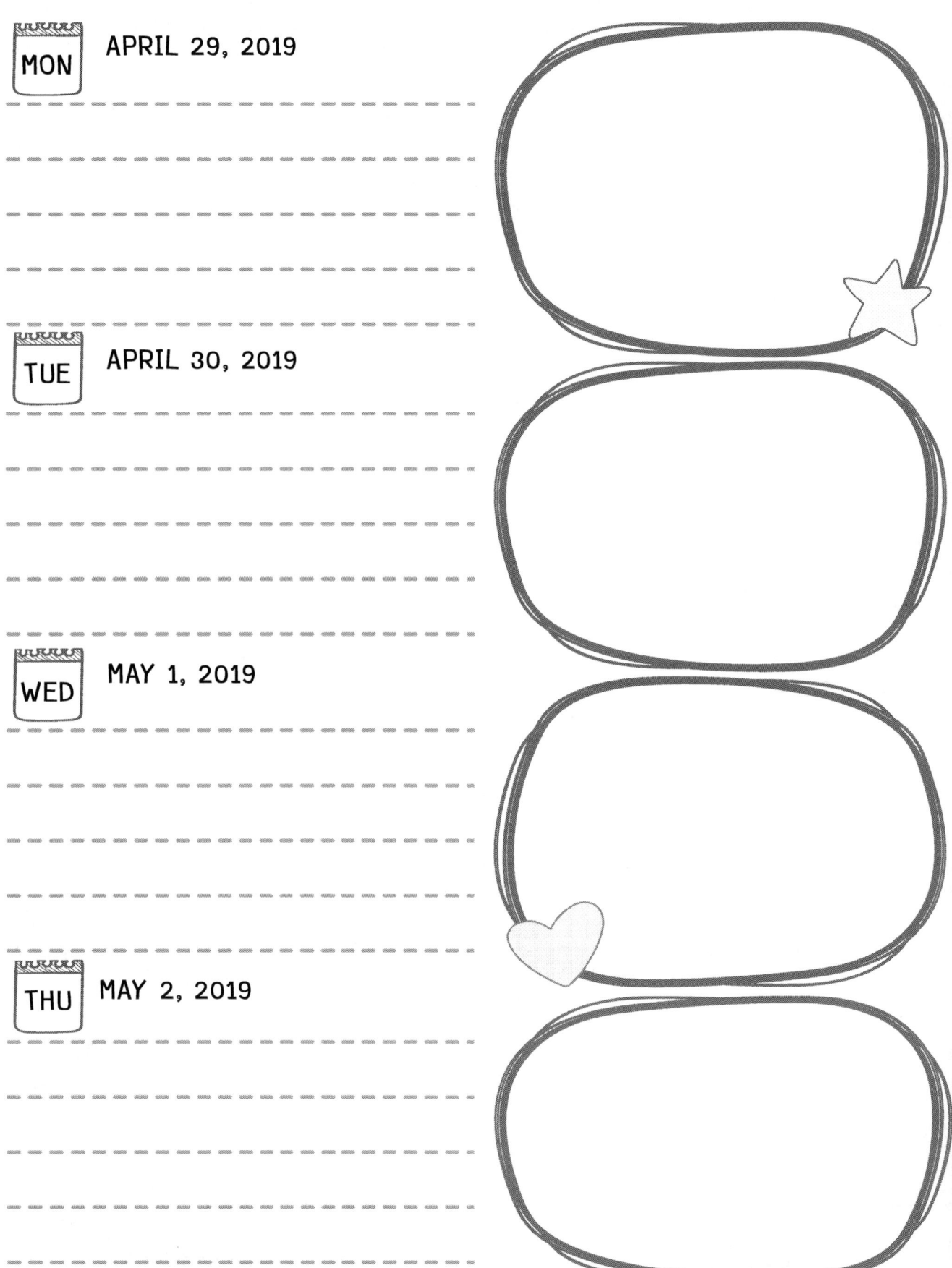

FRI | MAY 3, 2019

SAT | MAY 4, 2019

SUN | MAY 5, 2019

NOTES

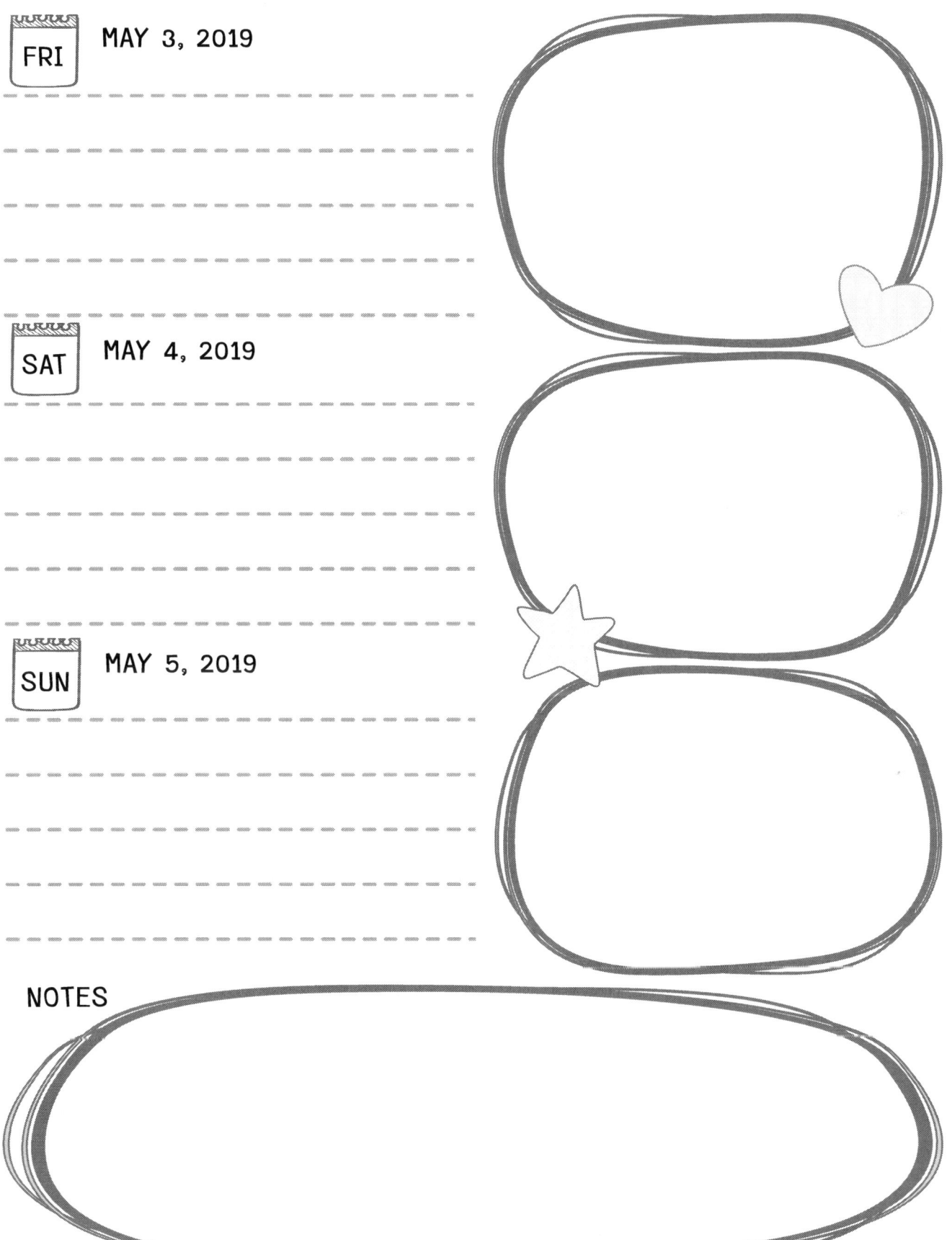

May 2019

Sunday	Monday	Tuesday	Wednesday
28	29	30	1
5	6	7	8
12	13	14	15
19	20	21	22
26	27	28	29

Thursday	Friday	Saturday	
2	3	4	
9	10	11	
16	17	18	
23	24	25	
30	31	1	

MON MAY 6, 2019

TUE MAY 7, 2019

WED MAY 8, 2019

THU MAY 9, 2019

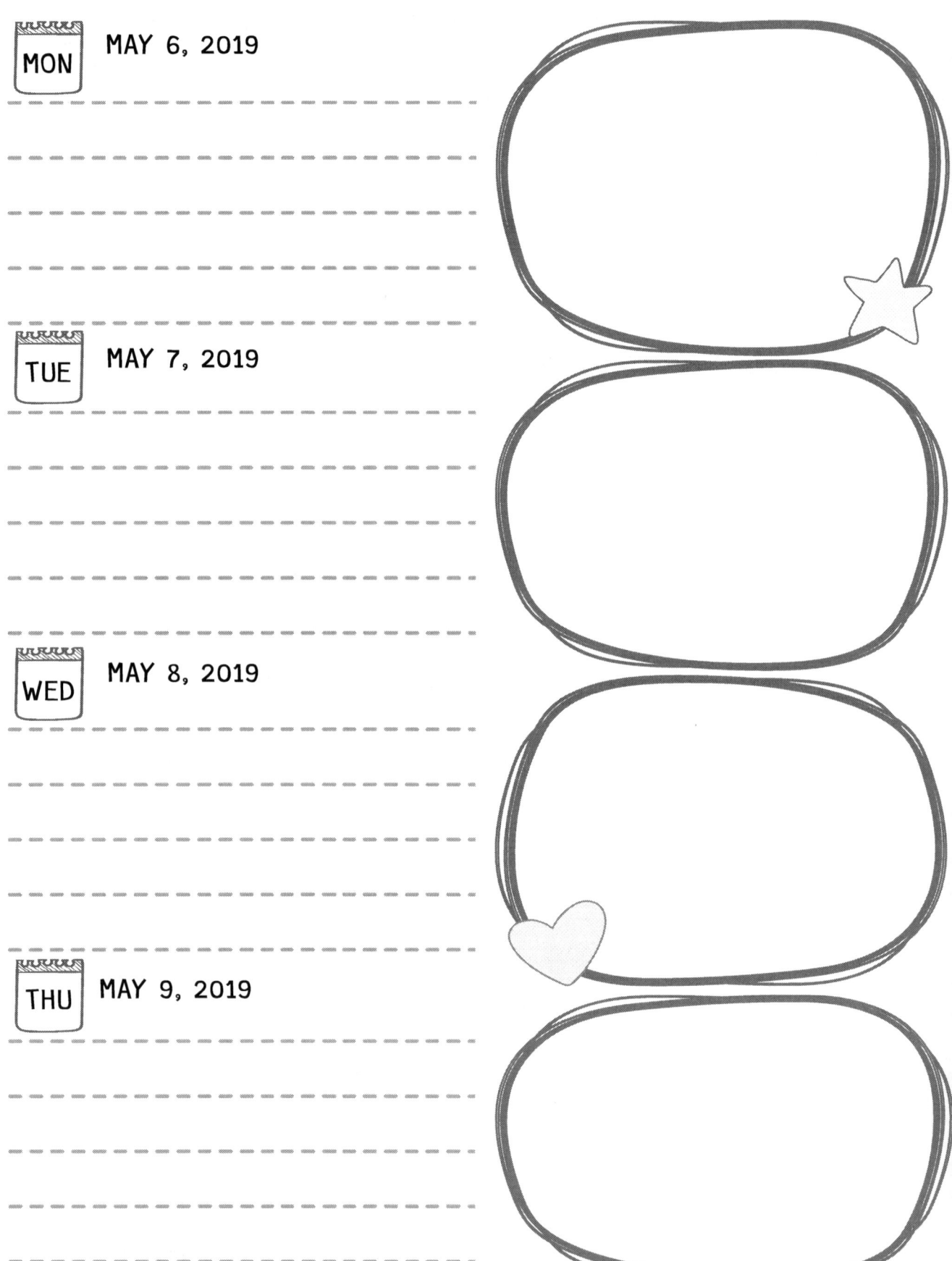

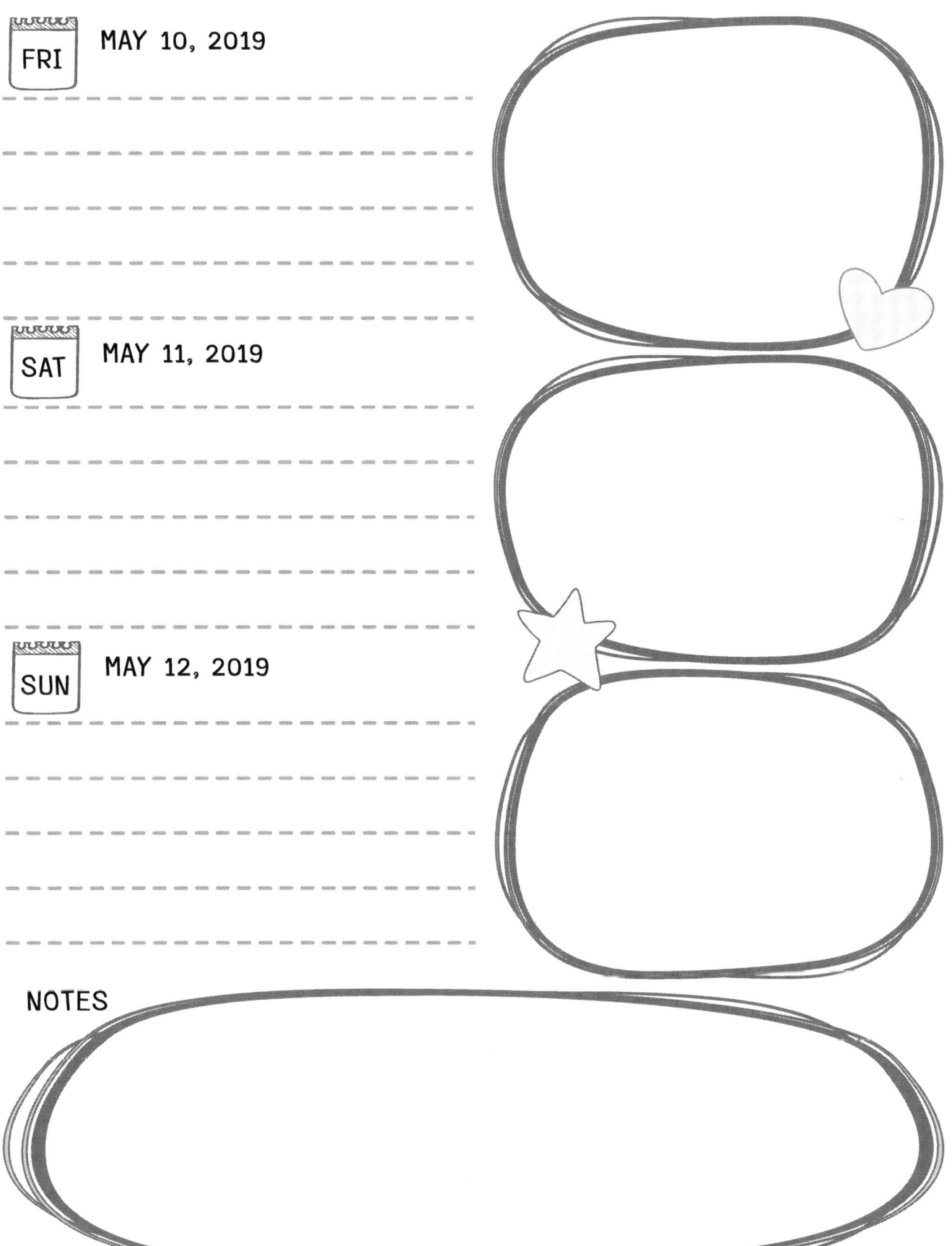

FRI MAY 10, 2019

SAT MAY 11, 2019

SUN MAY 12, 2019

NOTES

MON MAY 13, 2019

TUE MAY 14, 2019

WED MAY 15, 2019

THU MAY 16, 2019

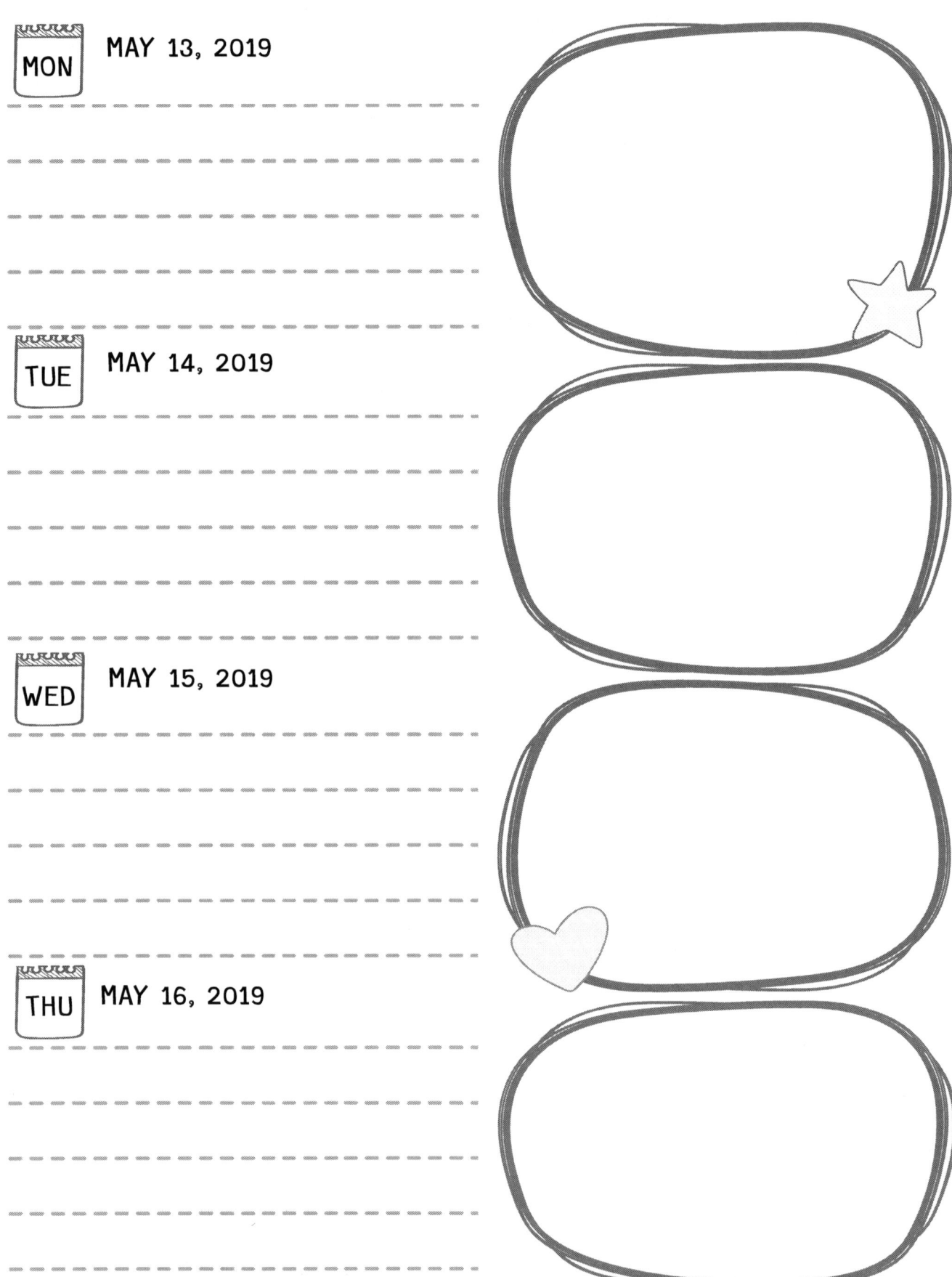

FRI MAY 17, 2019

SAT MAY 18, 2019

SUN MAY 19, 2019

NOTES

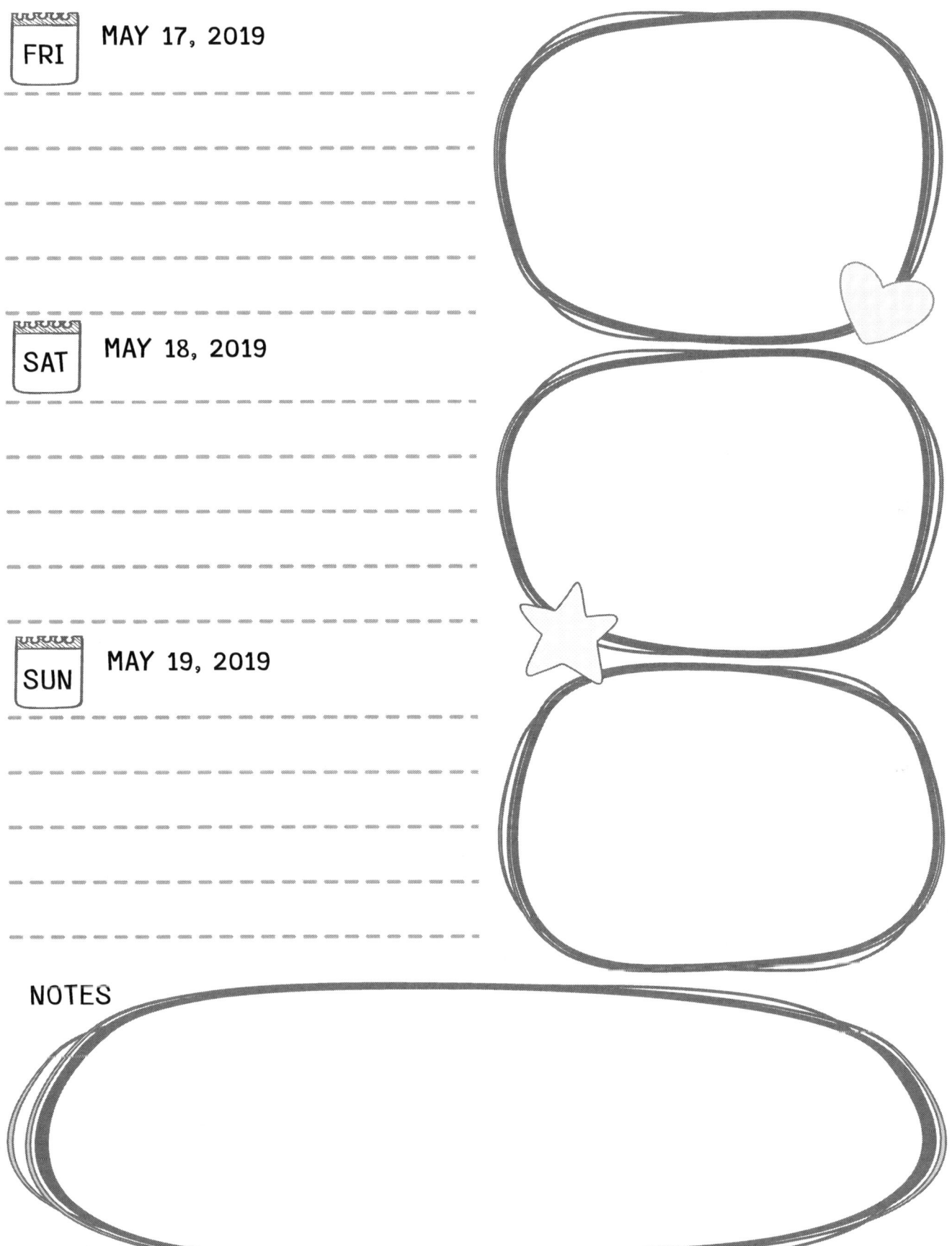

MON MAY 20, 2019

TUE MAY 21, 2019

WED MAY 22, 2019

THU MAY 23, 2019

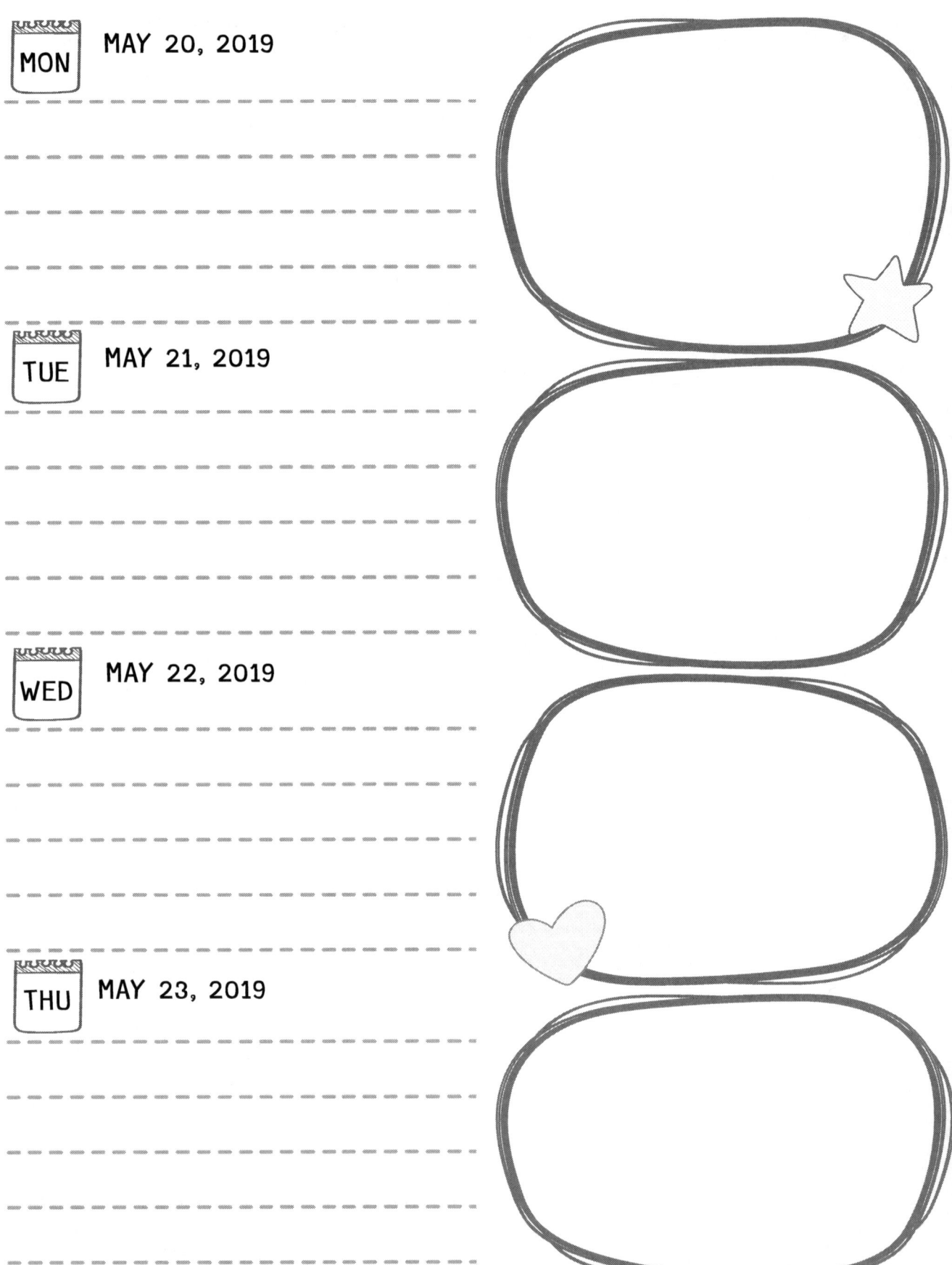

FRI MAY 24, 2019

SAT MAY 25, 2019

SUN MAY 26, 2019

NOTES

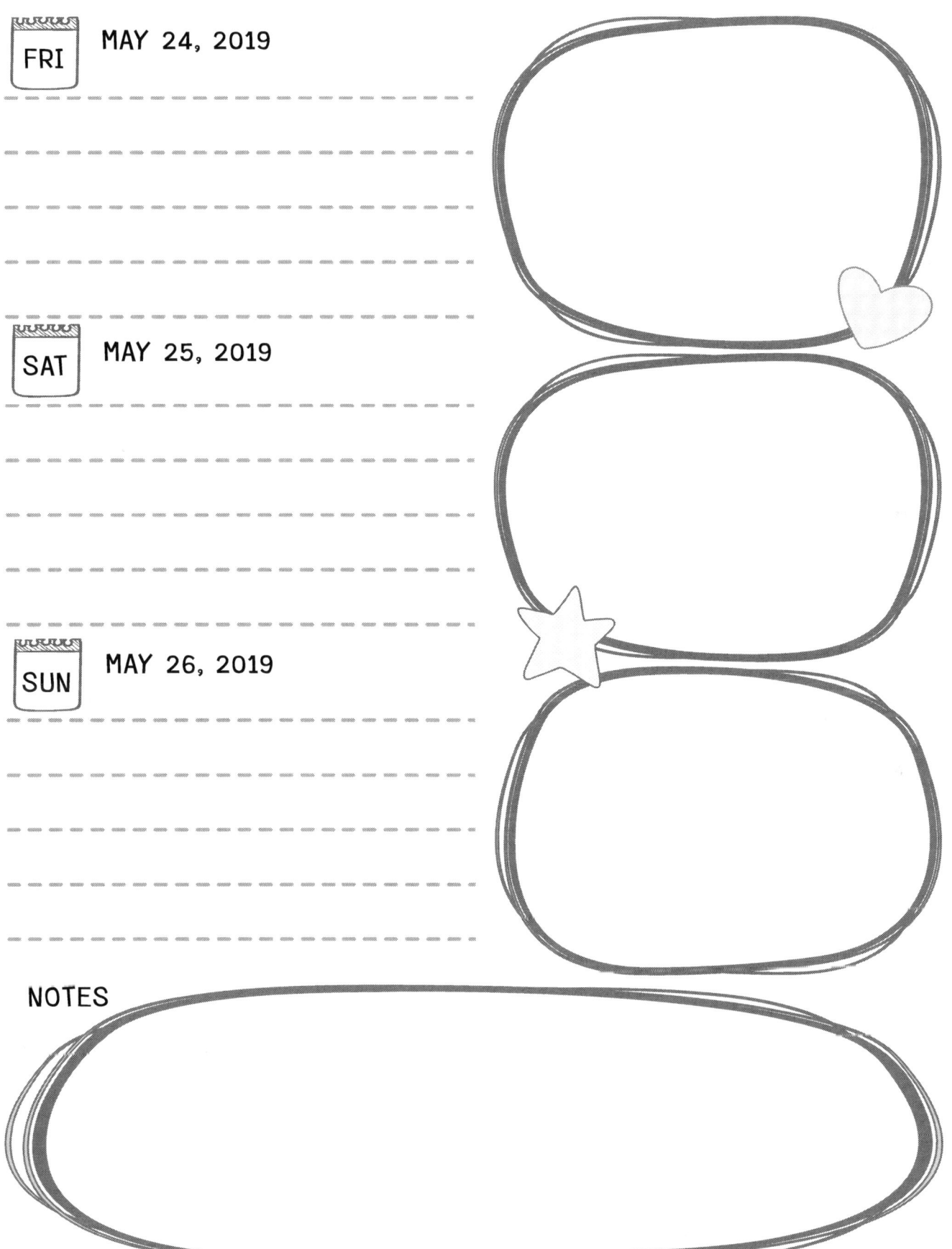

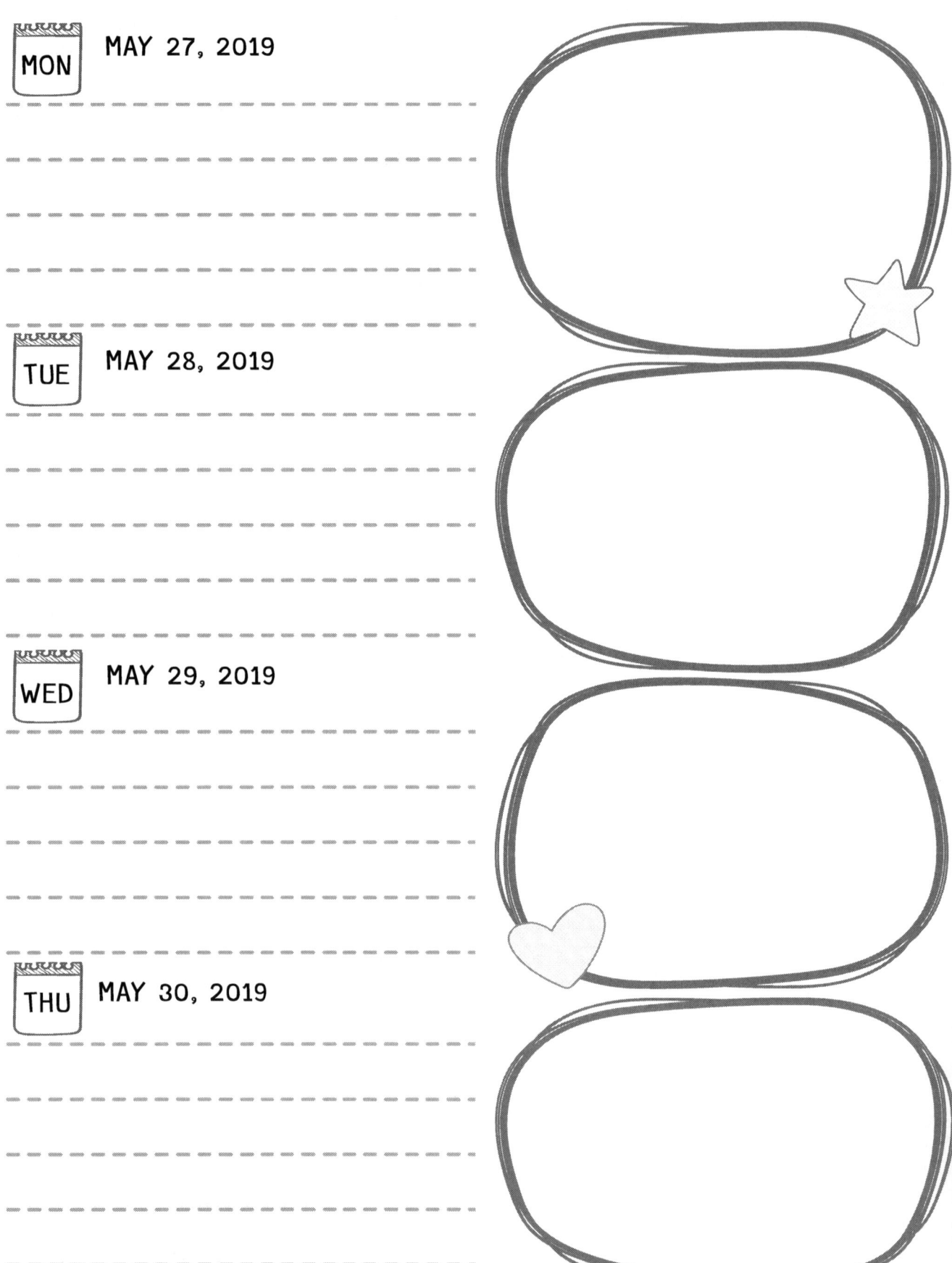

MON MAY 27, 2019

TUE MAY 28, 2019

WED MAY 29, 2019

THU MAY 30, 2019

FRI MAY 31, 2019

SAT JUNE 1, 2019

SUN JUNE 2, 2019

NOTES

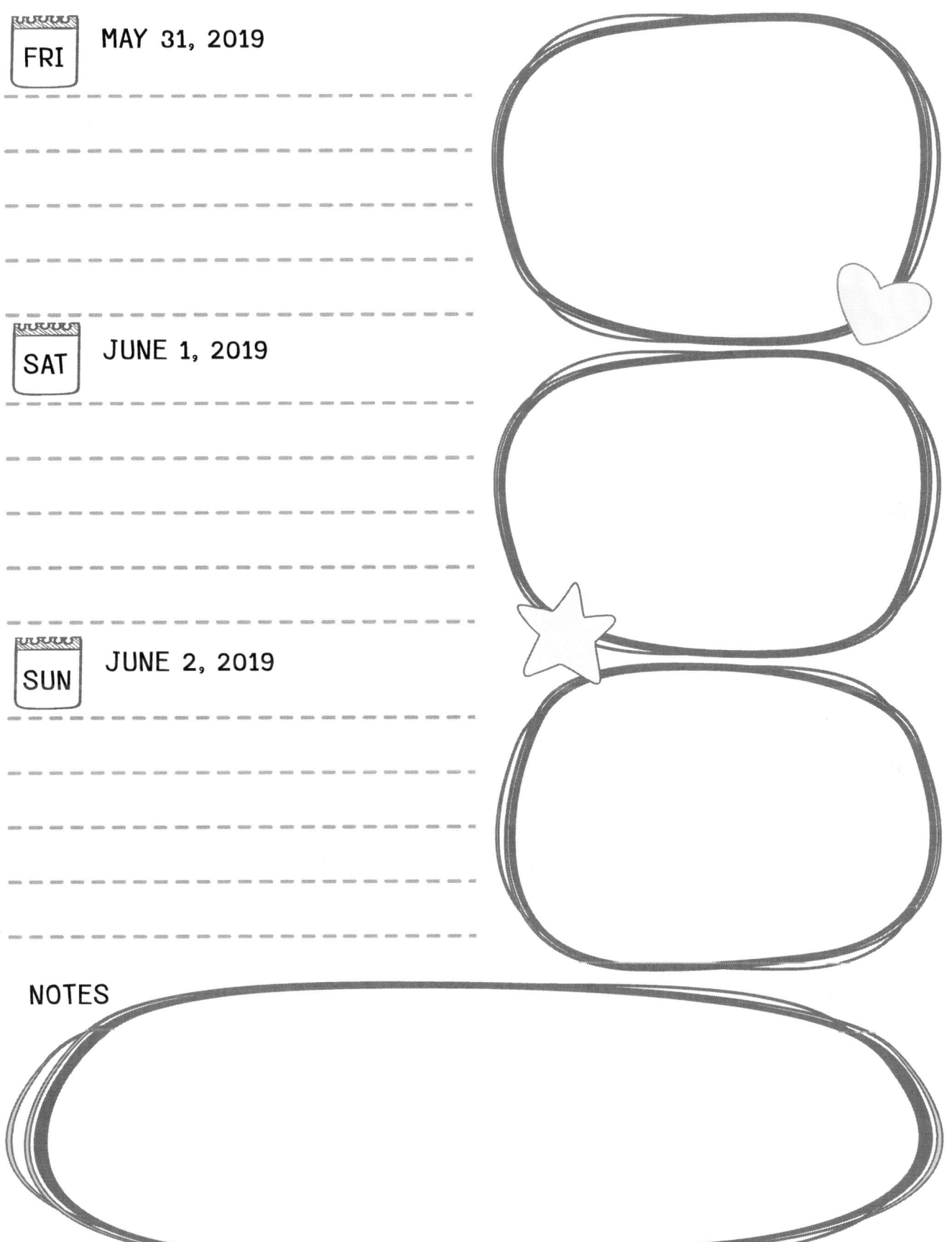

June 2019

Sunday	Monday	Tuesday	Wednesday
26	27	28	29
2	3	4	5
9	10	11	12
16	17	18	19
23	24	25	26
30	1	2	3

Thursday	Friday	Saturday	
30	31	1	
6	7	8	
13	14	15	
20	21	22	
27	28	29	
4	5	6	

MON JUNE 3, 2019

TUE JUNE 4, 2019

WED JUNE 5, 2019

THU JUNE 6, 2019

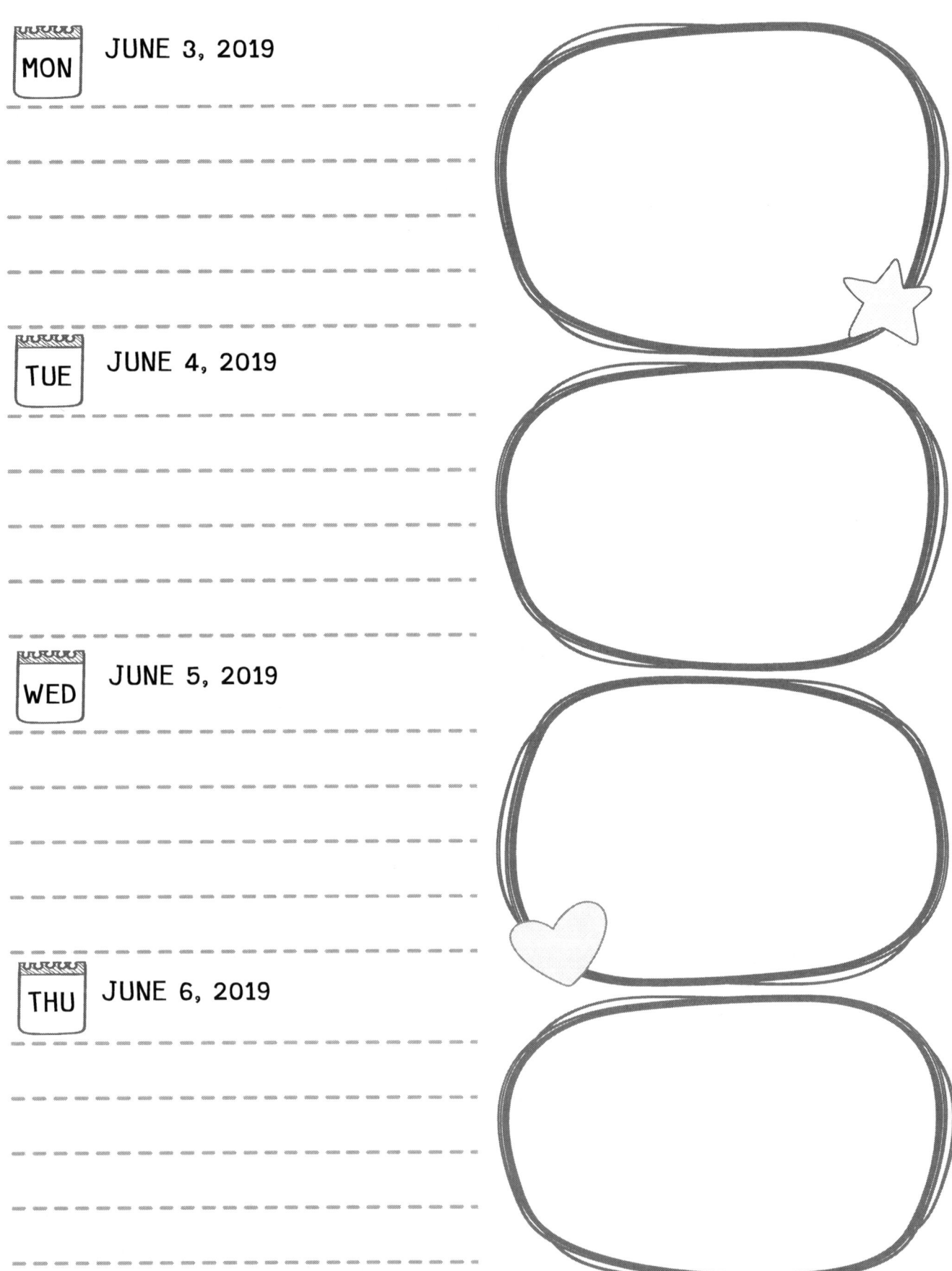

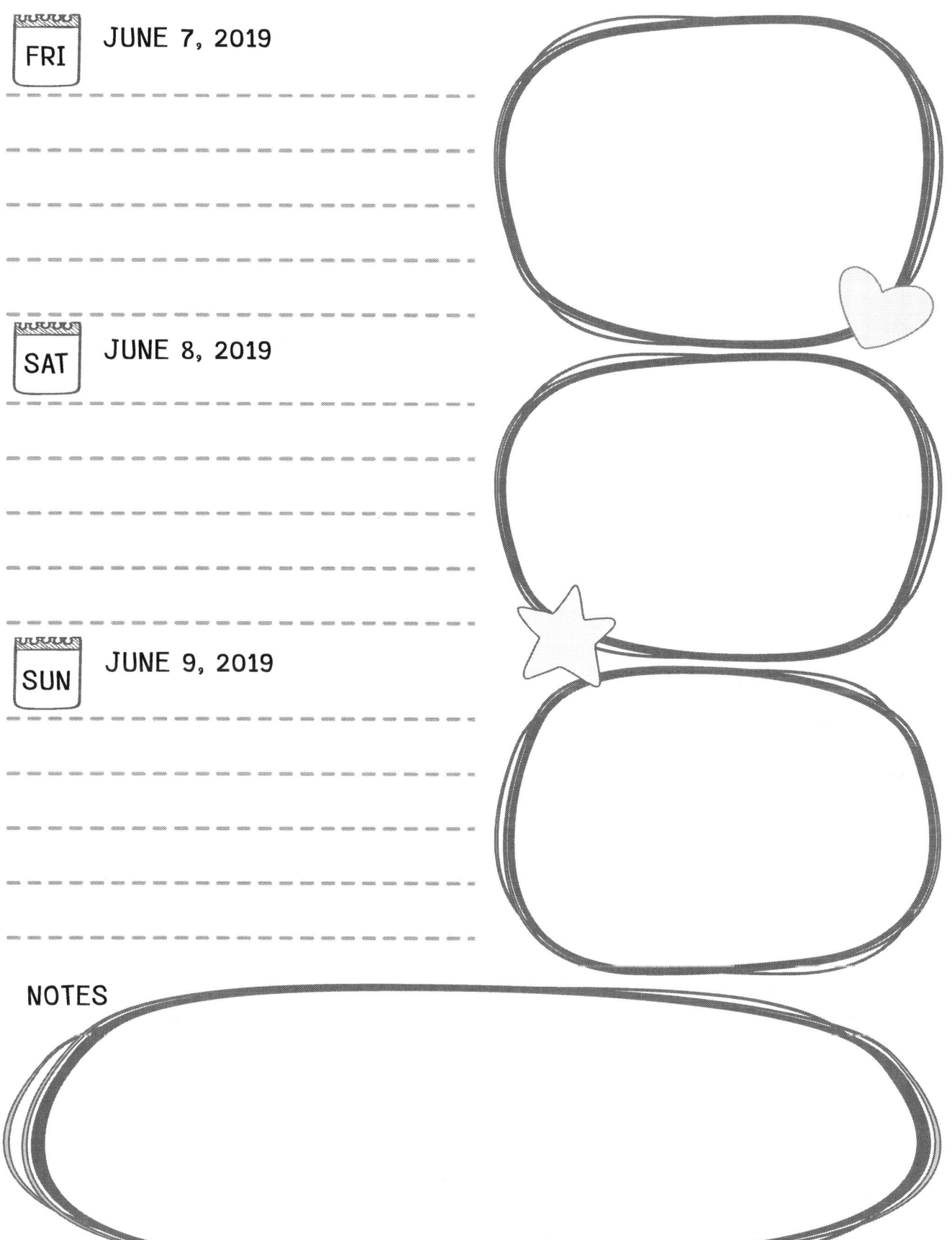

FRI   JUNE 7, 2019

SAT   JUNE 8, 2019

SUN   JUNE 9, 2019

NOTES

MON JUNE 10, 2019

TUE JUNE 11, 2019

WED JUNE 12, 2019

THU JUNE 13, 2019

FRI **JUNE 14, 2019**

SAT **JUNE 15, 2019**

SUN **JUNE 16, 2019**

NOTES

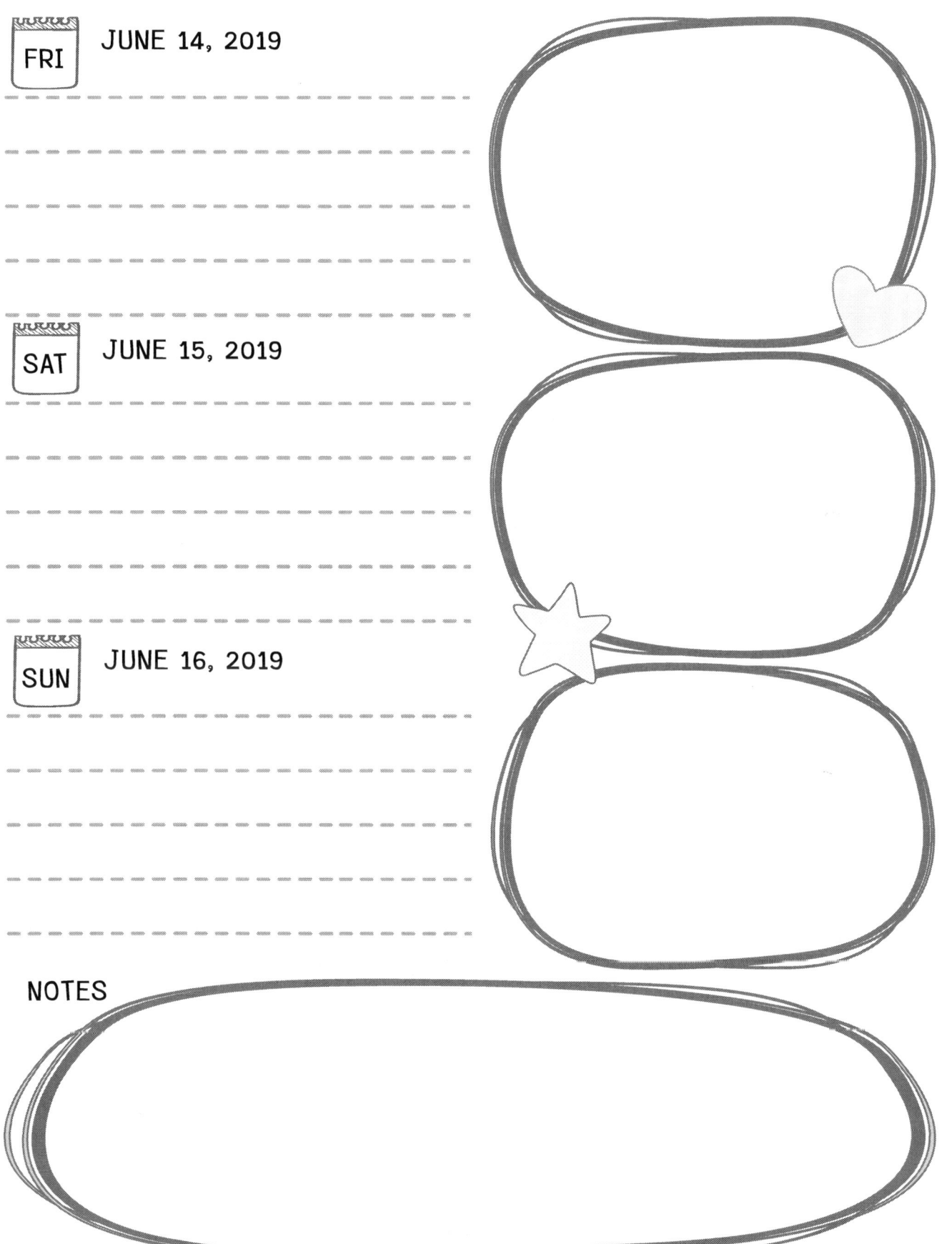

MON JUNE 17, 2019

TUE JUNE 18, 2019

WED JUNE 19, 2019

THU JUNE 20, 2019

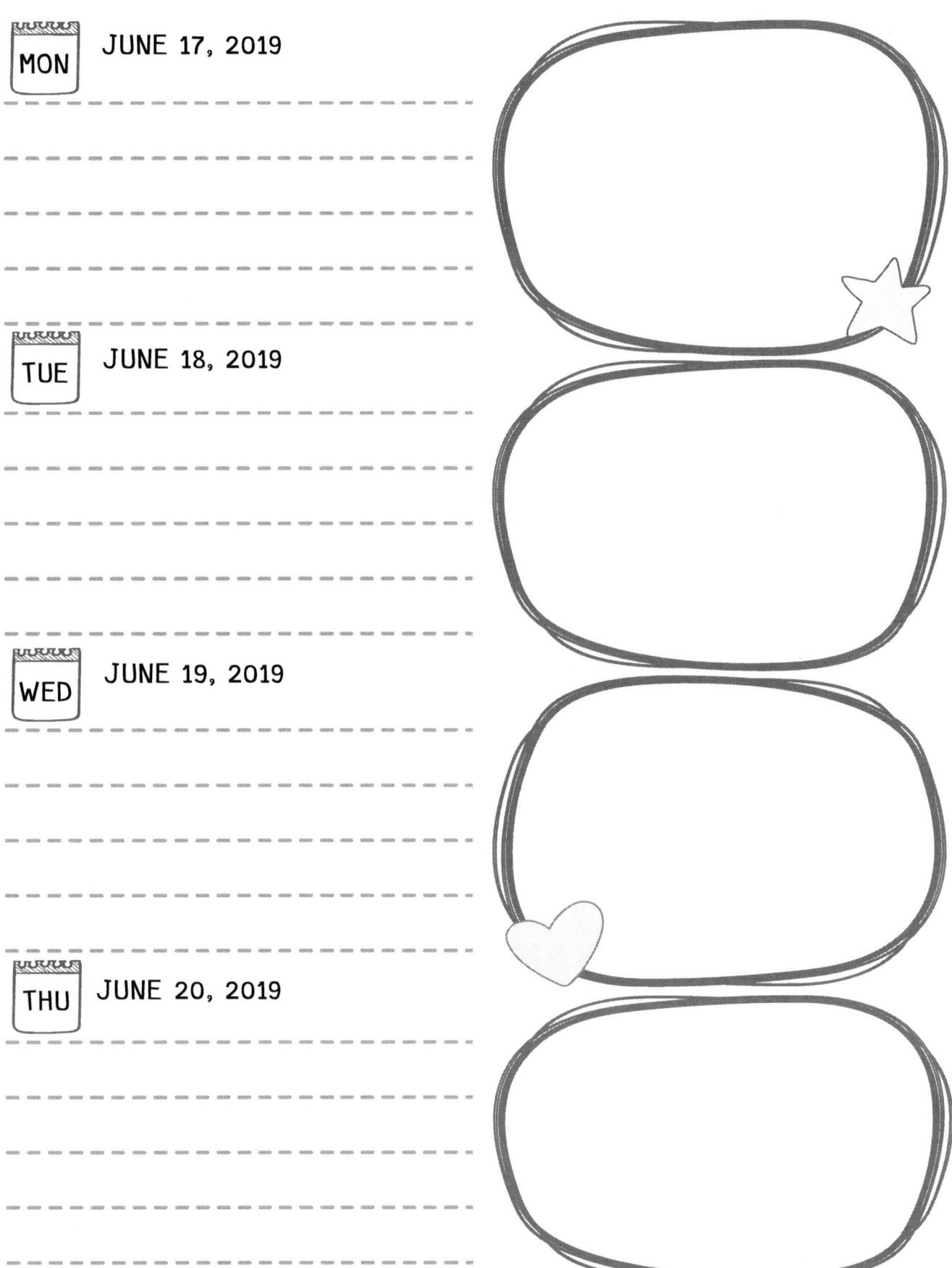

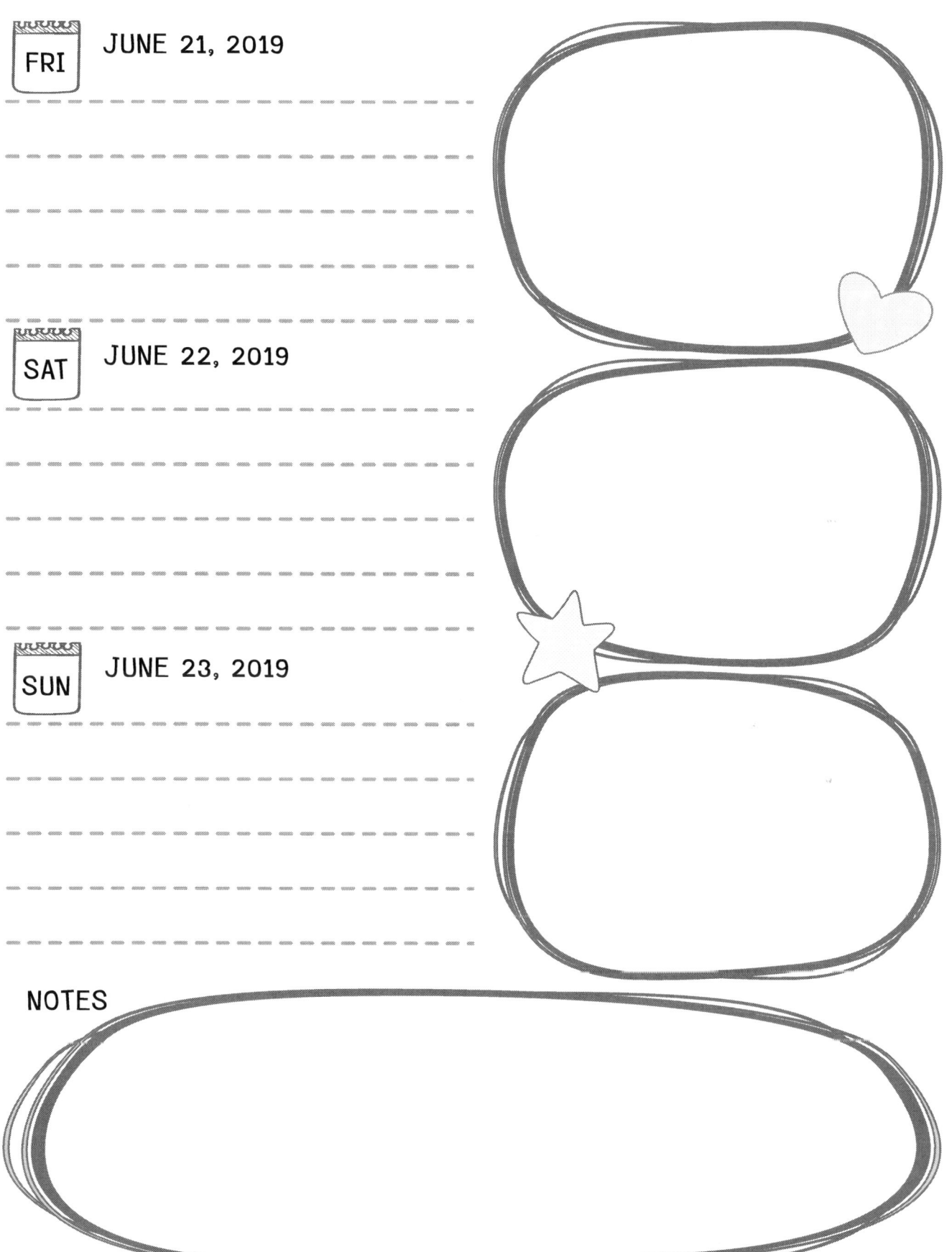

FRI JUNE 21, 2019

SAT JUNE 22, 2019

SUN JUNE 23, 2019

NOTES

MON JUNE 24, 2019

TUE JUNE 25, 2019

WED JUNE 26, 2019

THU JUNE 27, 2019

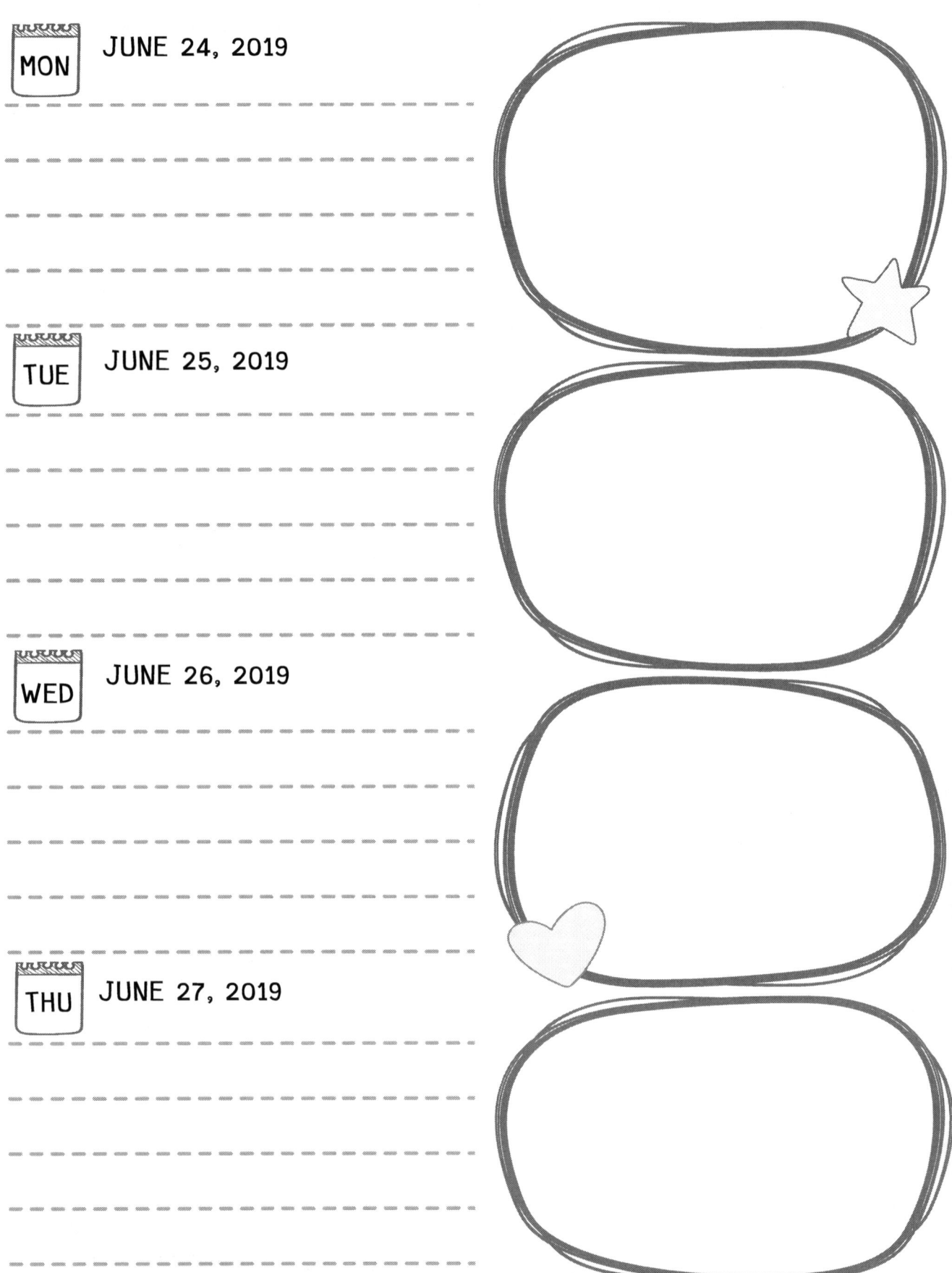

FRI JUNE 28, 2019

SAT JUNE 29, 2019

SUN JUNE 30, 2019

NOTES

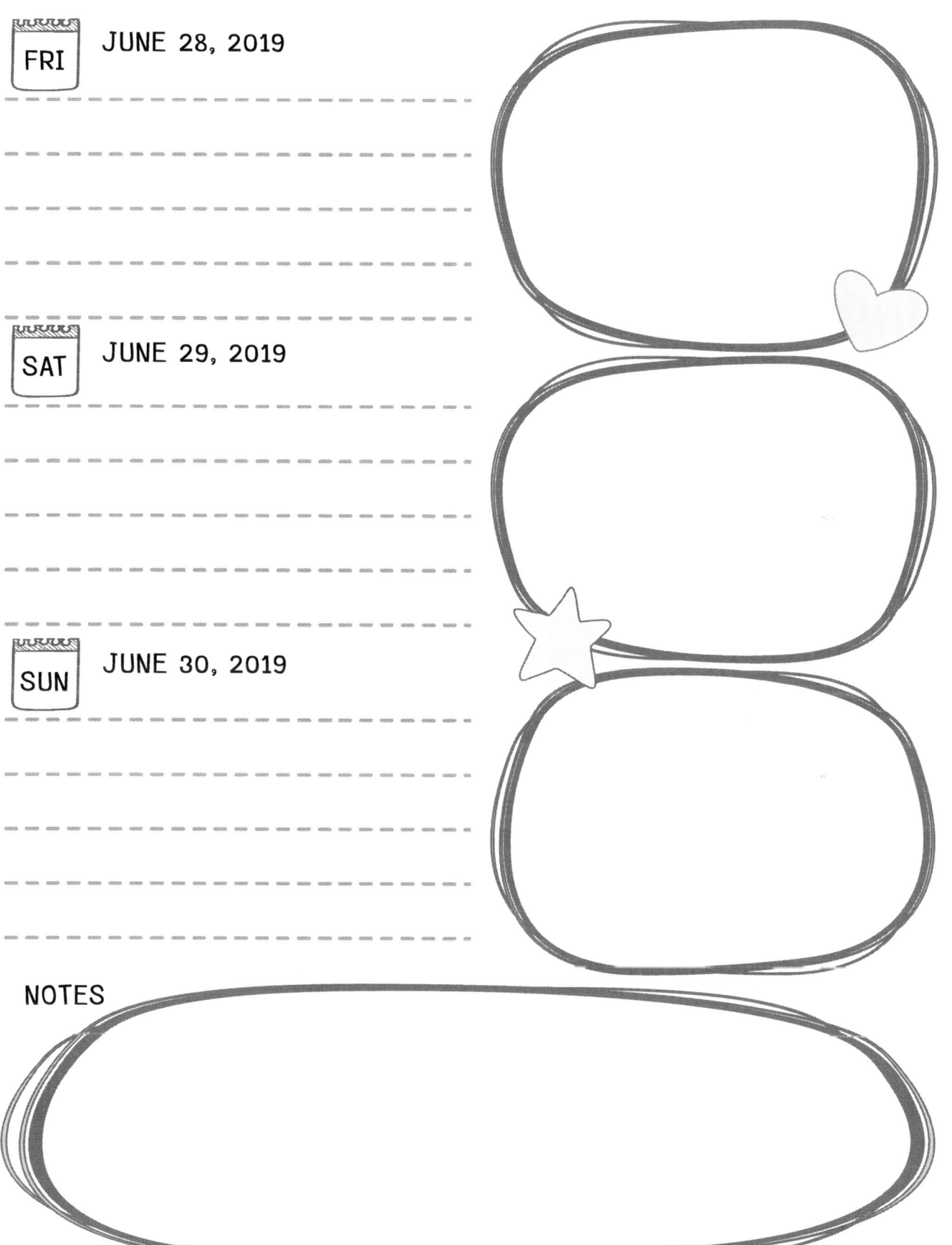

July 2019

Sunday	Monday	Tuesday	Wednesday
30	1	2	3
7	8	9	10
14	15	16	17
21	22	23	24
28	29	30	31

Thursday	Friday	Saturday	
4	5	6	
11	12	13	
18	19	20	
25	26	27	
1	2	3	

MON JULY 1, 2019

TUE JULY 2, 2019

WED JULY 3, 2019

THU JULY 4, 2019

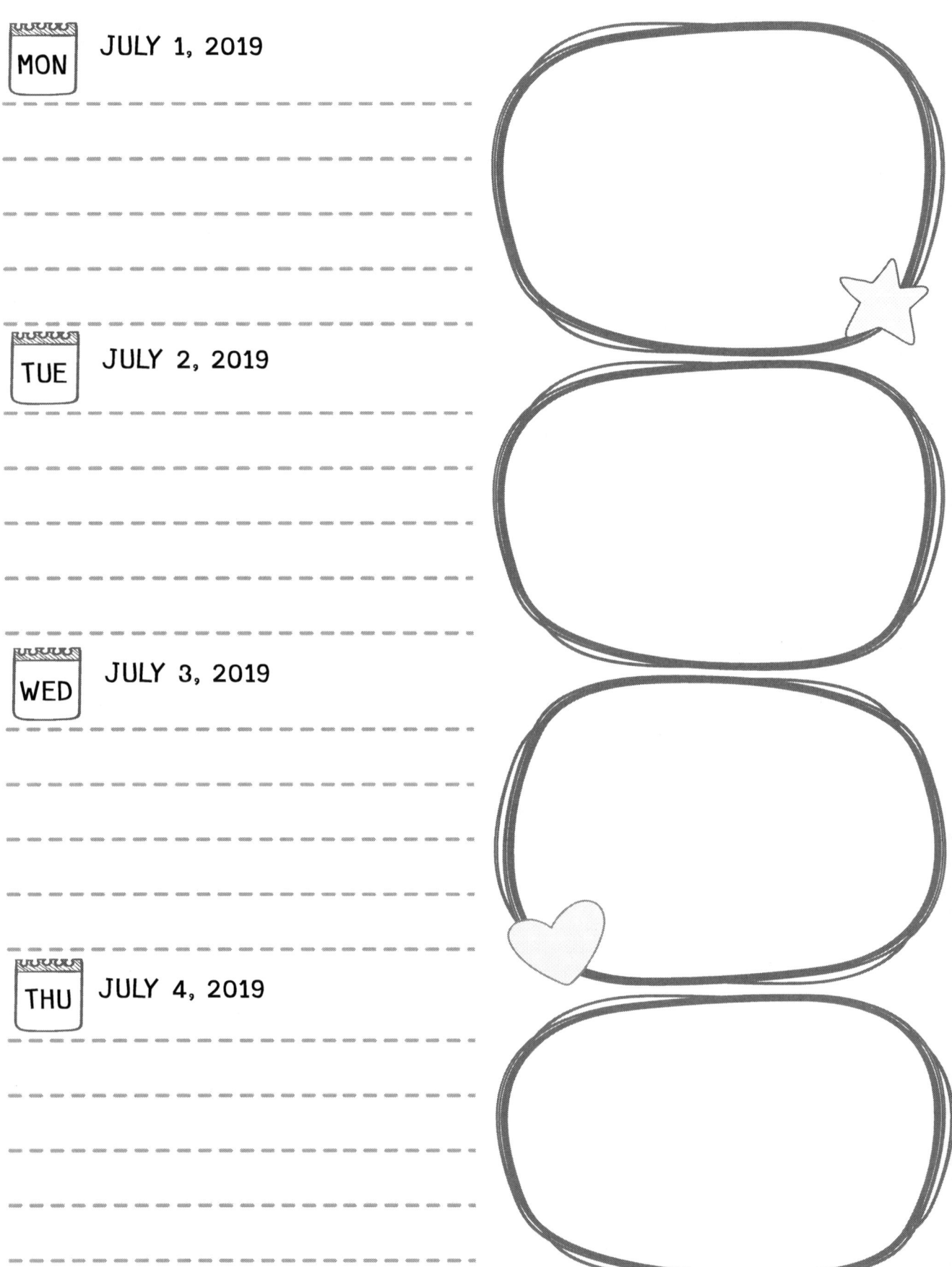

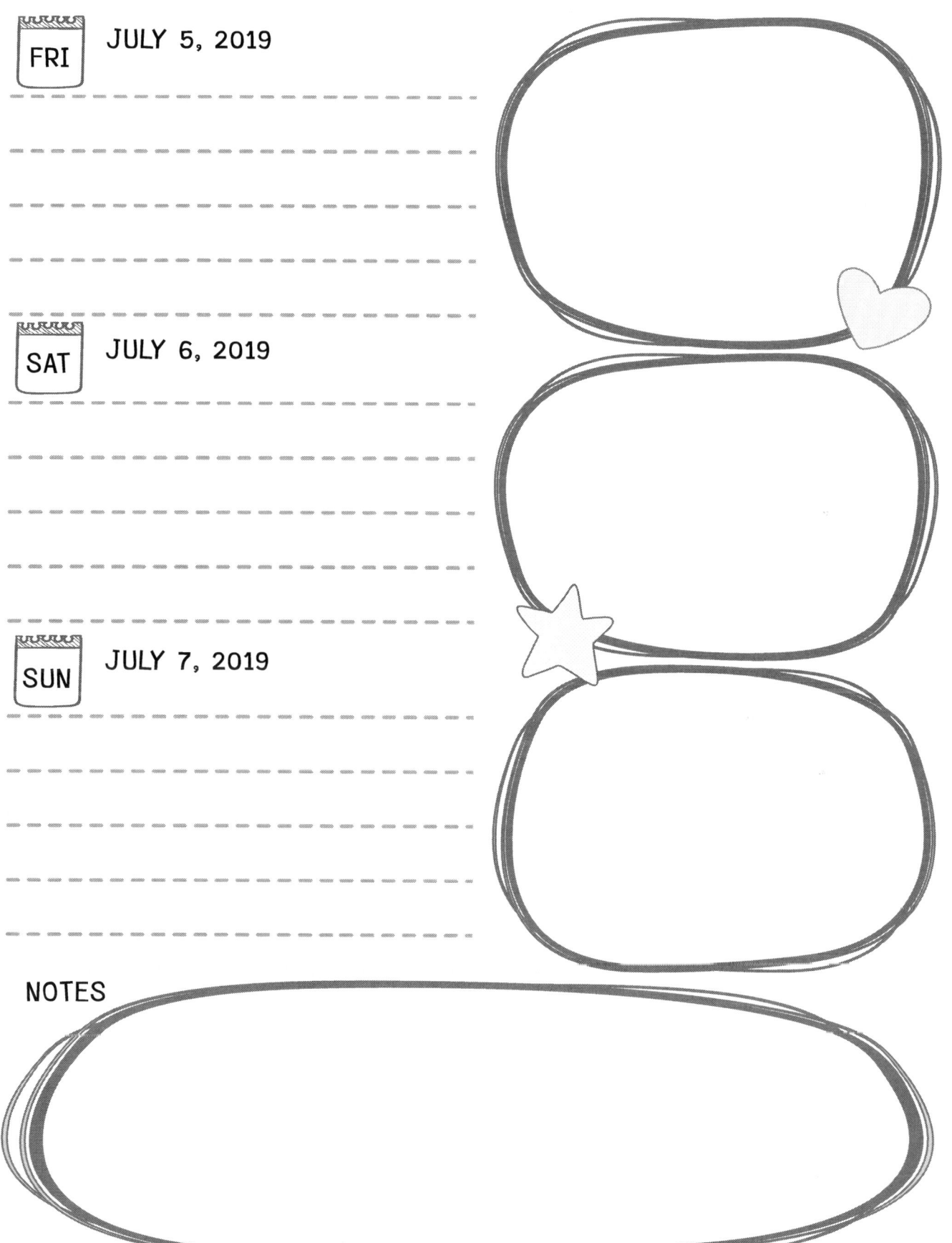

FRI JULY 5, 2019

SAT JULY 6, 2019

SUN JULY 7, 2019

NOTES

MON JULY 8, 2019

TUE JULY 9, 2019

WED JULY 10, 2019

THU JULY 11, 2019

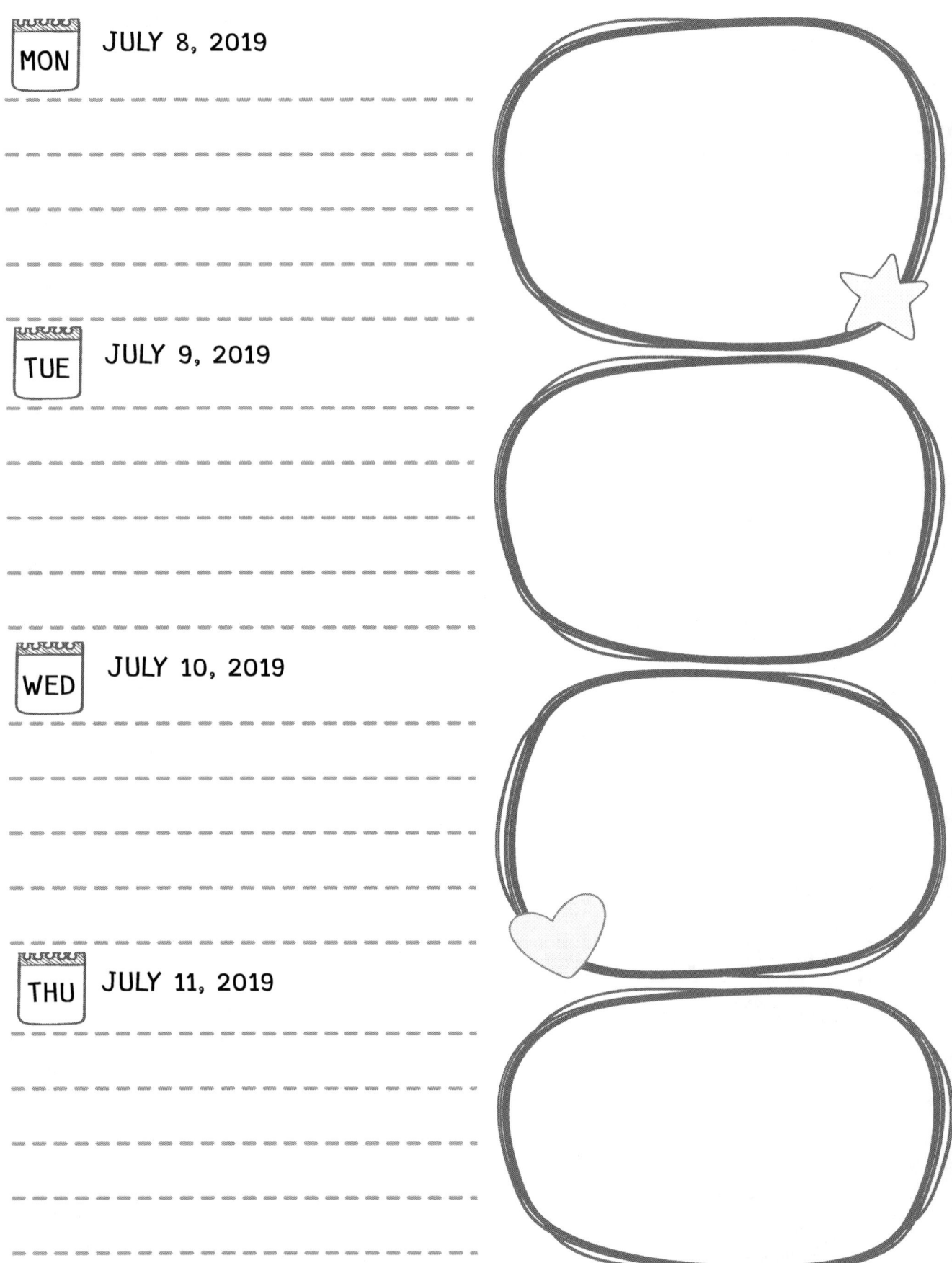

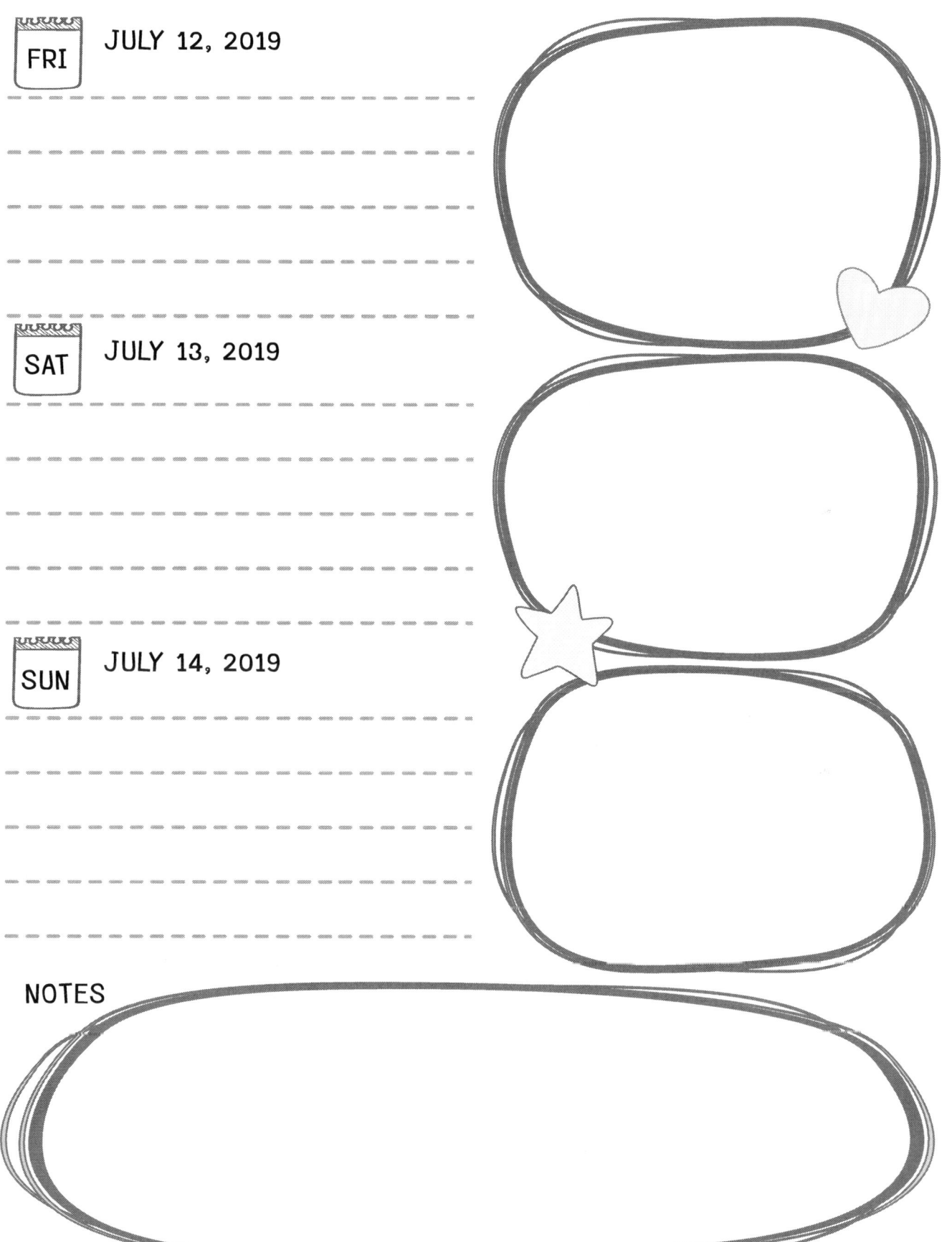

FRI JULY 12, 2019

SAT JULY 13, 2019

SUN JULY 14, 2019

NOTES

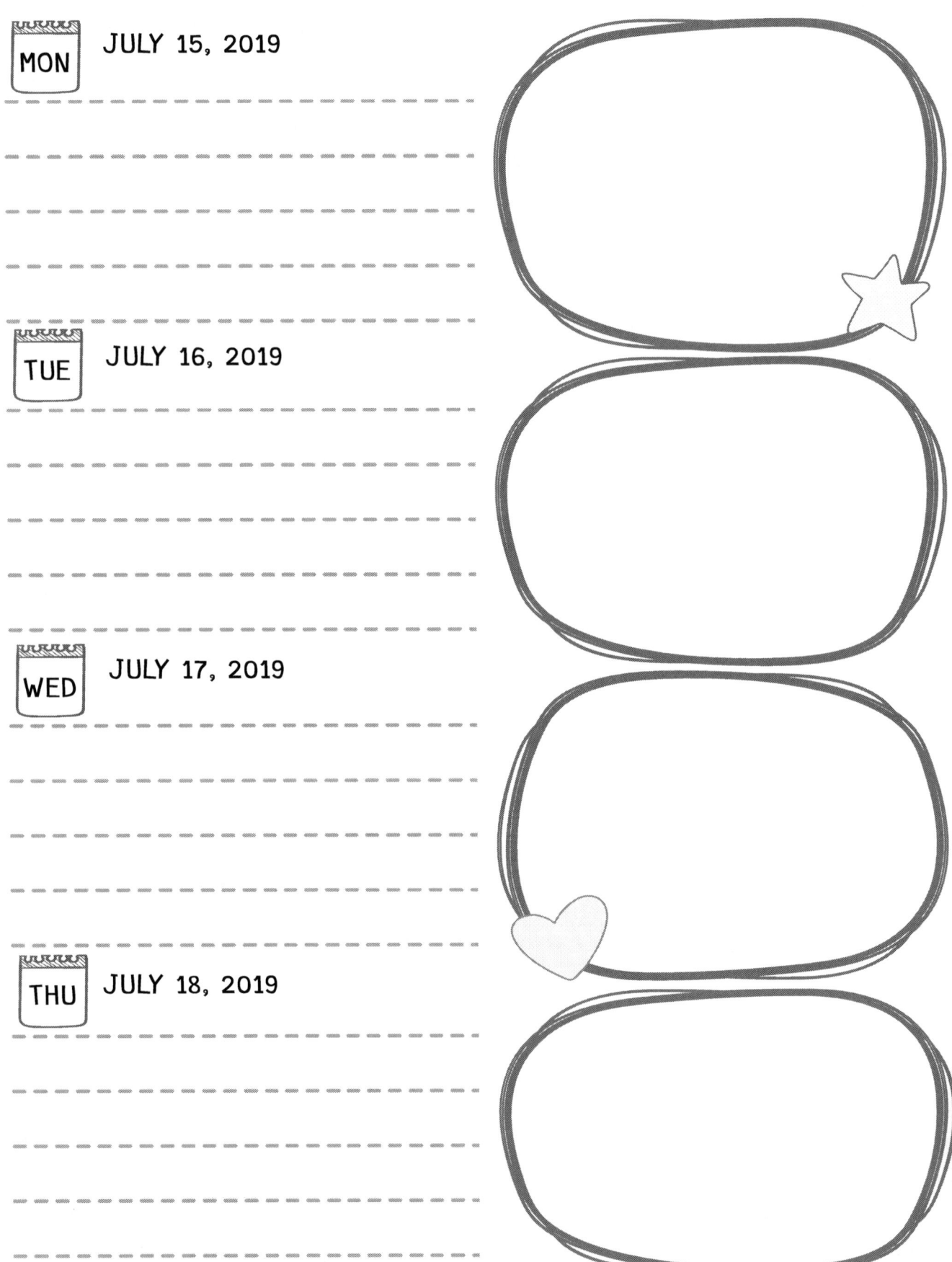

MON JULY 15, 2019

TUE JULY 16, 2019

WED JULY 17, 2019

THU JULY 18, 2019

FRI JULY 19, 2019

SAT JULY 20, 2019

SUN JULY 21, 2019

NOTES

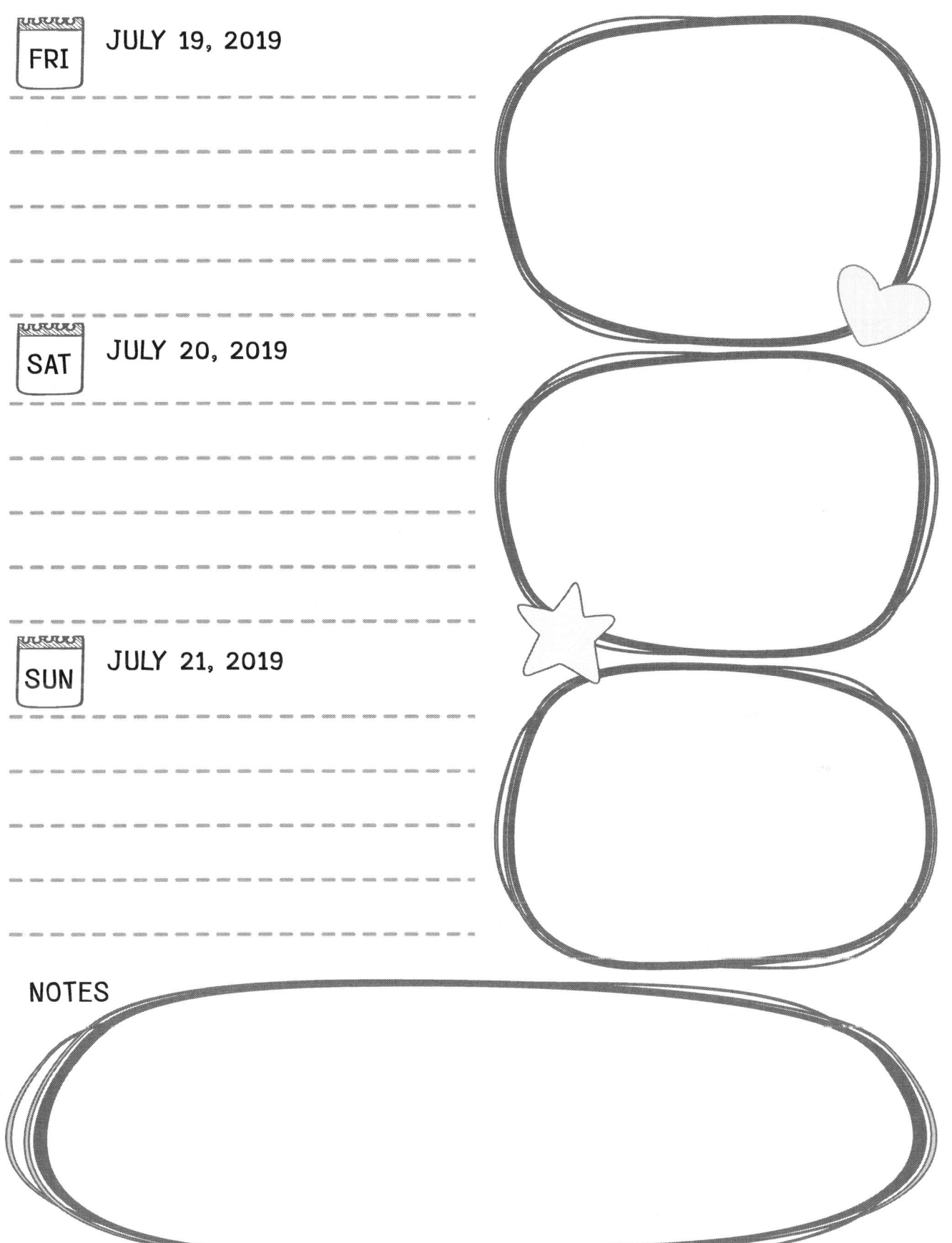

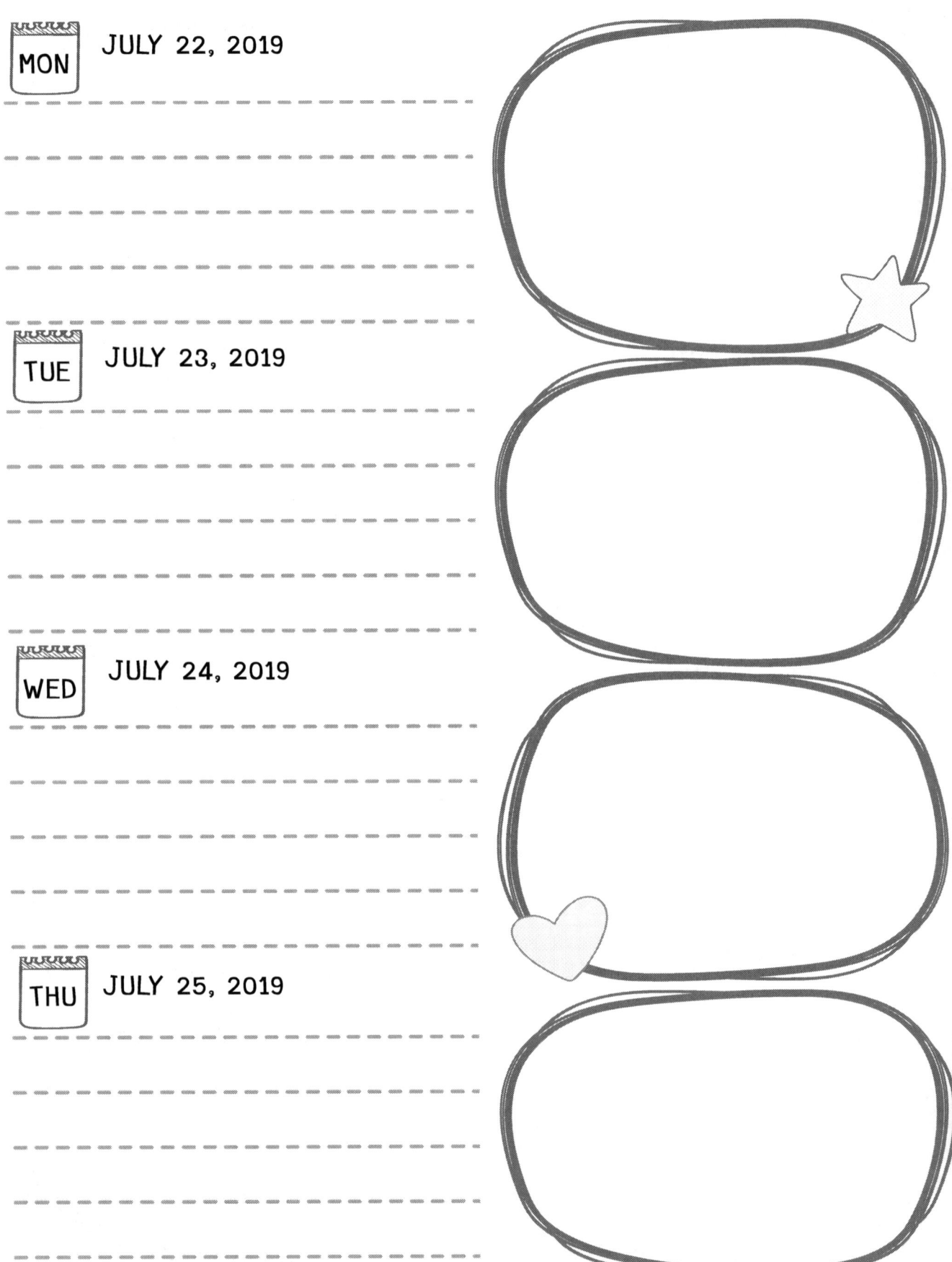

MON   JULY 22, 2019

TUE   JULY 23, 2019

WED   JULY 24, 2019

THU   JULY 25, 2019

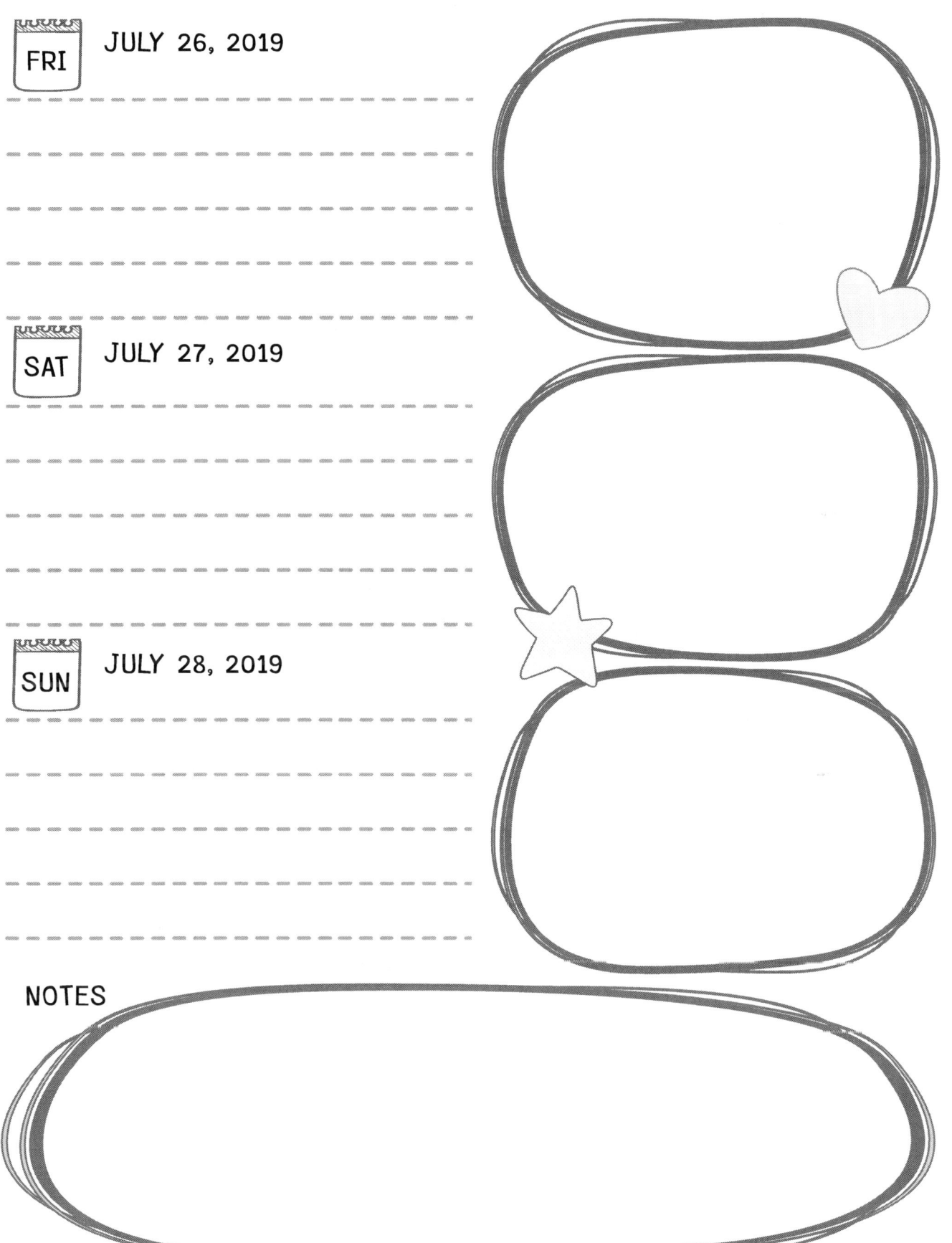

FRI JULY 26, 2019

SAT JULY 27, 2019

SUN JULY 28, 2019

NOTES

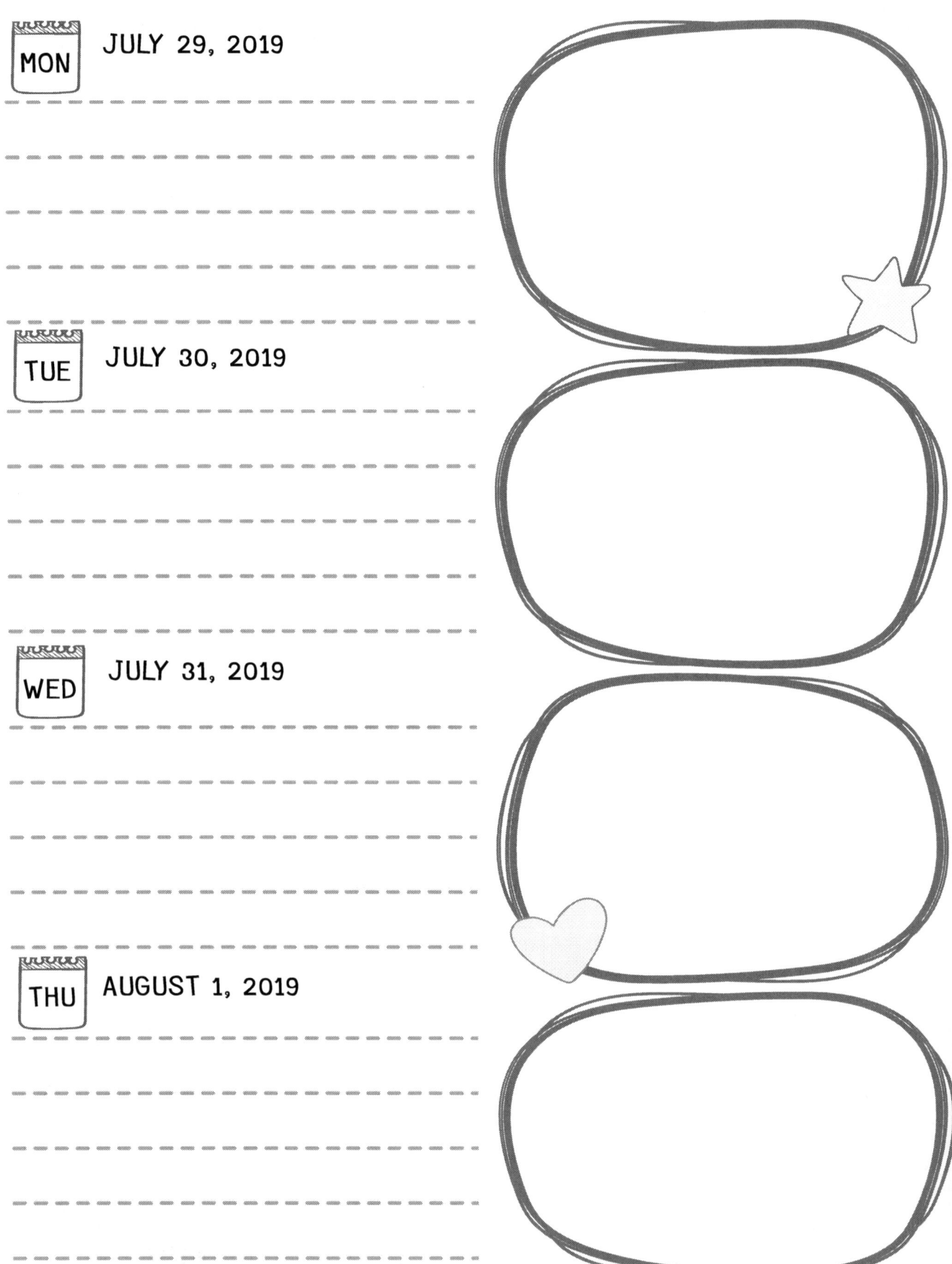

MON   JULY 29, 2019

TUE   JULY 30, 2019

WED   JULY 31, 2019

THU   AUGUST 1, 2019

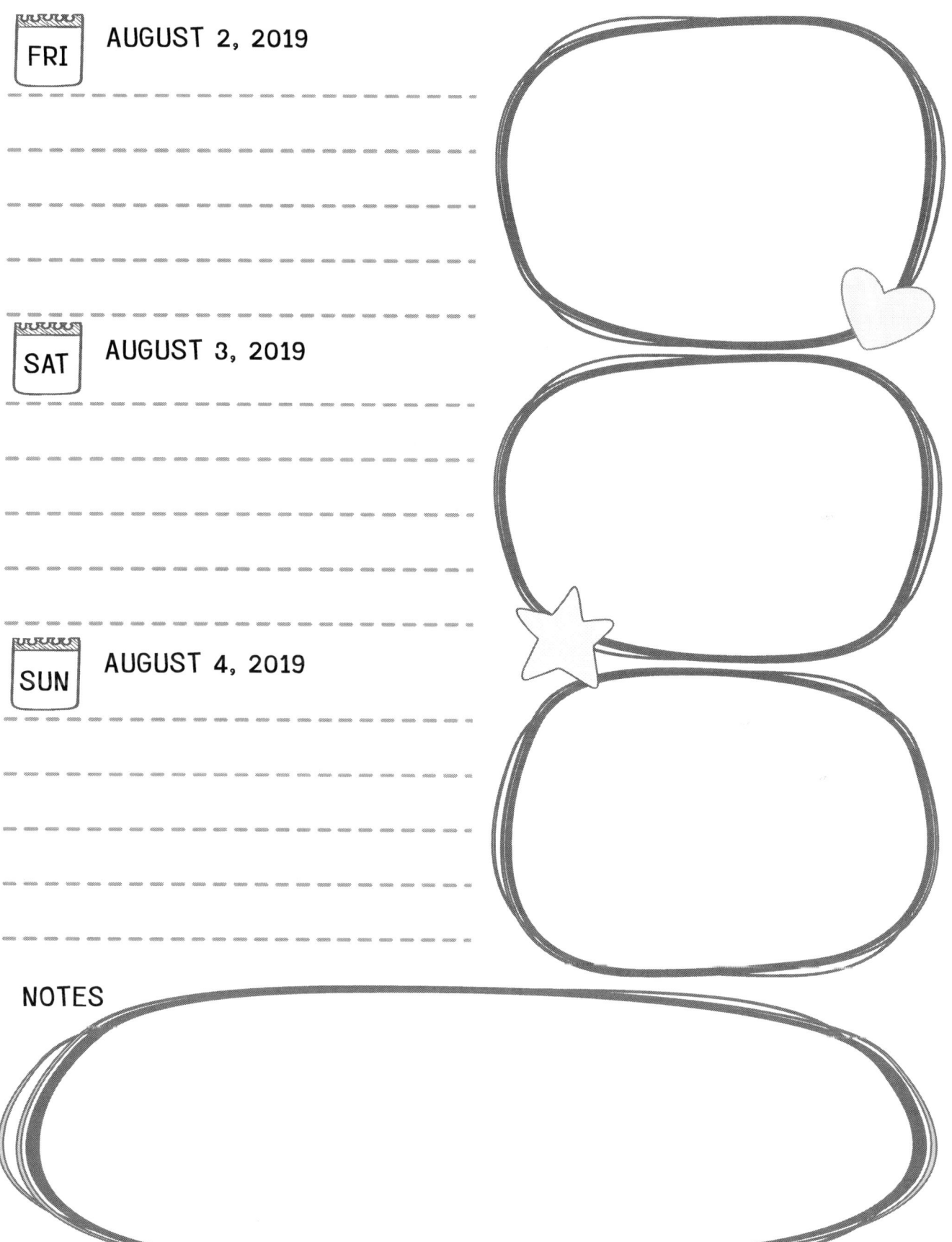

FRI AUGUST 2, 2019

SAT AUGUST 3, 2019

SUN AUGUST 4, 2019

NOTES

August 2019

Sunday	Monday	Tuesday	Wednesday
28	29	30	31
4	5	6	7
11	12	13	14
18	19	20	21
25	26	27	28

Thursday	Friday	Saturday	
1	2	3	
8	9	10	
15	16	17	
22	23	24	
29	30	31	

MON AUGUST 5, 2019

TUE AUGUST 6, 2019

WED AUGUST 7, 2019

THU AUGUST 8, 2019

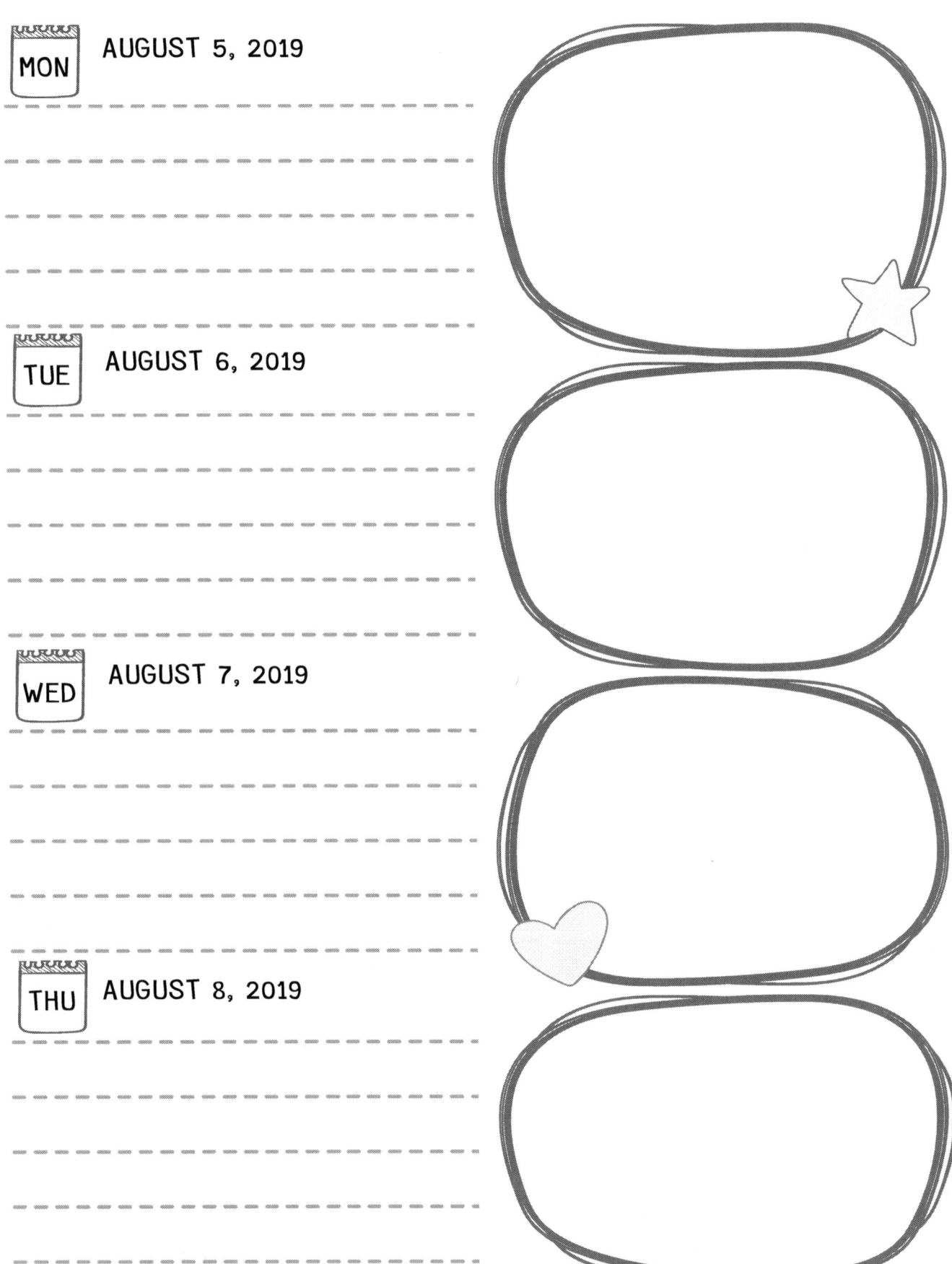

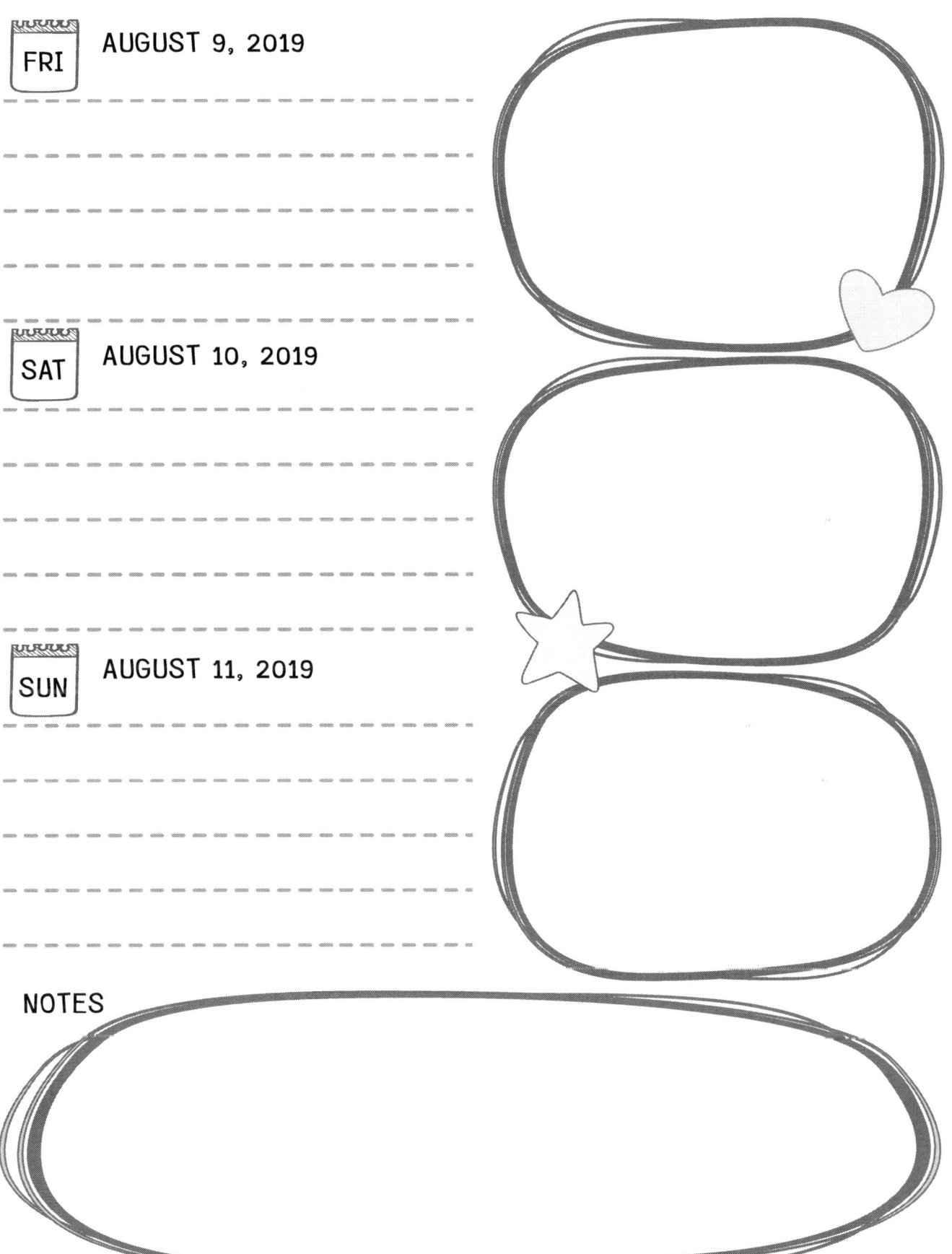

FRI
AUGUST 9, 2019

SAT
AUGUST 10, 2019

SUN
AUGUST 11, 2019

NOTES

MON AUGUST 12, 2019

TUE AUGUST 13, 2019

WED AUGUST 14, 2019

THU AUGUST 15, 2019

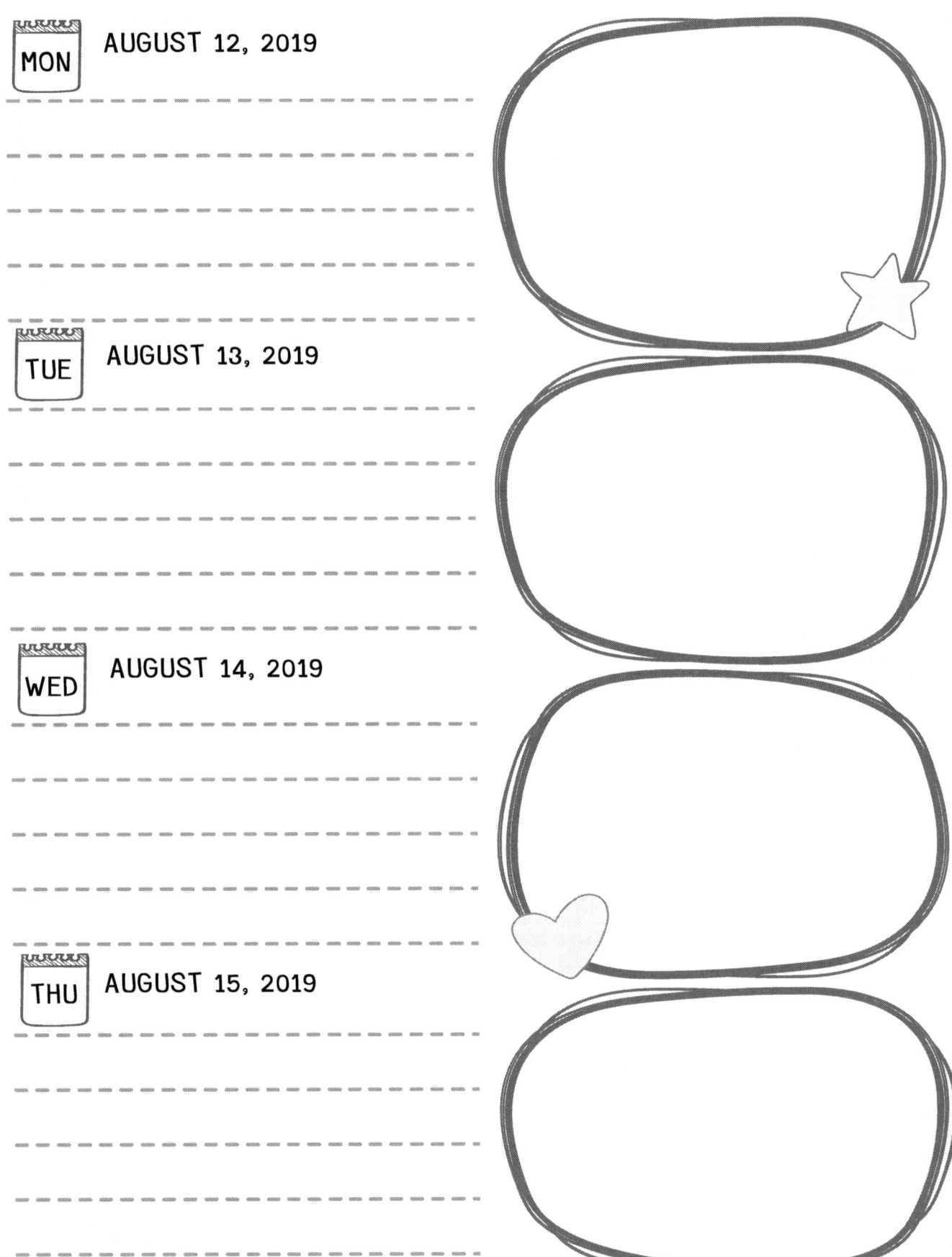

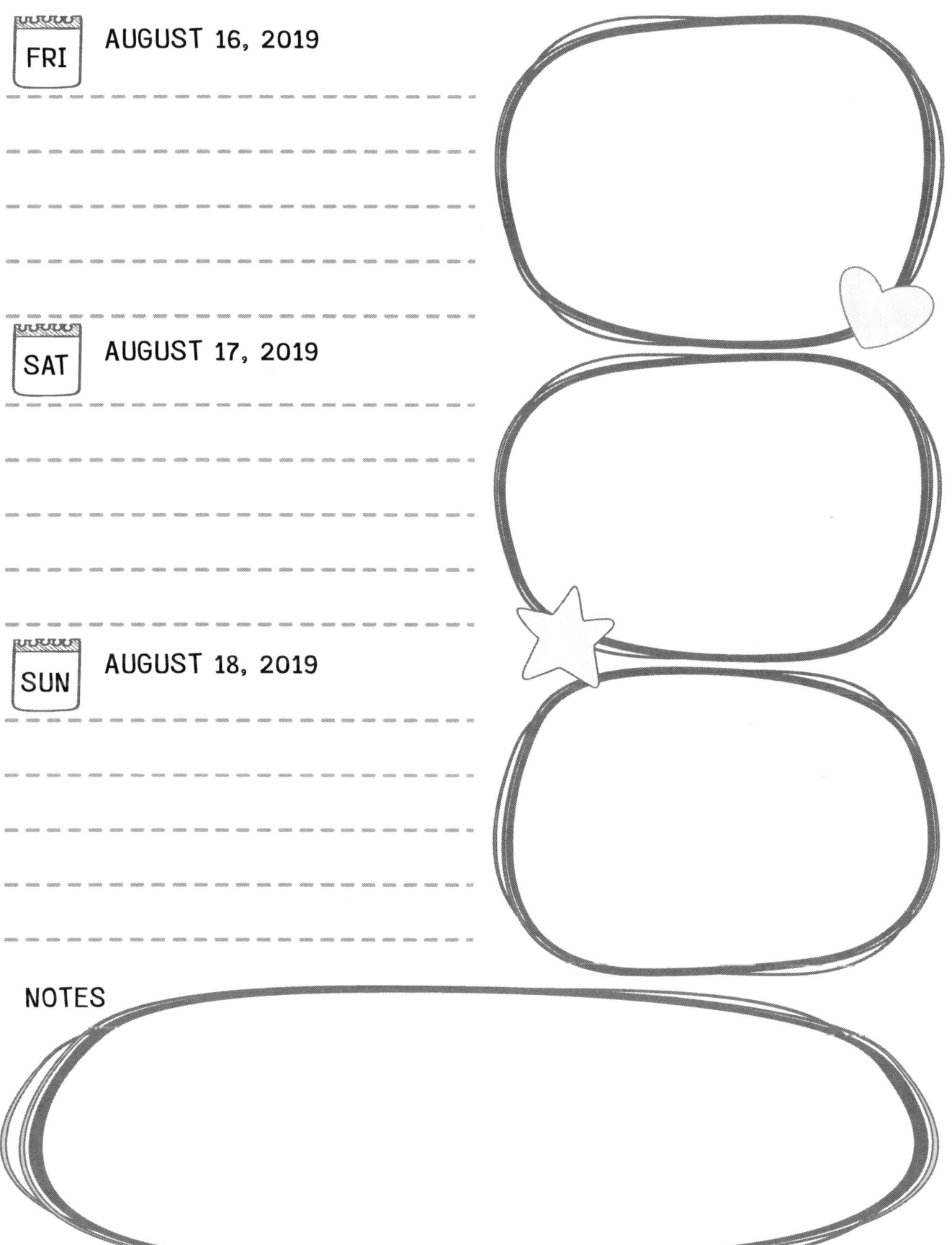

FRI AUGUST 16, 2019

SAT AUGUST 17, 2019

SUN AUGUST 18, 2019

NOTES

MON AUGUST 19, 2019

TUE AUGUST 20, 2019

WED AUGUST 21, 2019

THU AUGUST 22, 2019

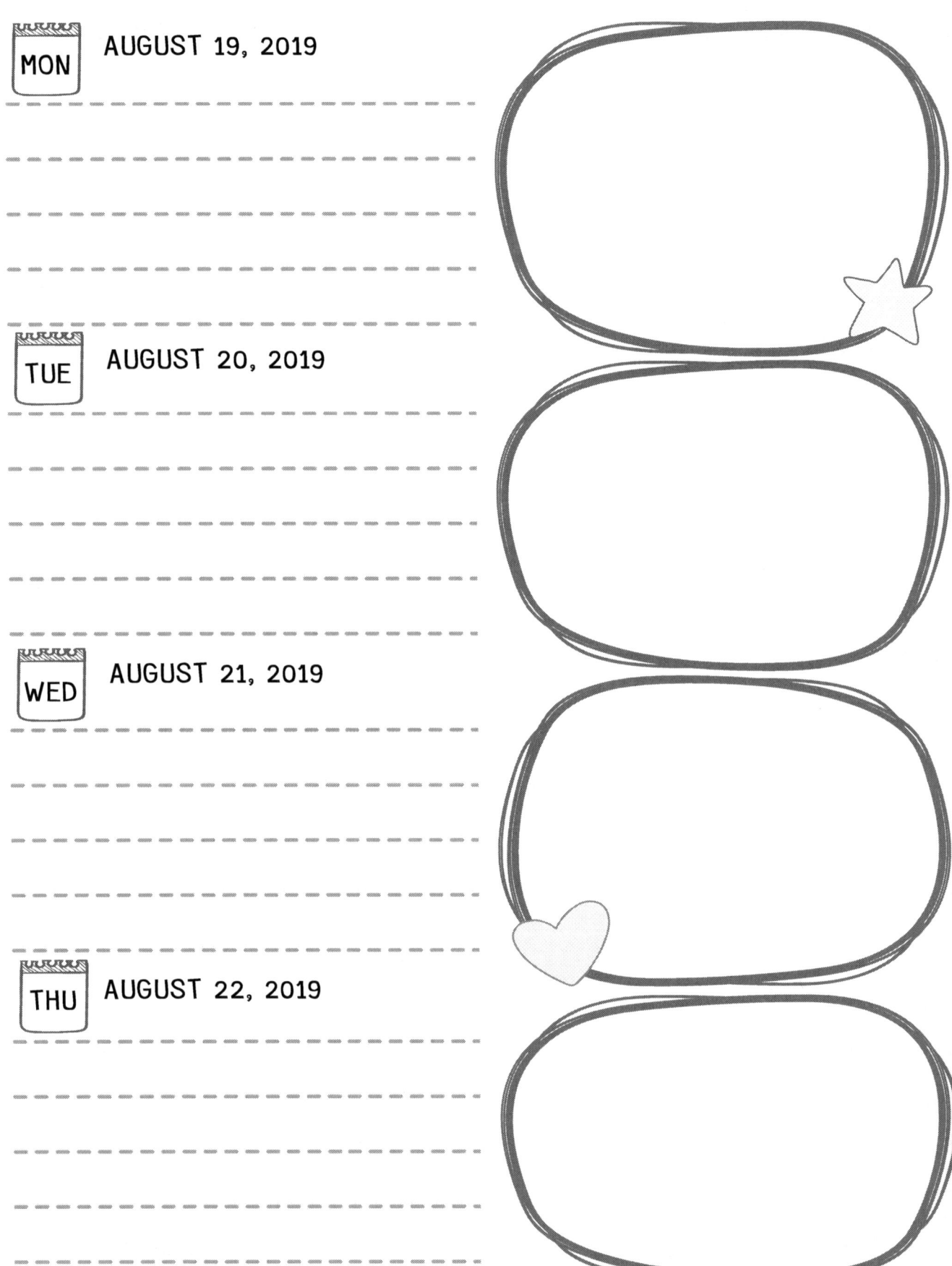

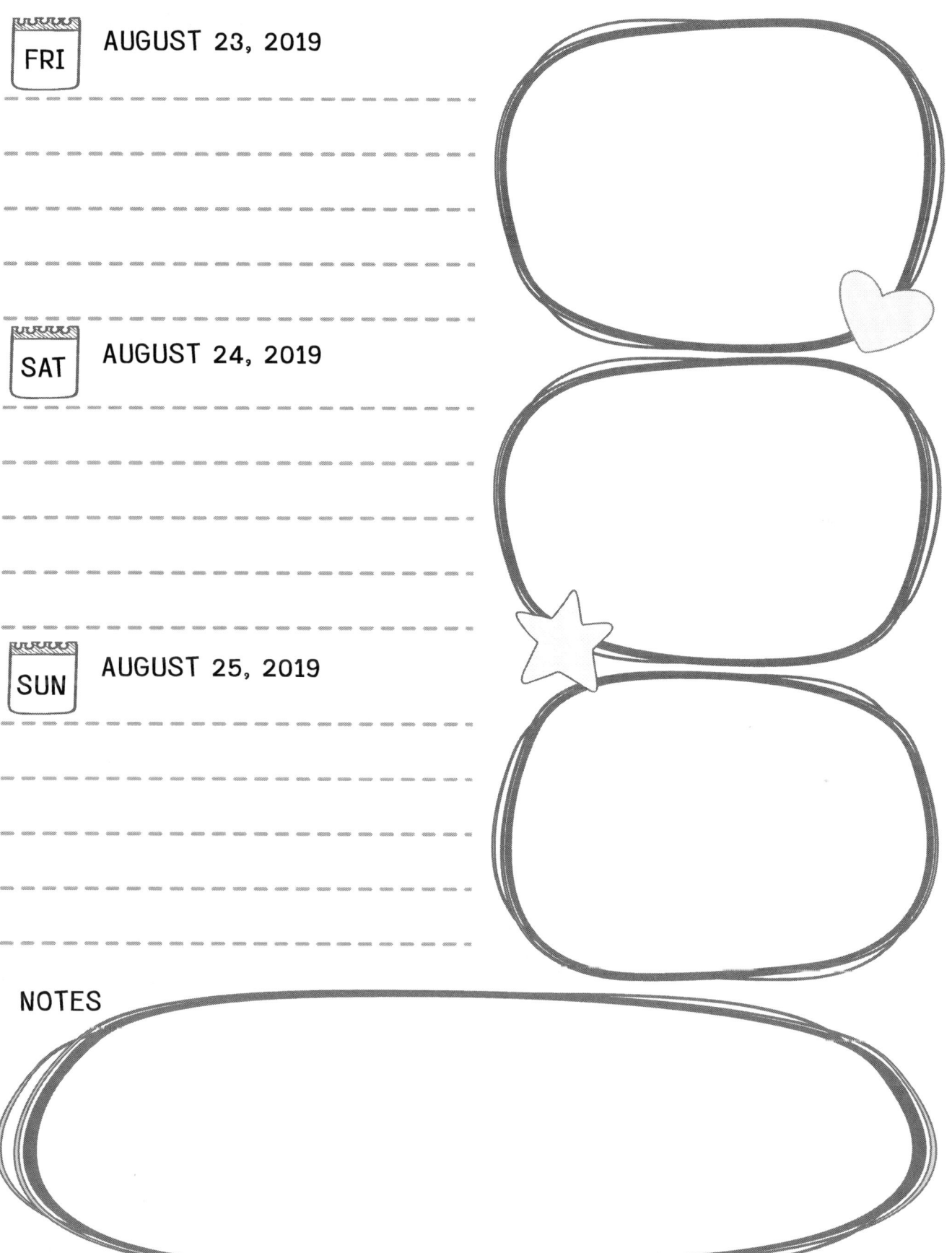

FRI AUGUST 23, 2019

SAT AUGUST 24, 2019

SUN AUGUST 25, 2019

NOTES

MON AUGUST 26, 2019

TUE AUGUST 27, 2019

WED AUGUST 28, 2019

THU AUGUST 29, 2019

FRI AUGUST 30, 2019

SAT AUGUST 31, 2019

SUN SEPTEMBER 1, 2019

NOTES

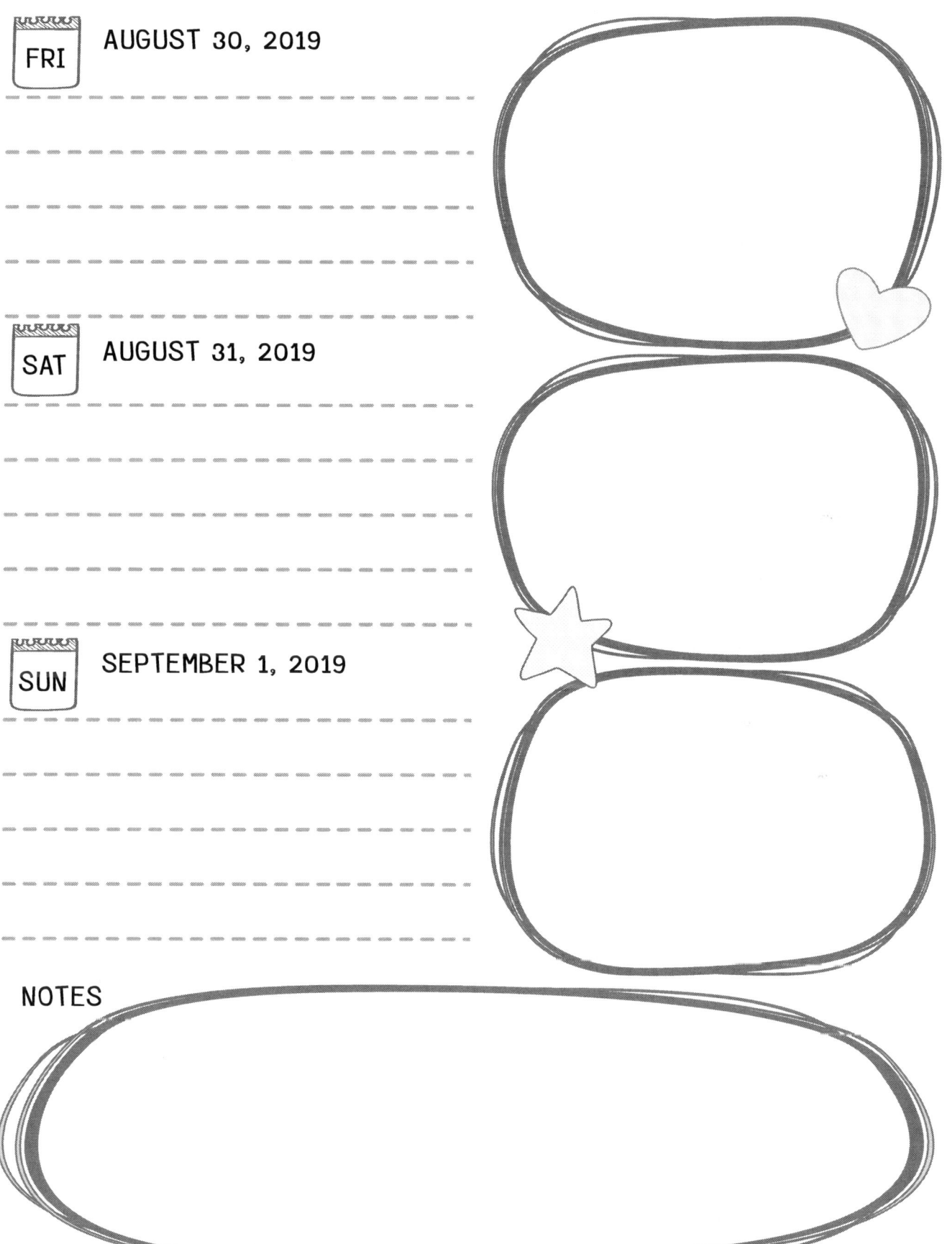

September 2019

Sunday	Monday	Tuesday	Wednesday
1	2	3	4
8	9	10	11
15	16	17	18
22	23	24	25
29	30	1	2

Thursday	Friday	Saturday	
5	6	7	
12	13	14	
19	20	21	
26	27	28	
3	4	5	

MON SEPTEMBER 2, 2019

TUE SEPTEMBER 3, 2019

WED SEPTEMBER 4, 2019

THU SEPTEMBER 5, 2019

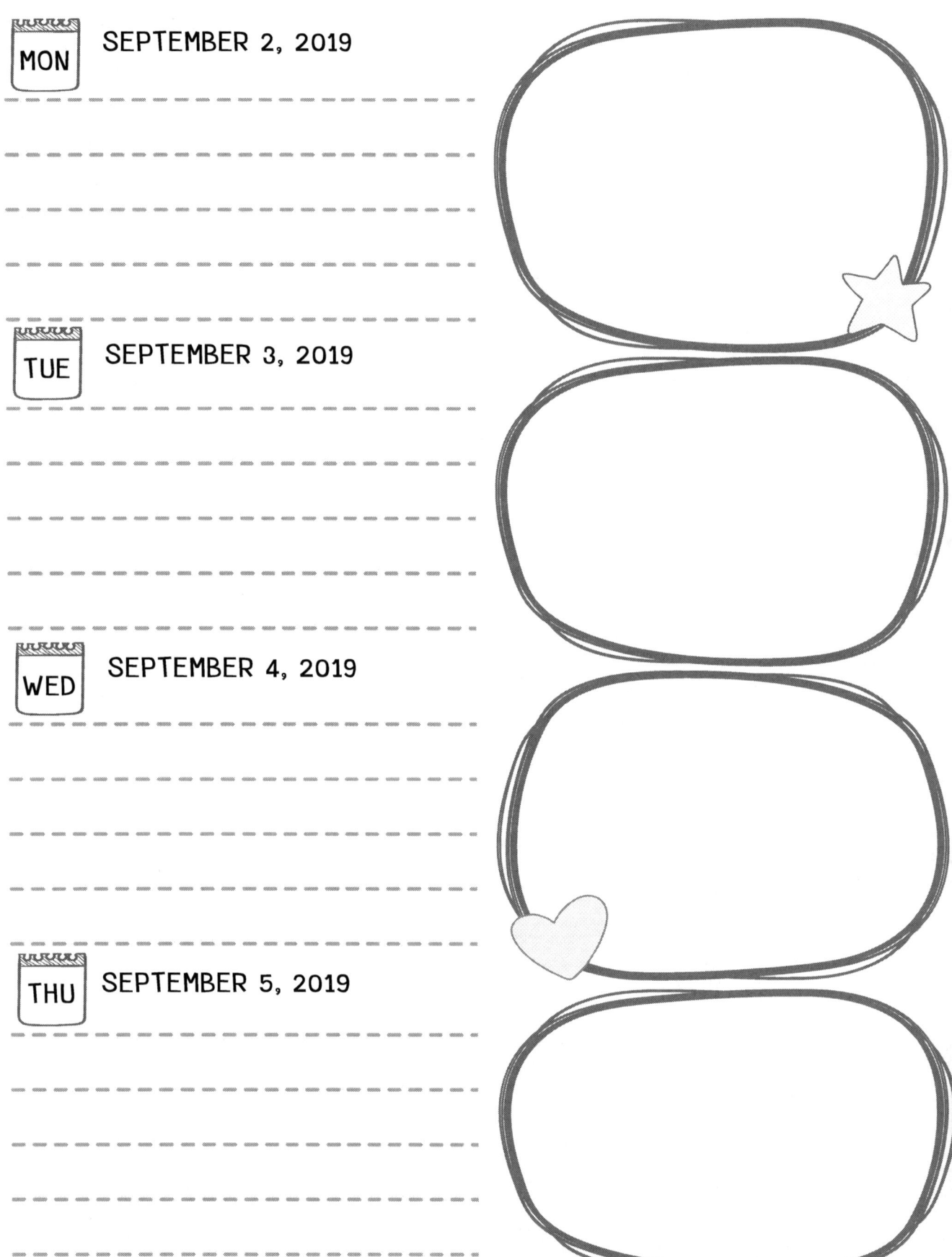

FRI **SEPTEMBER 6, 2019**

SAT **SEPTEMBER 7, 2019**

SUN **SEPTEMBER 8, 2019**

NOTES

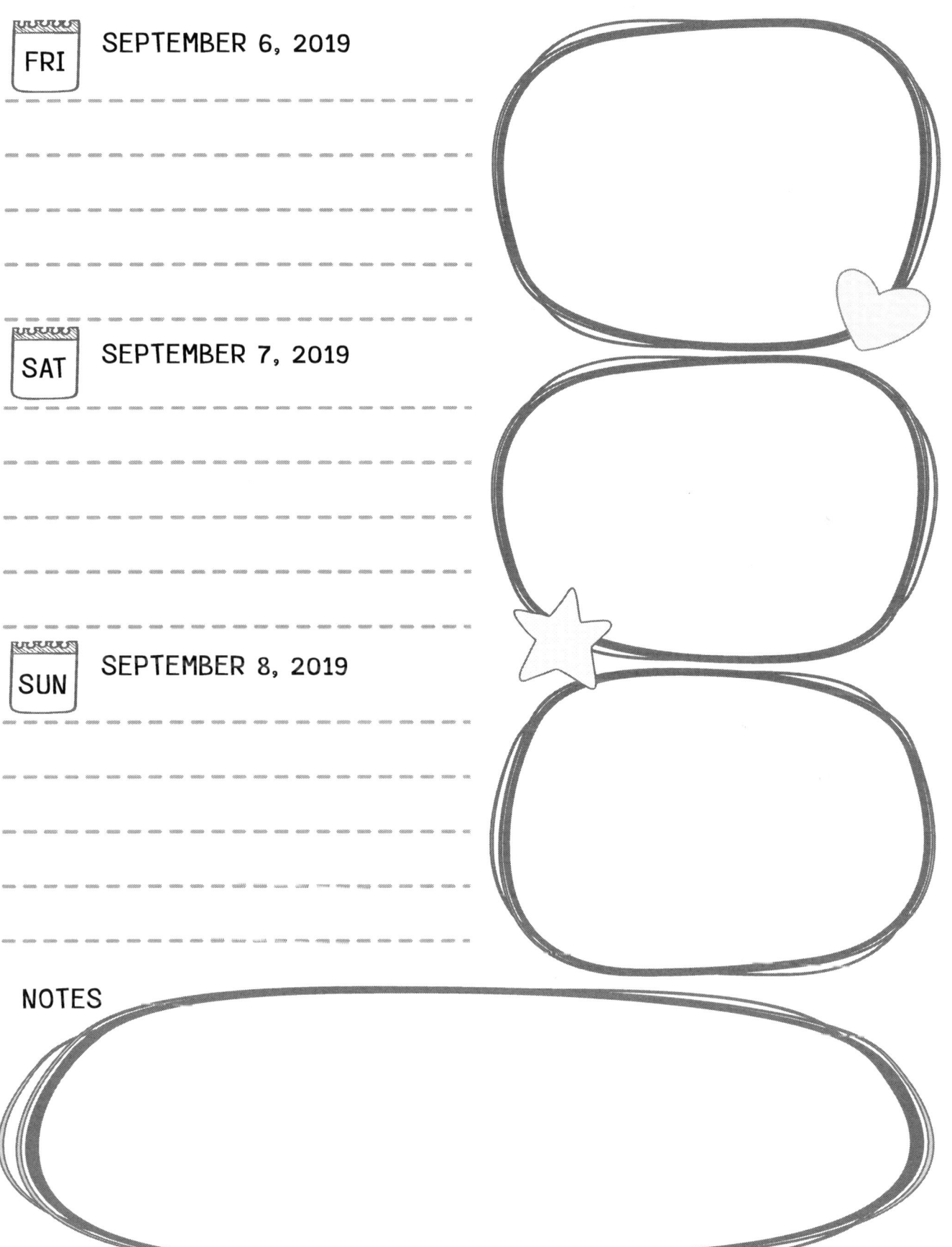

MON SEPTEMBER 9, 2019

TUE SEPTEMBER 10, 2019

WED SEPTEMBER 11, 2019

THU SEPTEMBER 12, 2019

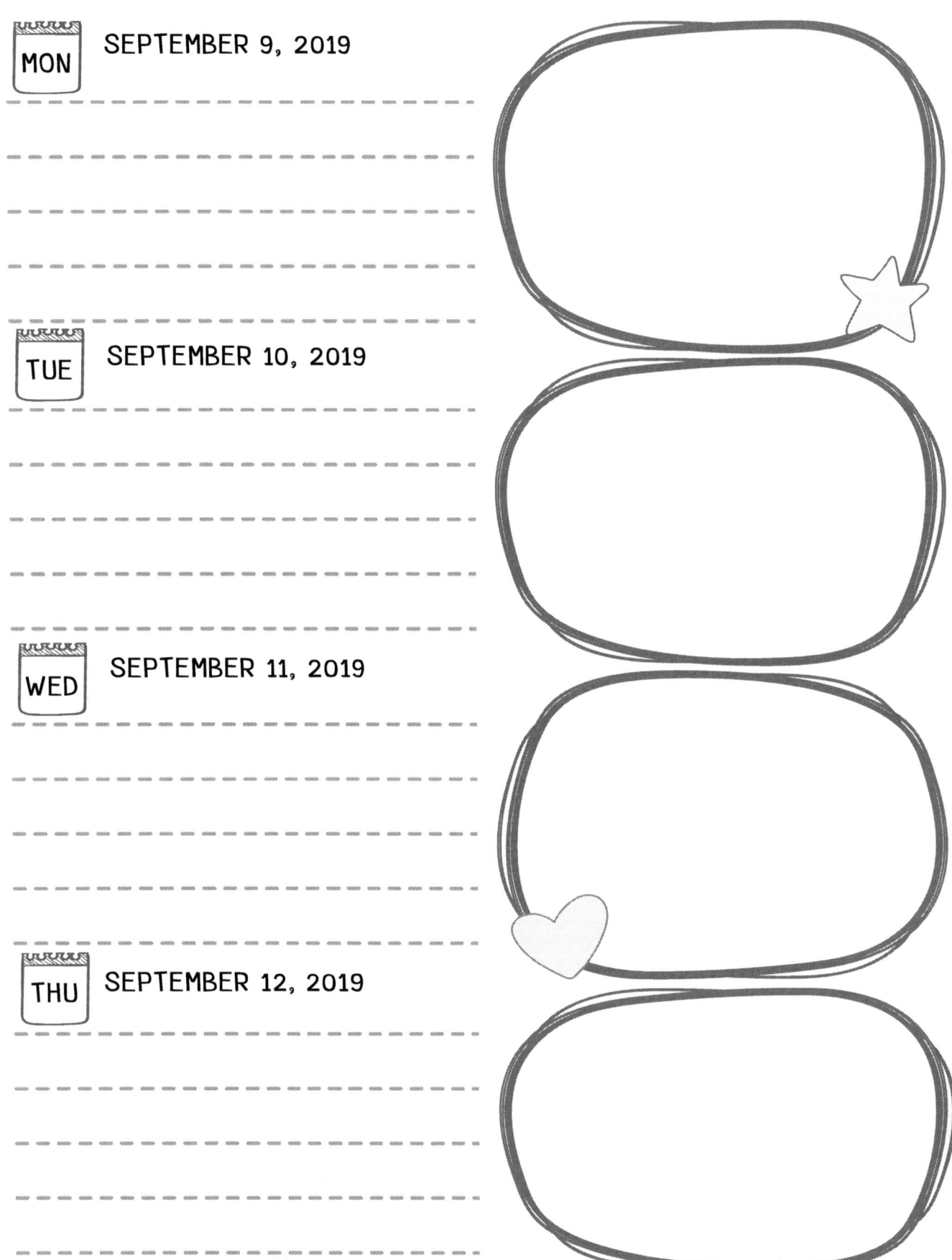

FRI SEPTEMBER 13, 2019

SAT SEPTEMBER 14, 2019

SUN SEPTEMBER 15, 2019

NOTES

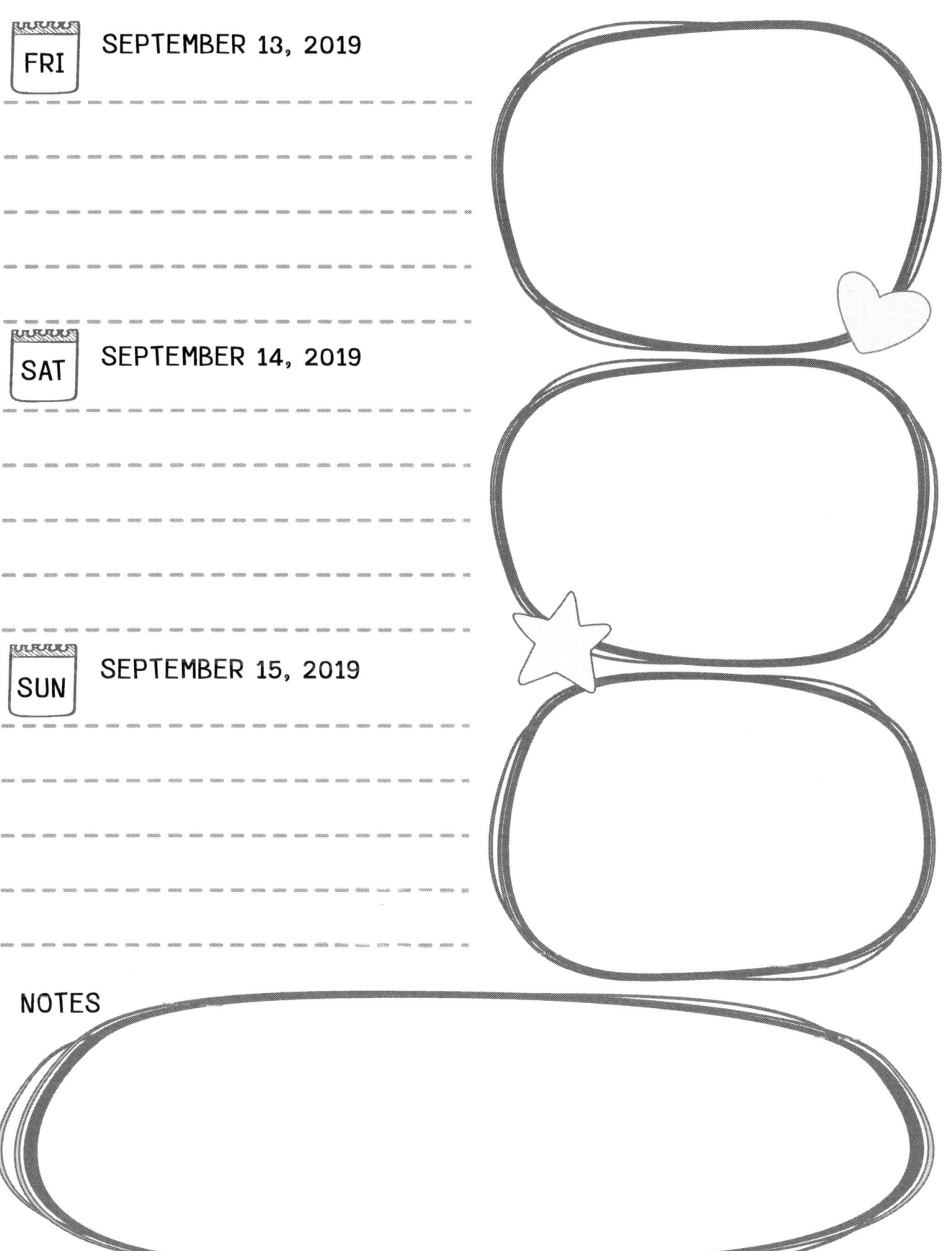

MON SEPTEMBER 16, 2019

TUE SEPTEMBER 17, 2019

WED SEPTEMBER 18, 2019

THU SEPTEMBER 19, 2019

FRI SEPTEMBER 20, 2019

SAT SEPTEMBER 21, 2019

SUN SEPTEMBER 22, 2019

NOTES

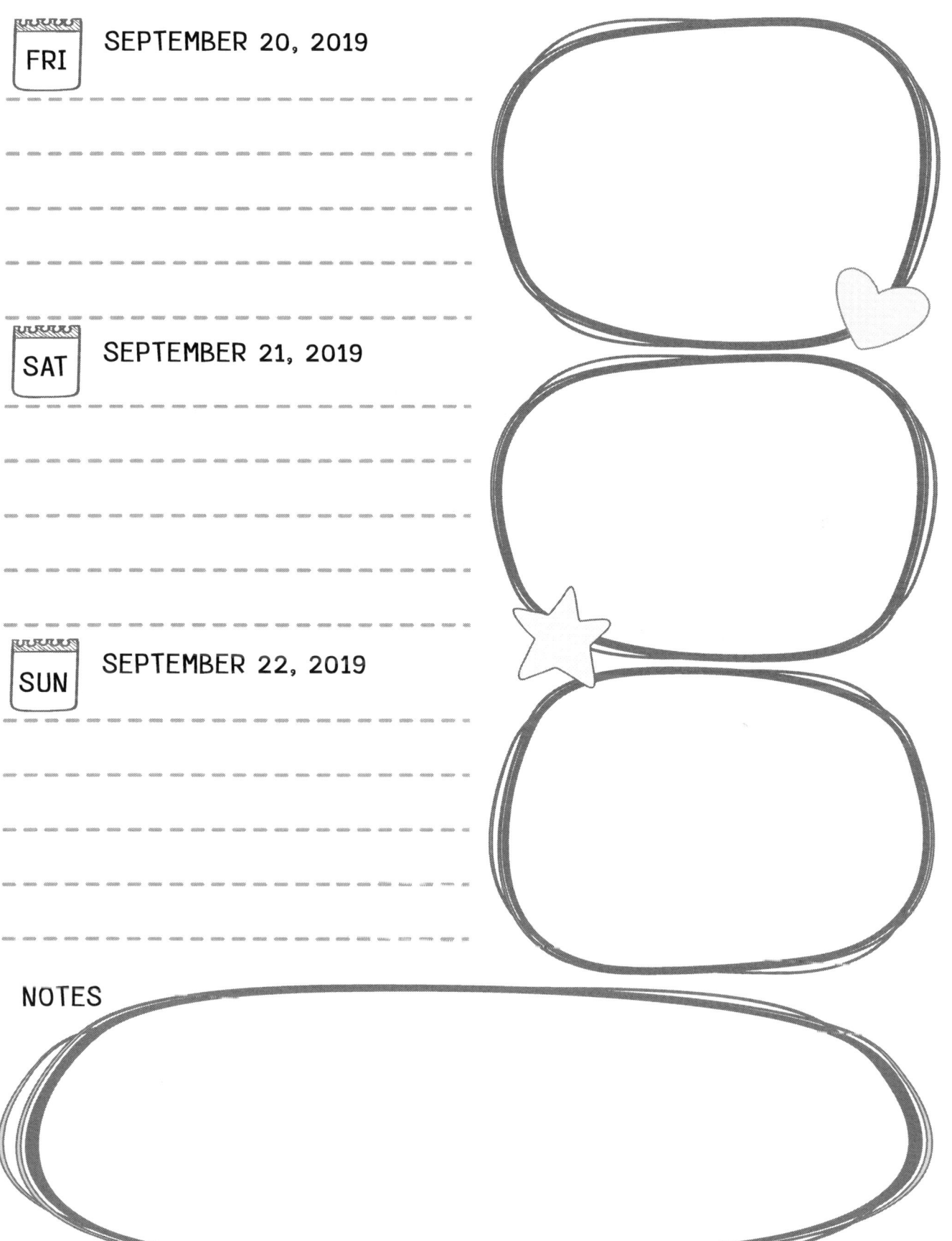

MON SEPTEMBER 23, 2019

TUE SEPTEMBER 24, 2019

WED SEPTEMBER 25, 2019

THU SEPTEMBER 26, 2019

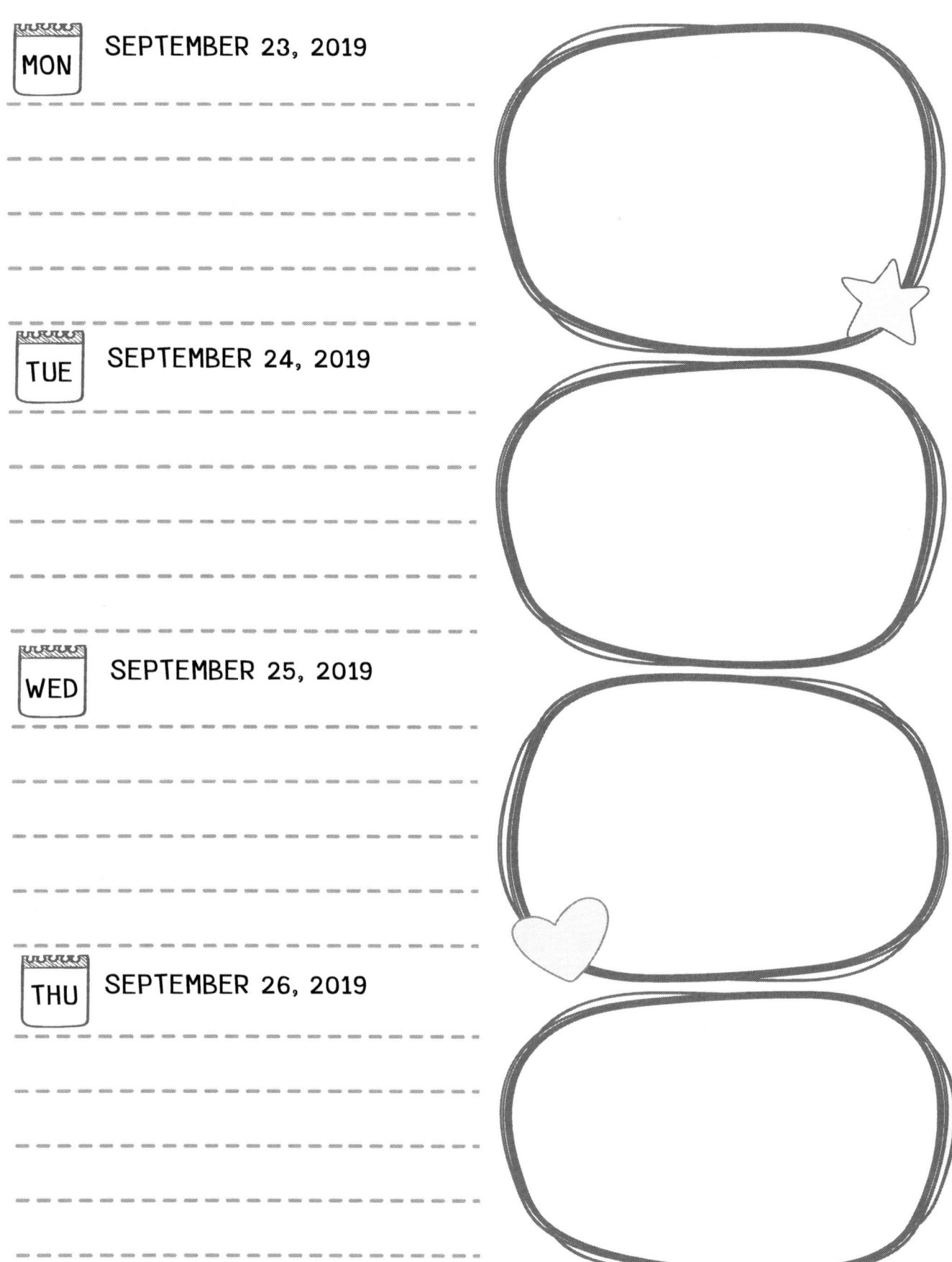

FRI SEPTEMBER 27, 2019

SAT SEPTEMBER 28, 2019

SUN SEPTEMBER 29, 2019

NOTES

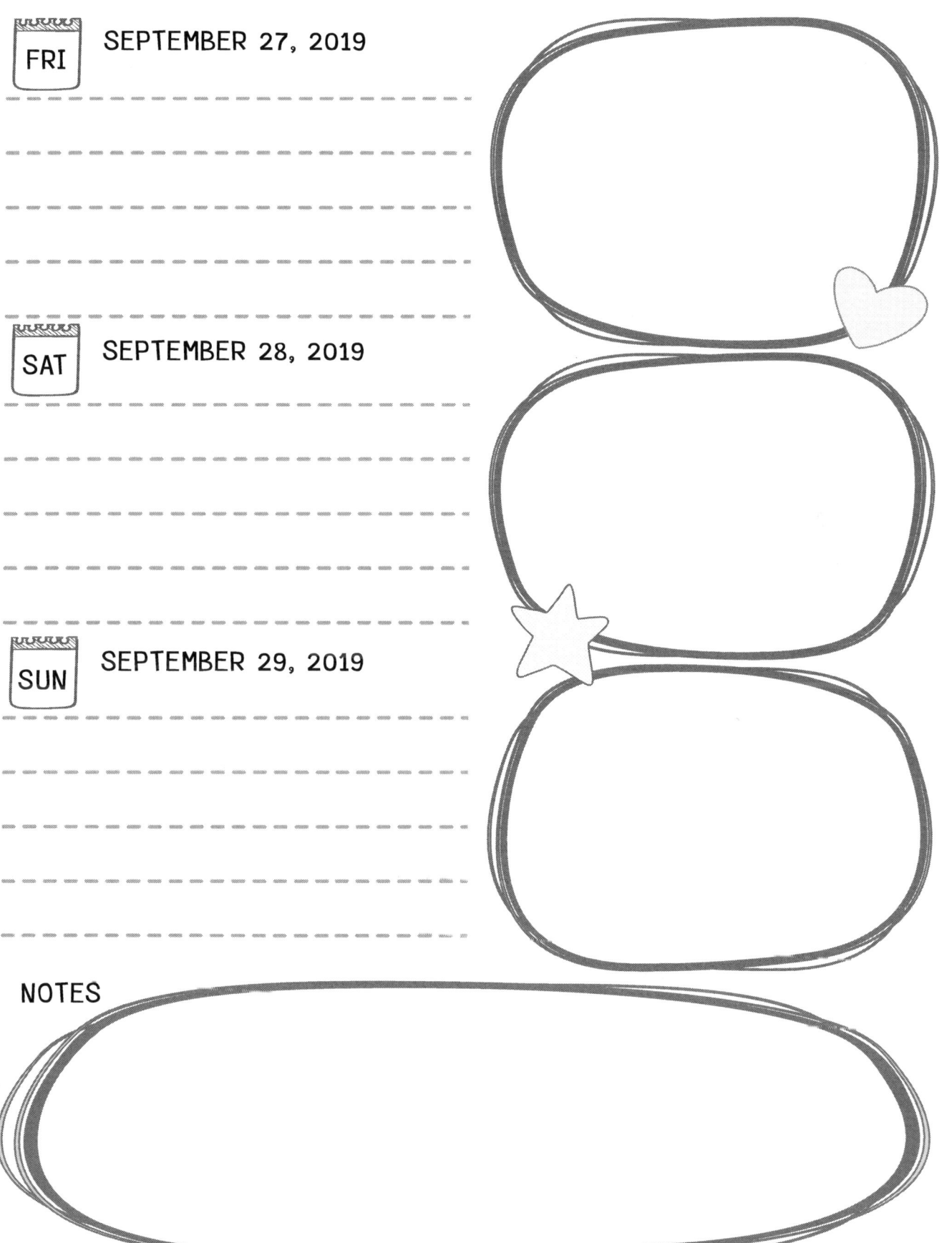

MON SEPTEMBER 30, 2019

TUE OCTOBER 1, 2019

WED OCTOBER 2, 2019

THU OCTOBER 3, 2019

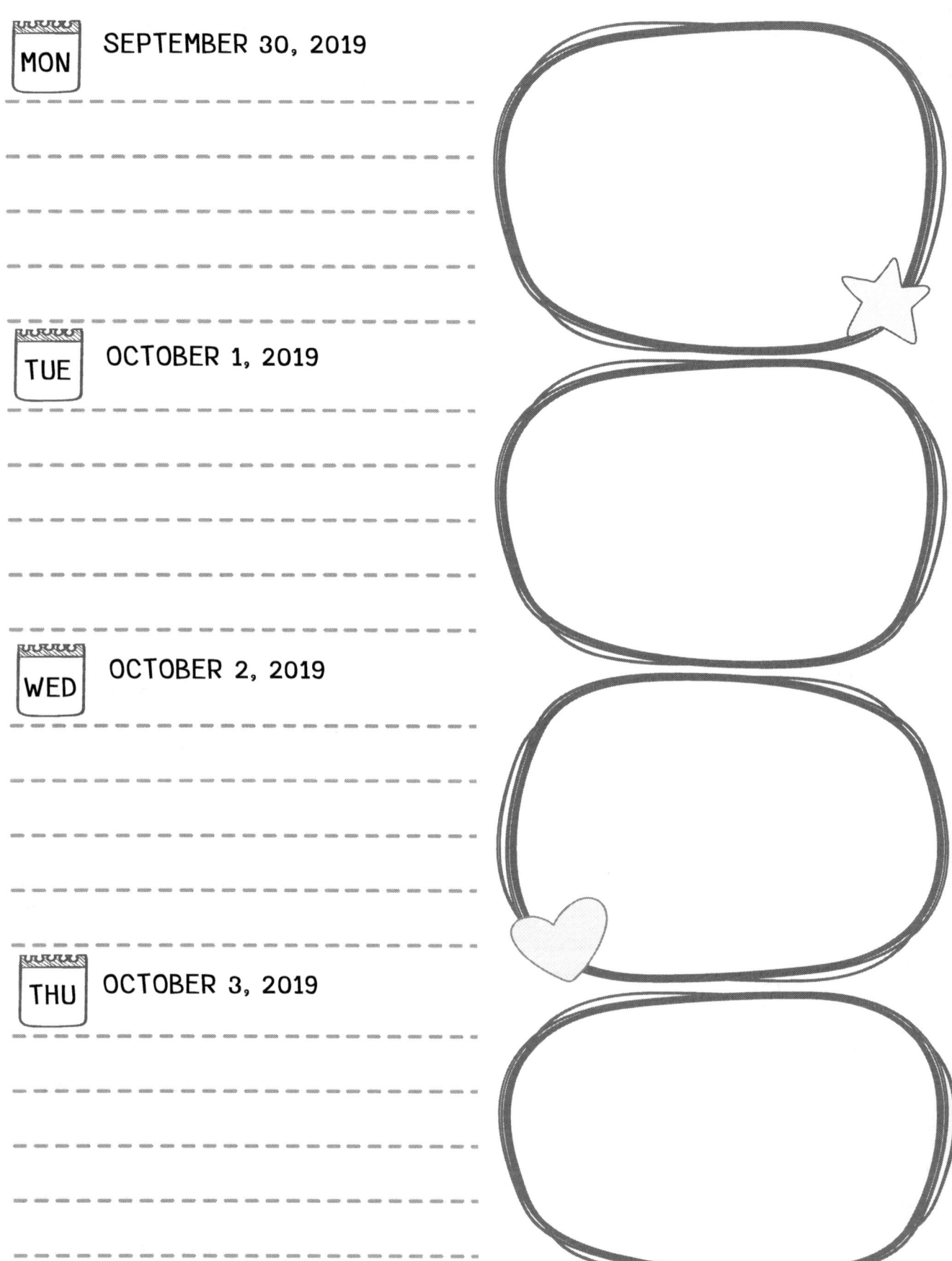

FRI OCTOBER 4, 2019

SAT OCTOBER 5, 2019

SUN OCTOBER 6, 2019

NOTES

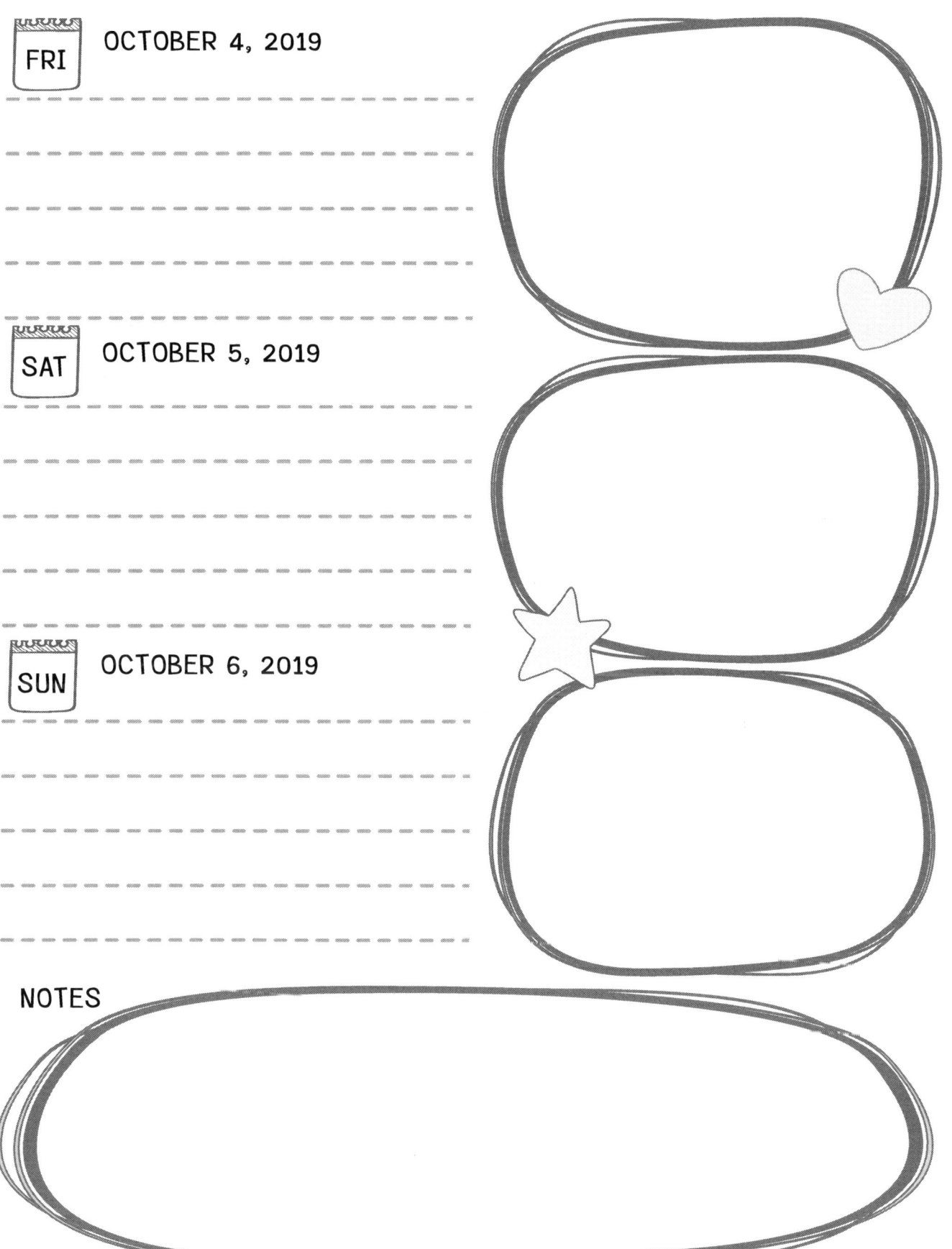

October 2019

Sunday	Monday	Tuesday	Wednesday
29	30	1	2
6	7	8	9
13	14	15	16
20	21	22	23
27	28	29	30

Thursday	Friday	Saturday	
3	4	5	
10	11	12	
17	18	19	
24	25	26	
31	1	2	

MON OCTOBER 7, 2019

TUE OCTOBER 8, 2019

WED OCTOBER 9, 2019

THU OCTOBER 10, 2019

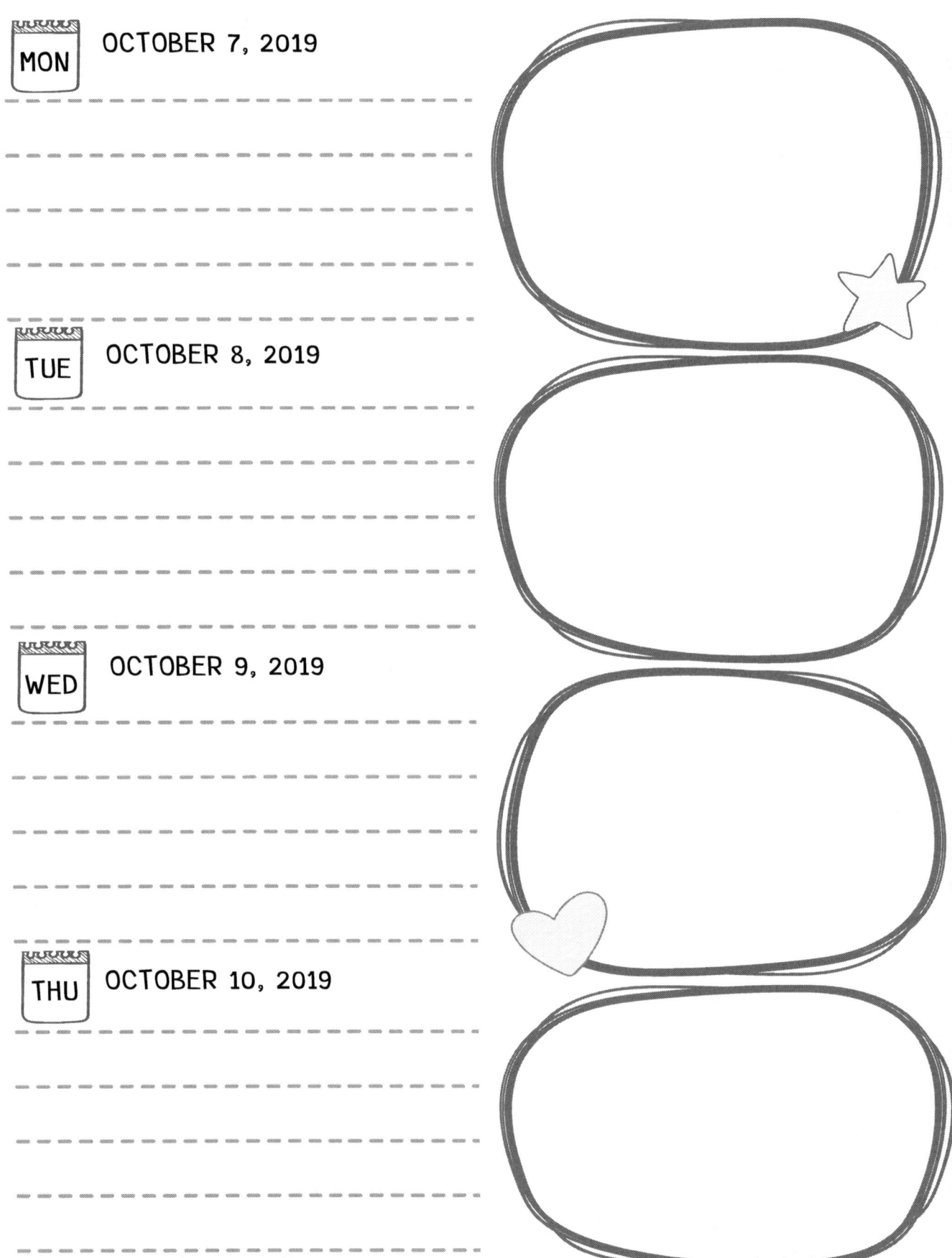

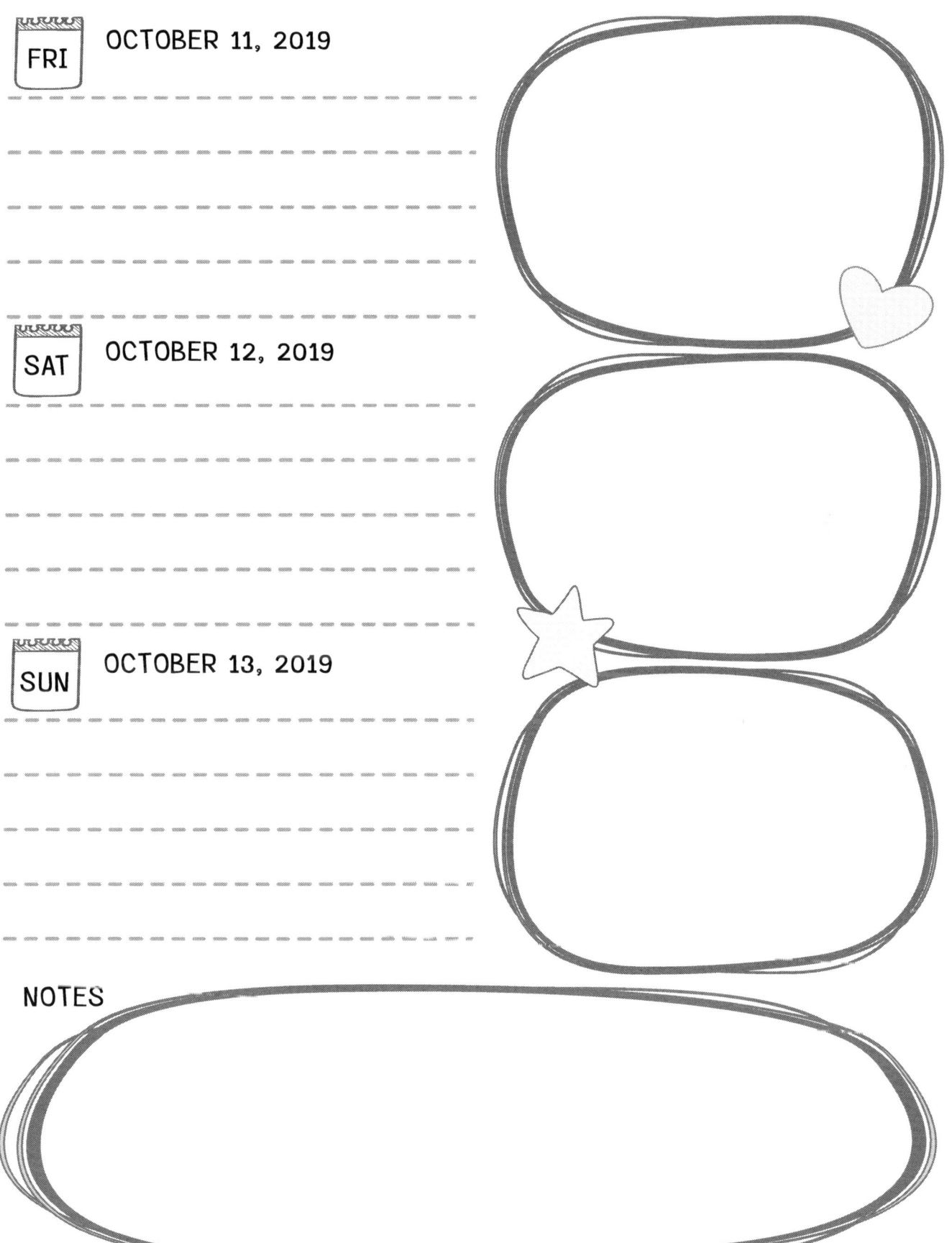

FRI OCTOBER 11, 2019

SAT OCTOBER 12, 2019

SUN OCTOBER 13, 2019

NOTES

MON OCTOBER 14, 2019

TUE OCTOBER 15, 2019

WED OCTOBER 16, 2019

THU OCTOBER 17, 2019

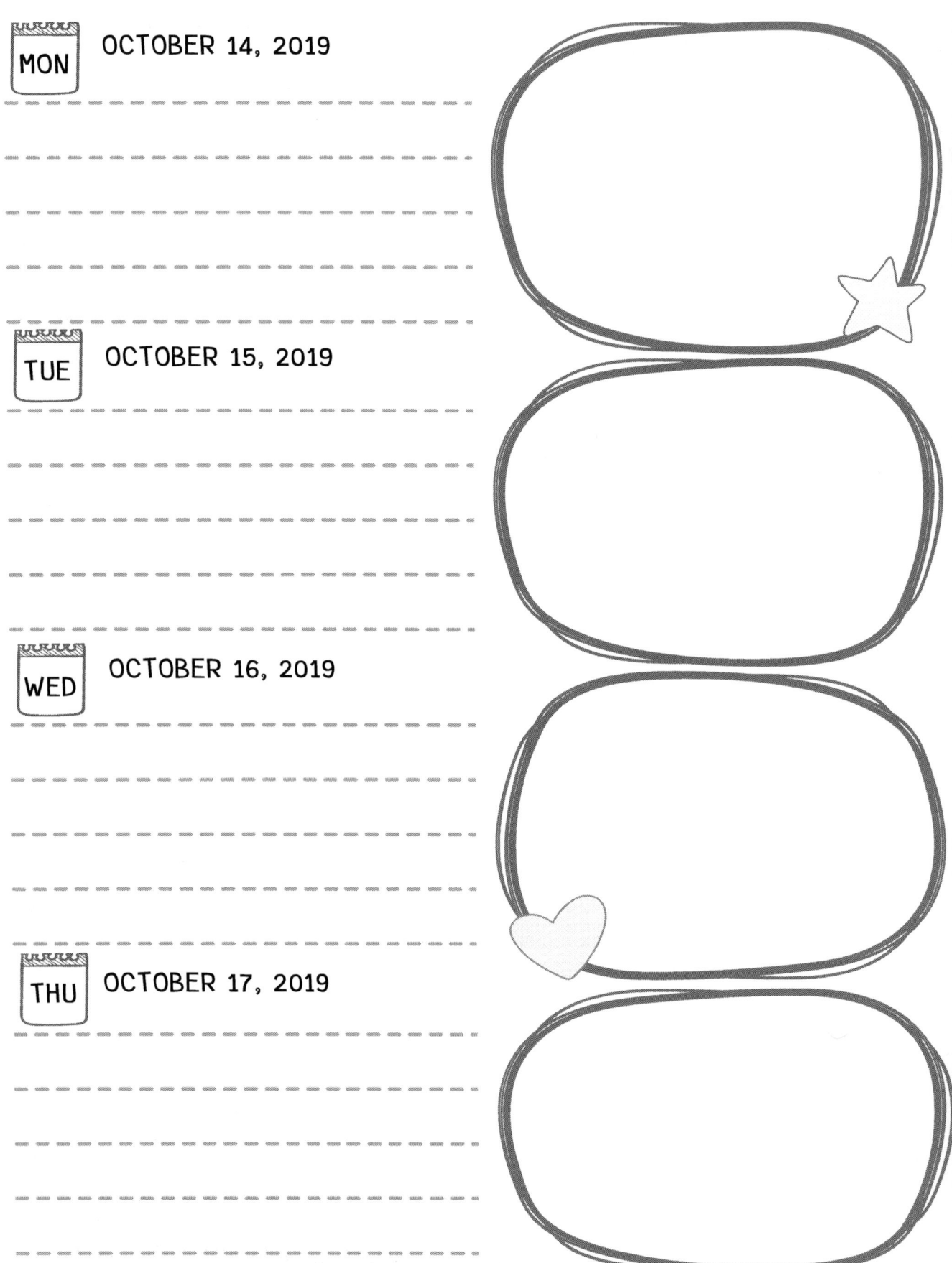

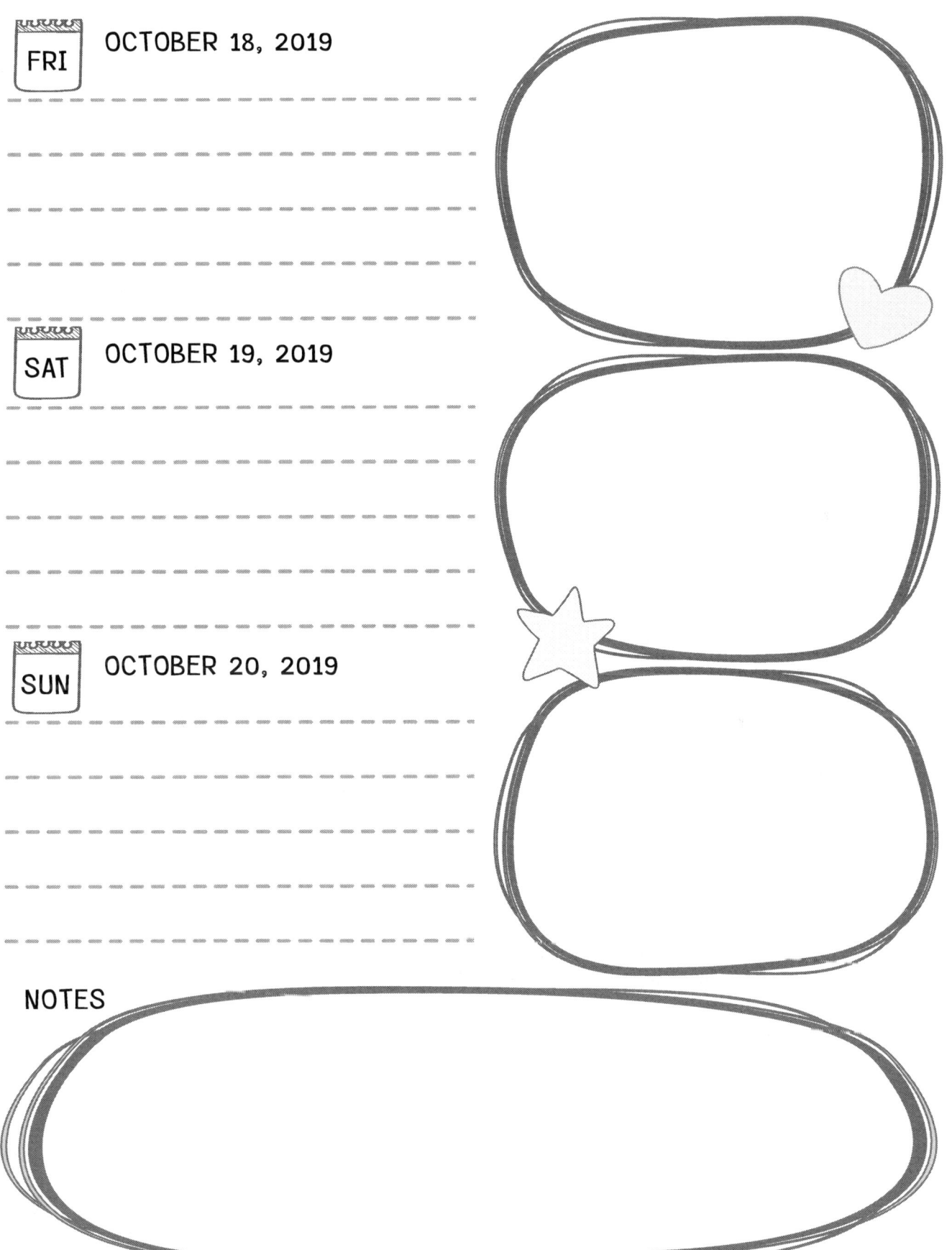

FRI OCTOBER 18, 2019

SAT OCTOBER 19, 2019

SUN OCTOBER 20, 2019

NOTES

MON OCTOBER 21, 2019

TUE OCTOBER 22, 2019

WED OCTOBER 23, 2019

THU OCTOBER 24, 2019

FRI OCTOBER 25, 2019

SAT OCTOBER 26, 2019

SUN OCTOBER 27, 2019

NOTES

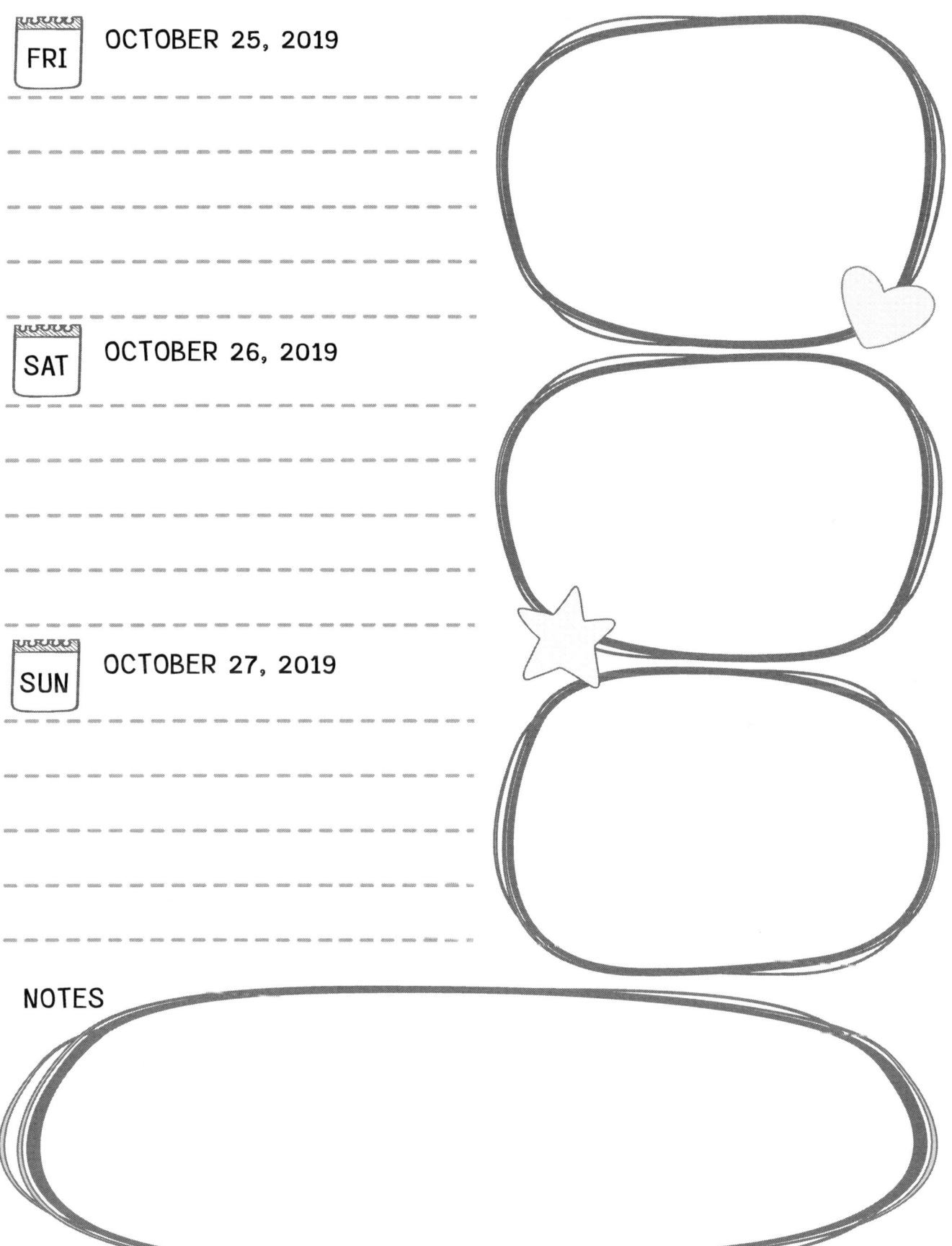

MON OCTOBER 28, 2019

TUE OCTOBER 29, 2019

WED OCTOBER 30, 2019

THU OCTOBER 31, 2019

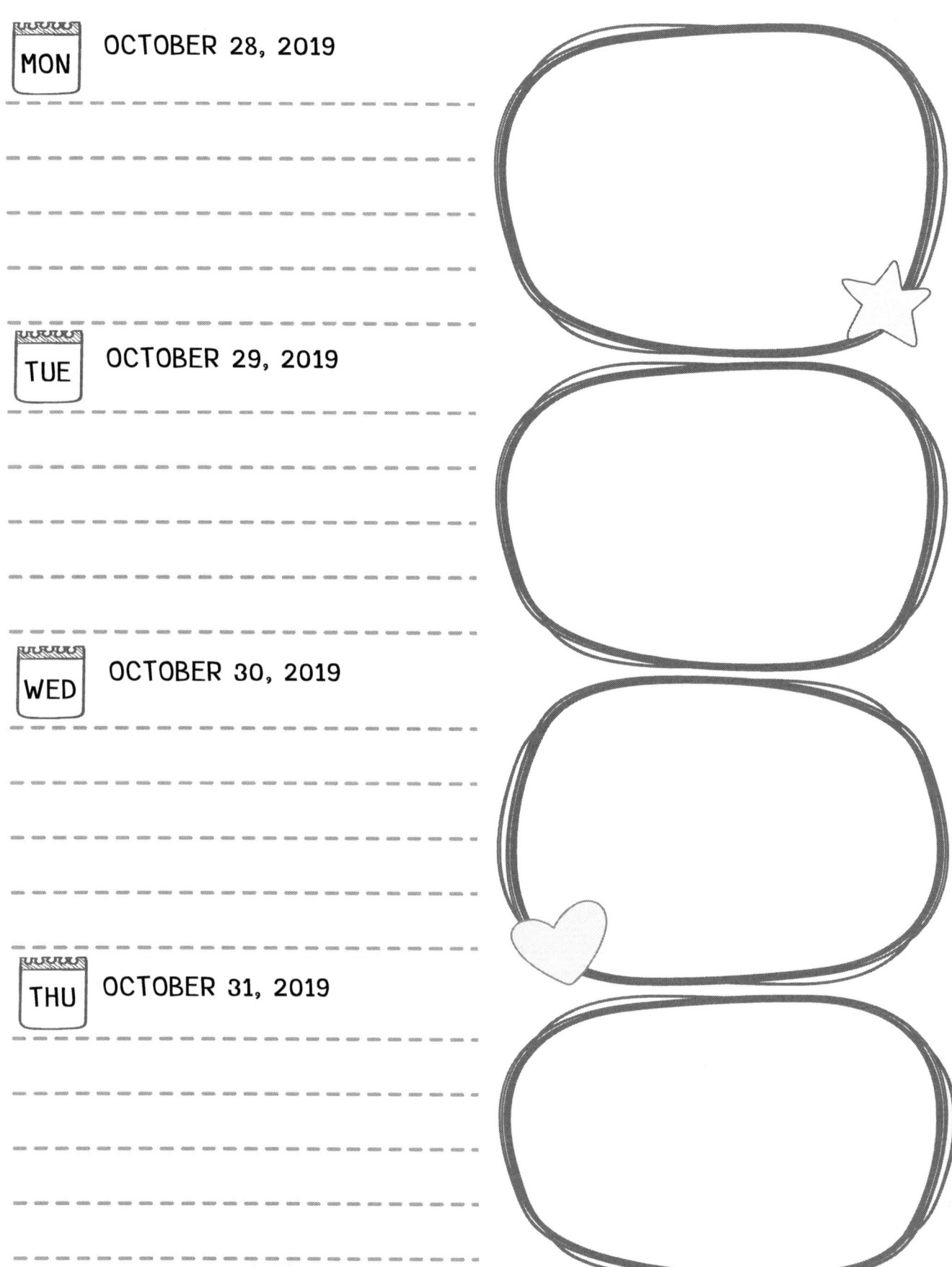

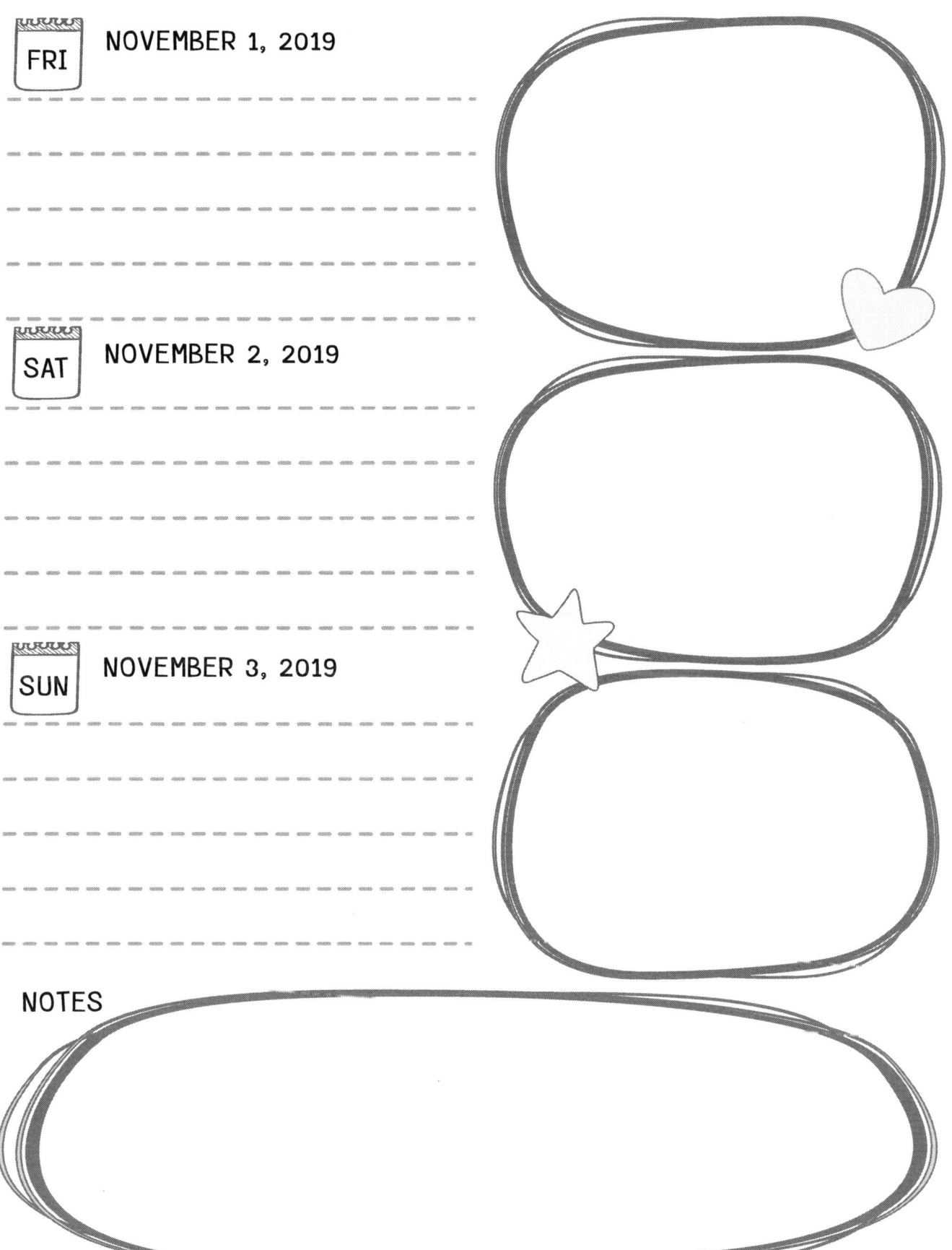

FRI NOVEMBER 1, 2019

SAT NOVEMBER 2, 2019

SUN NOVEMBER 3, 2019

NOTES

November 2019

Sunday	Monday	Tuesday	Wednesday
27	28	29	30
3	4	5	6
10	11	12	13
17	18	19	20
24	25	26	27

Thursday	Friday	Saturday
31	1	2
7	8	9
14	15	16
21	22	23
28	29	30

MON NOVEMBER 4, 2019

TUE NOVEMBER 5, 2019

WED NOVEMBER 6, 2019

THU NOVEMBER 7, 2019

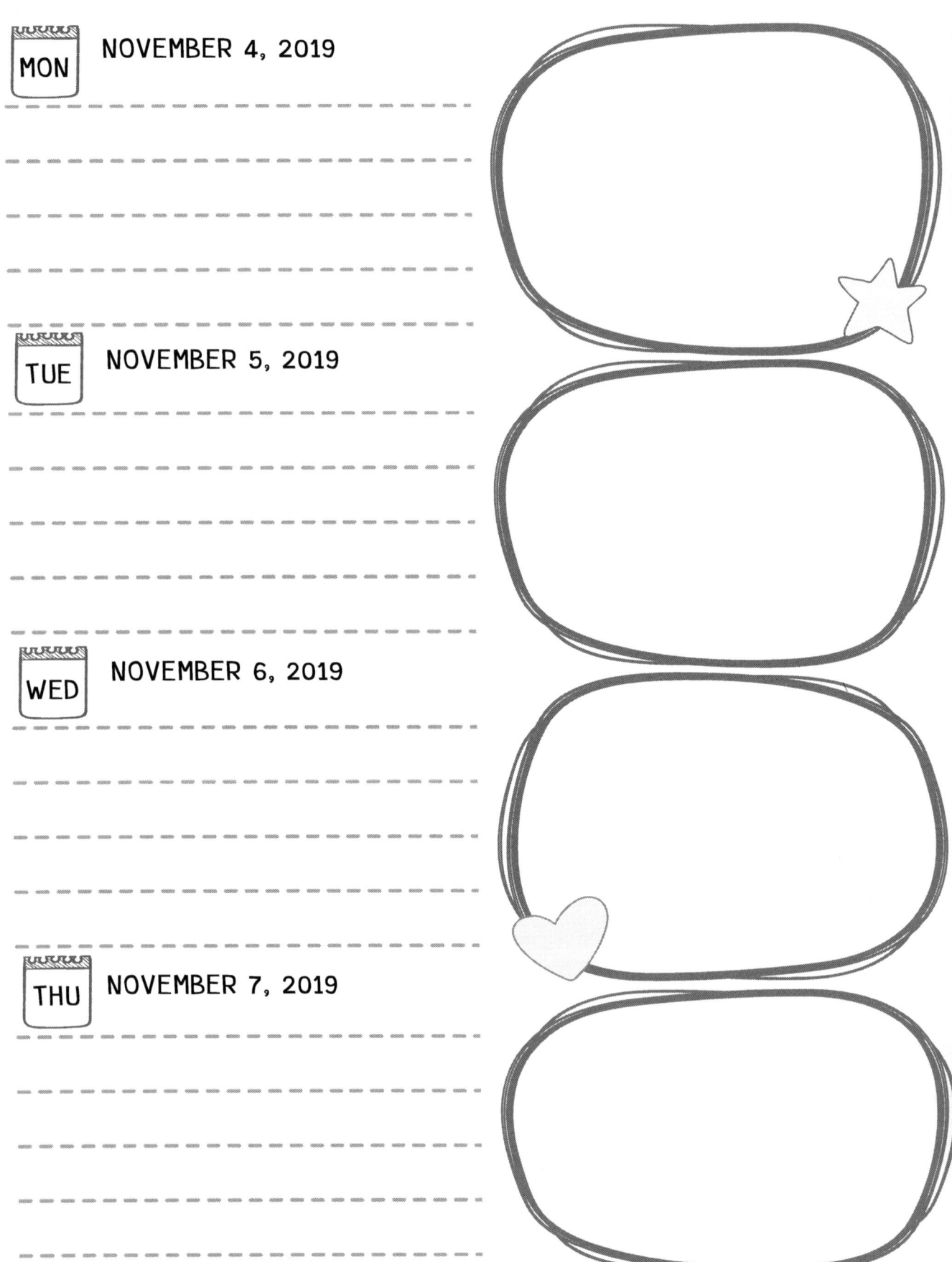

FRI NOVEMBER 8, 2019

SAT NOVEMBER 9, 2019

SUN NOVEMBER 10, 2019

NOTES

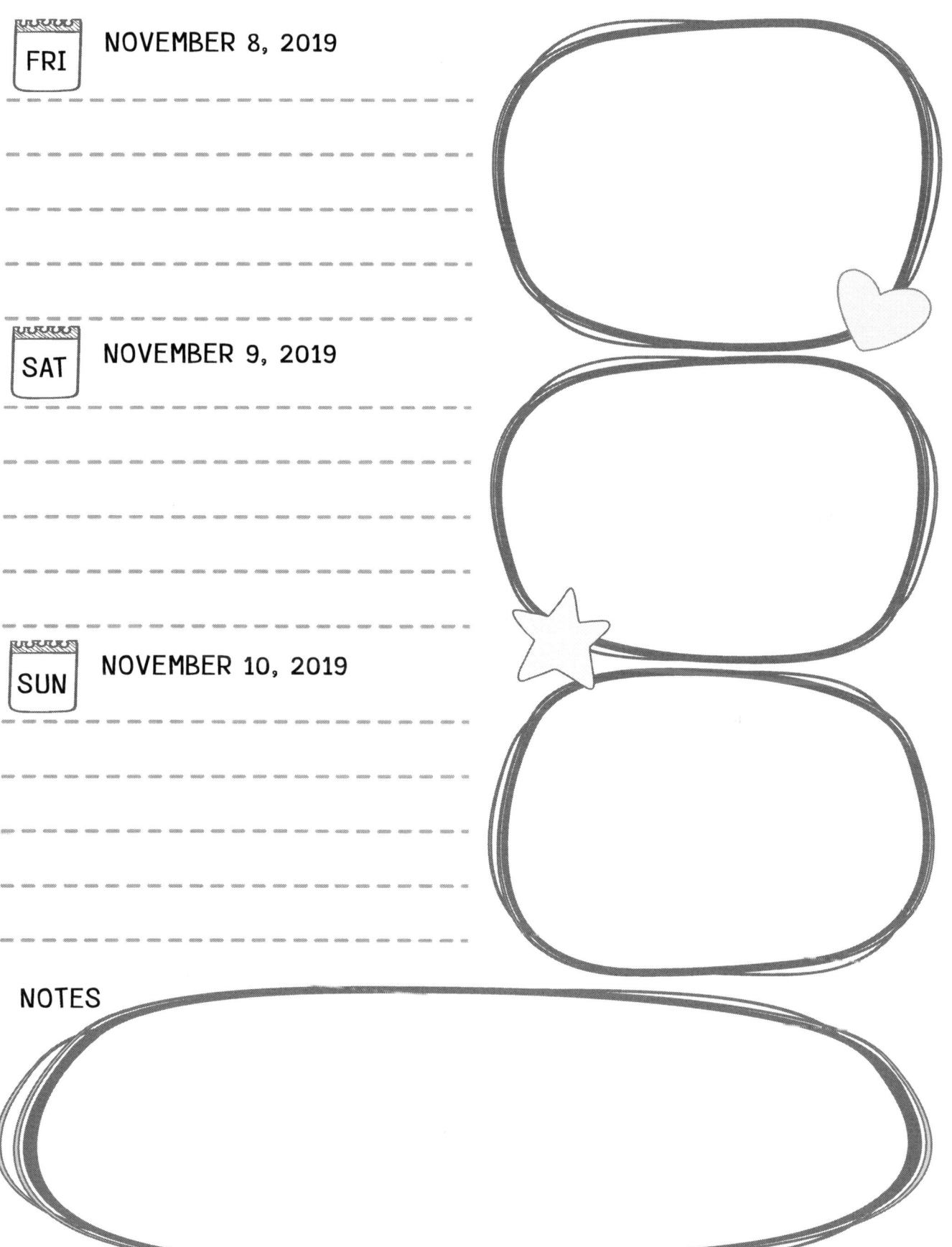

MON NOVEMBER 11, 2019

TUE NOVEMBER 12, 2019

WED NOVEMBER 13, 2019

THU NOVEMBER 14, 2019

FRI **NOVEMBER 15, 2019**

SAT **NOVEMBER 16, 2019**

SUN **NOVEMBER 17, 2019**

NOTES

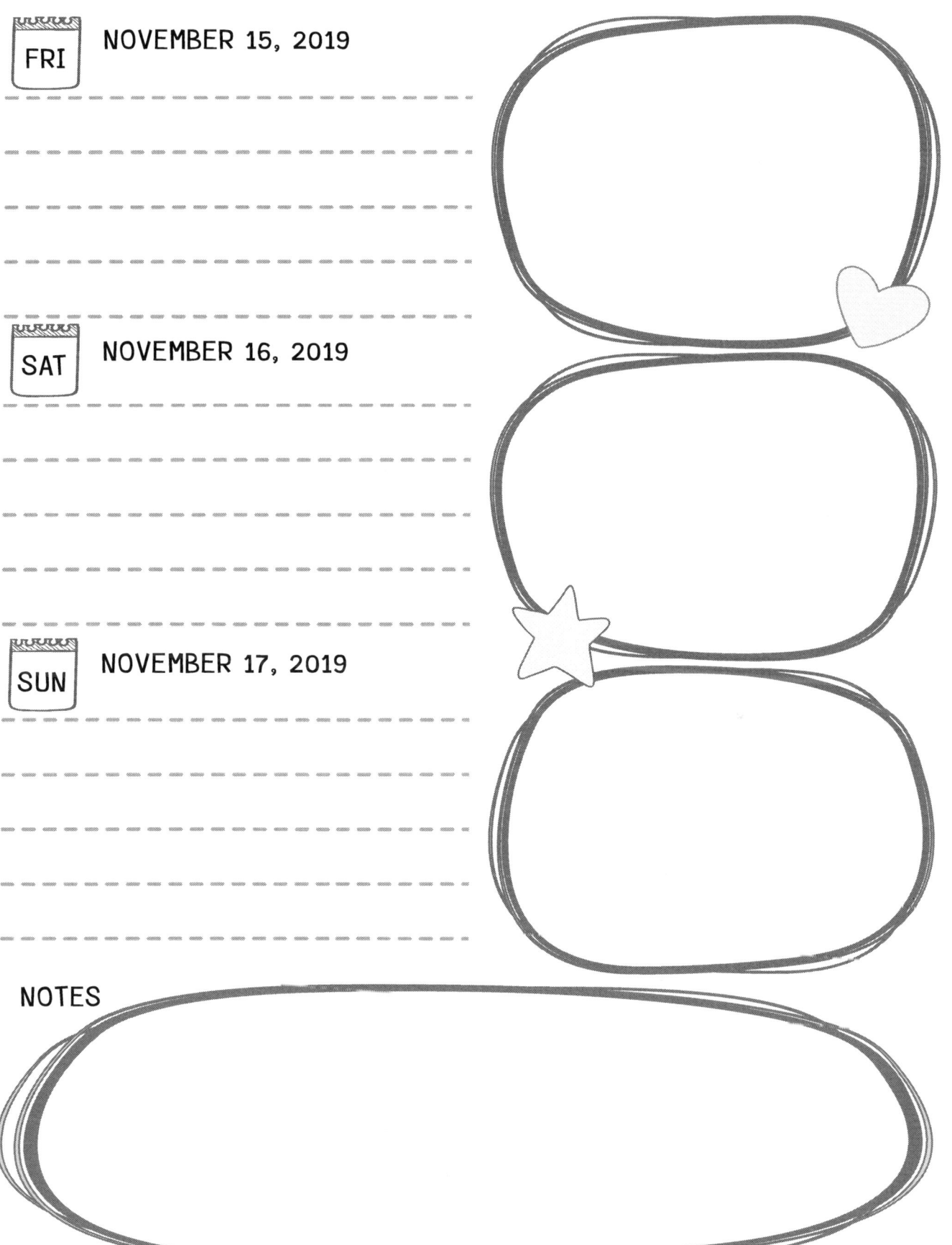

MON NOVEMBER 18, 2019

TUE NOVEMBER 19, 2019

WED NOVEMBER 20, 2019

THU NOVEMBER 21, 2019

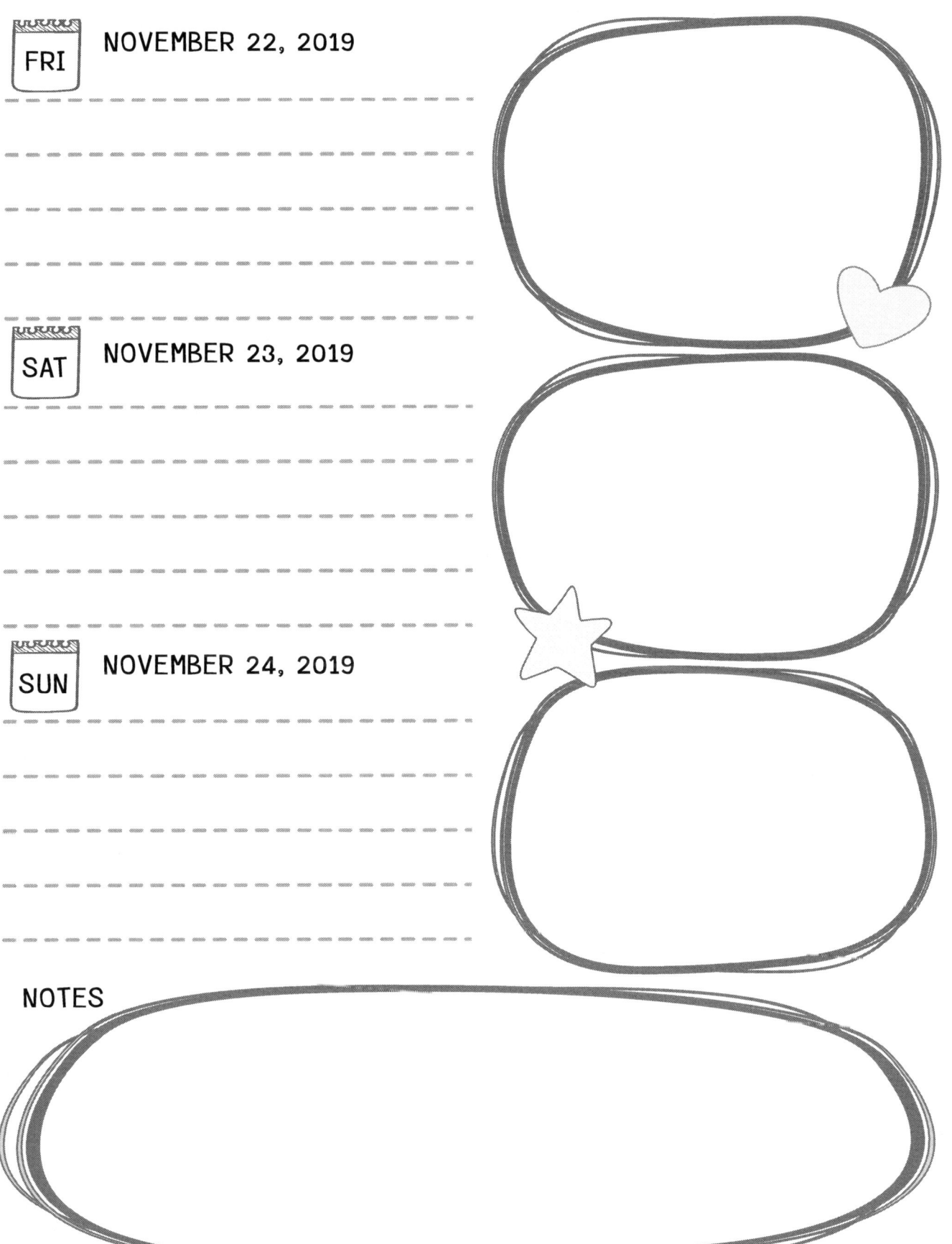

FRI NOVEMBER 22, 2019

SAT NOVEMBER 23, 2019

SUN NOVEMBER 24, 2019

NOTES

MON NOVEMBER 25, 2019

TUE NOVEMBER 26, 2019

WED NOVEMBER 27, 2019

THU NOVEMBER 28, 2019

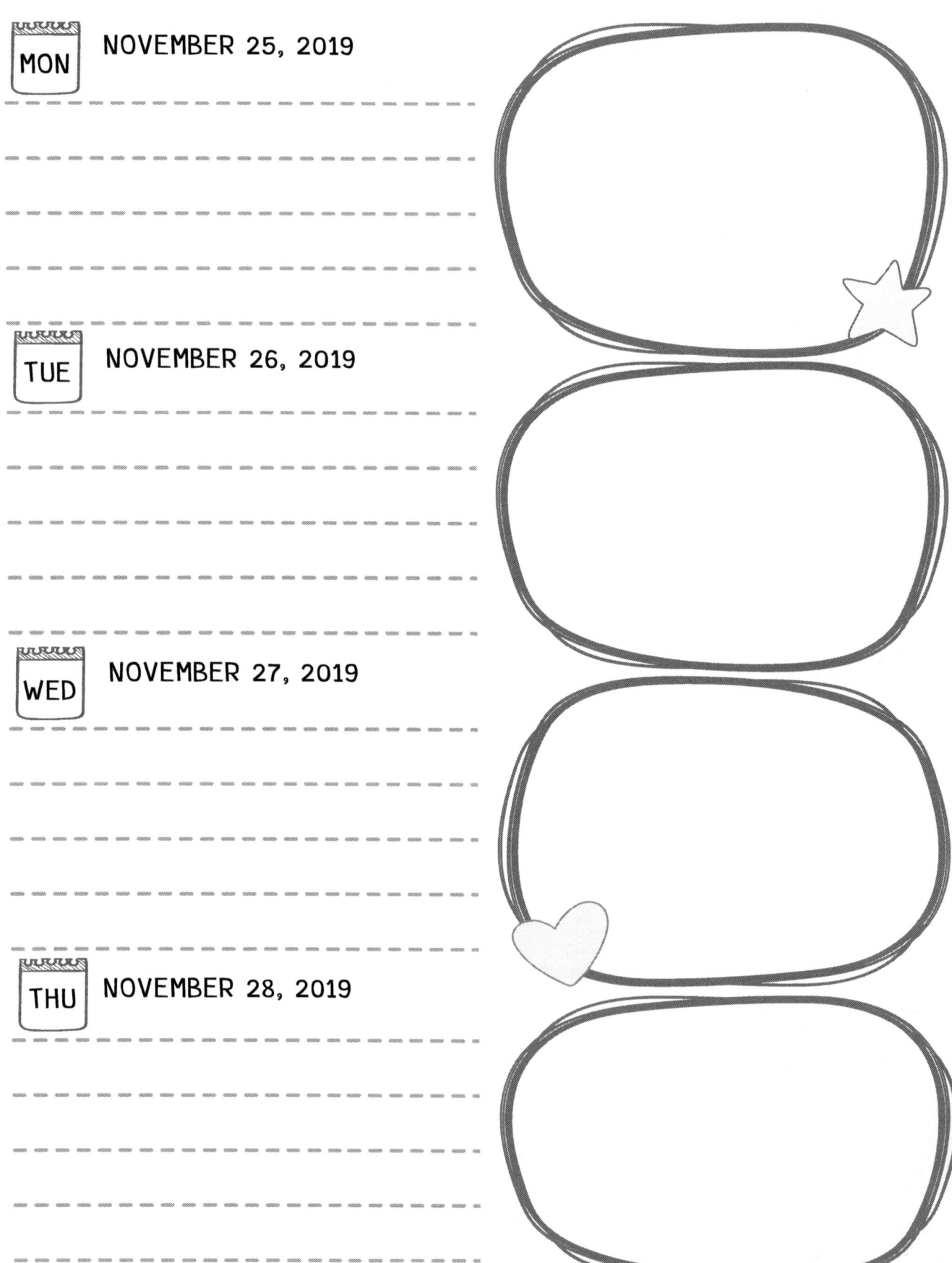

FRI NOVEMBER 29, 2019

SAT NOVEMBER 30, 2019

SUN DECEMBER 1, 2019

NOTES

December 2019

Sunday	Monday	Tuesday	Wednesday
1	2	3	4
8	9	10	11
15	16	17	18
22	23	24	25
29	30	31	1

Thursday	Friday	Saturday	
5	6	7	
12	13	14	
19	20	21	
26	27	28	
2	3	4	

MON DECEMBER 2, 2019

TUE DECEMBER 3, 2019

WED DECEMBER 4, 2019

THU DECEMBER 5, 2019

FRI DECEMBER 6, 2019

SAT DECEMBER 7, 2019

SUN DECEMBER 8, 2019

NOTES

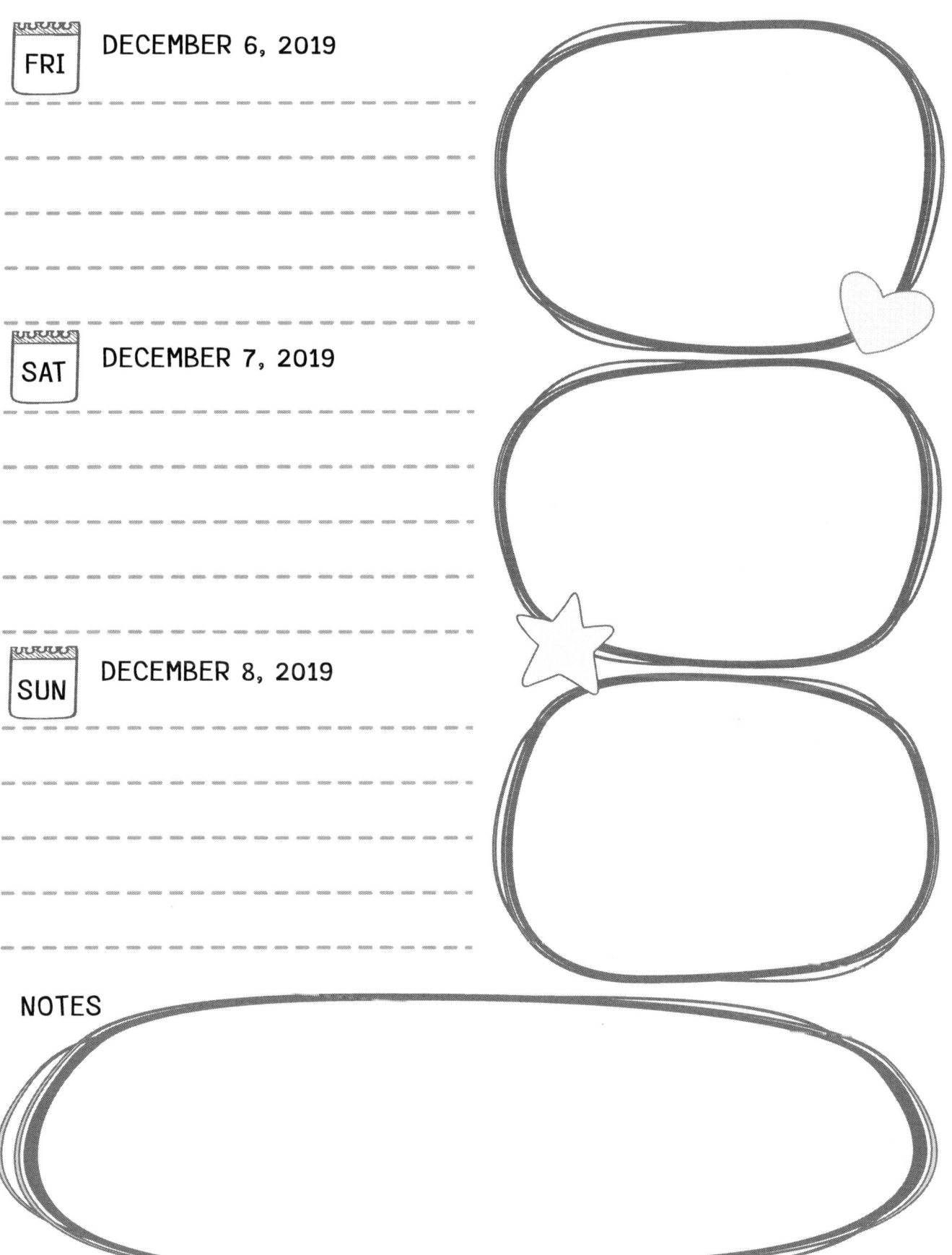

MON DECEMBER 9, 2019

TUE DECEMBER 10, 2019

WED DECEMBER 11, 2019

THU DECEMBER 12, 2019

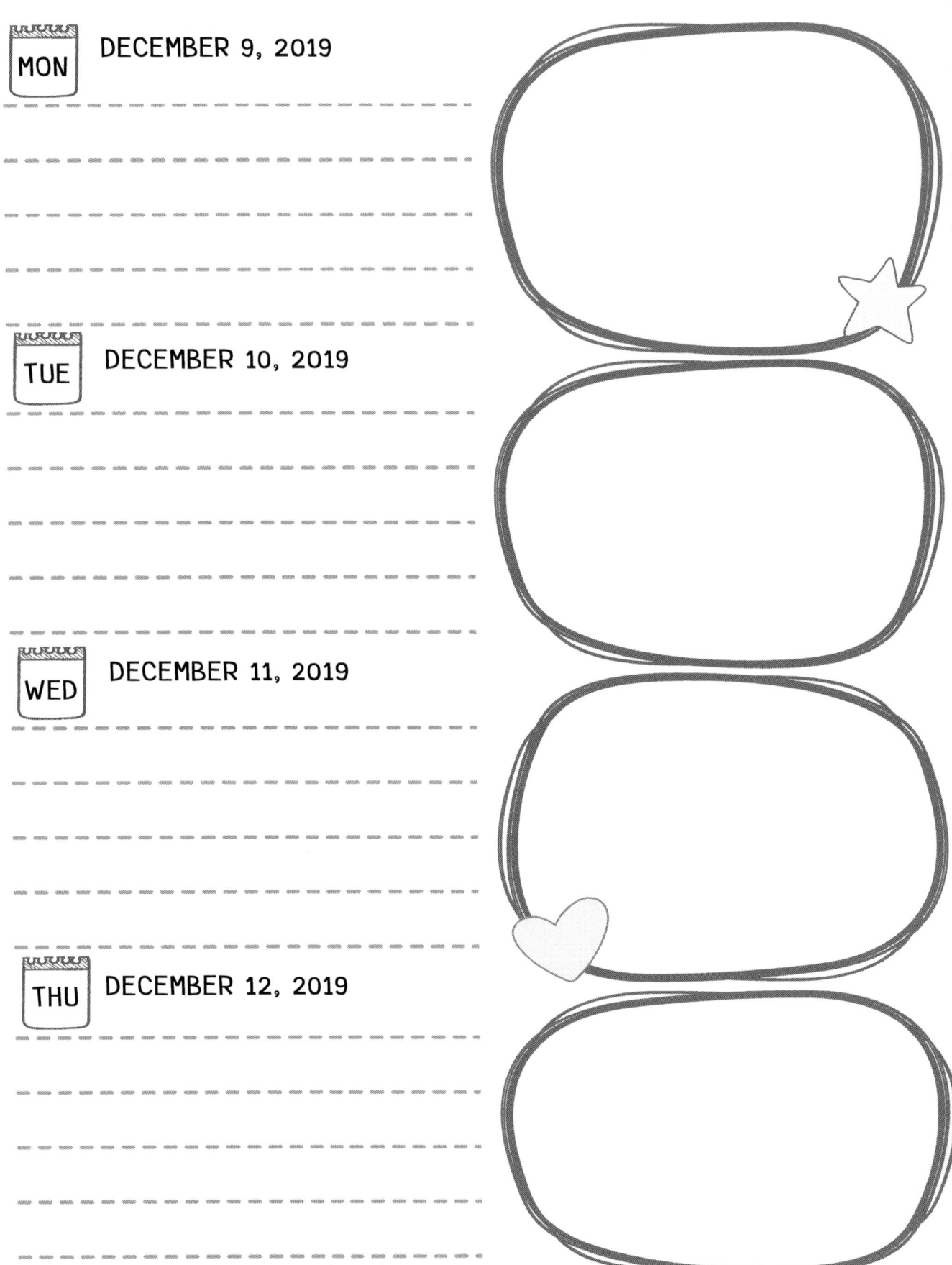

FRI DECEMBER 13, 2019

SAT DECEMBER 14, 2019

SUN DECEMBER 15, 2019

NOTES

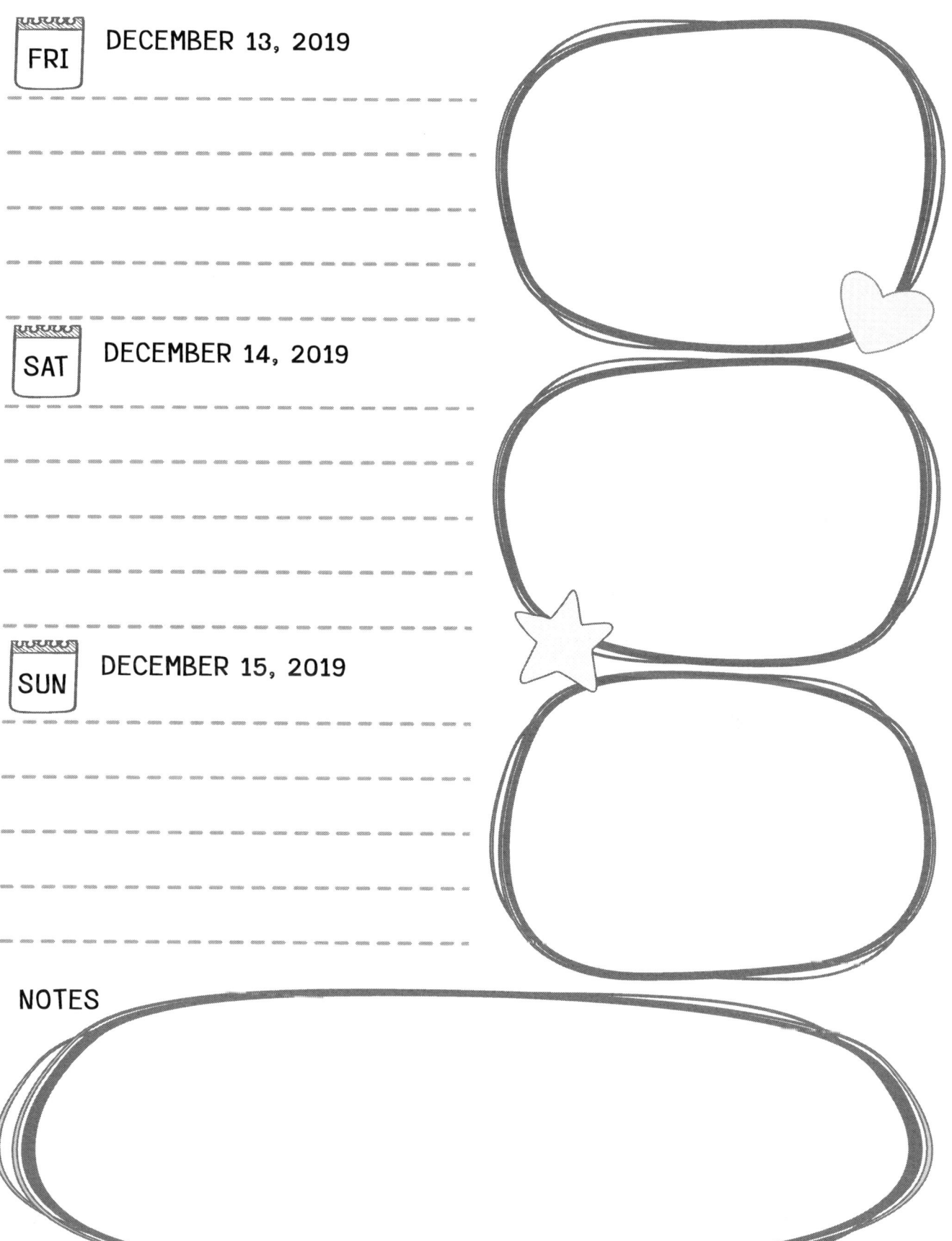

MON DECEMBER 16, 2019

TUE DECEMBER 17, 2019

WED DECEMBER 18, 2019

THU DECEMBER 19, 2019

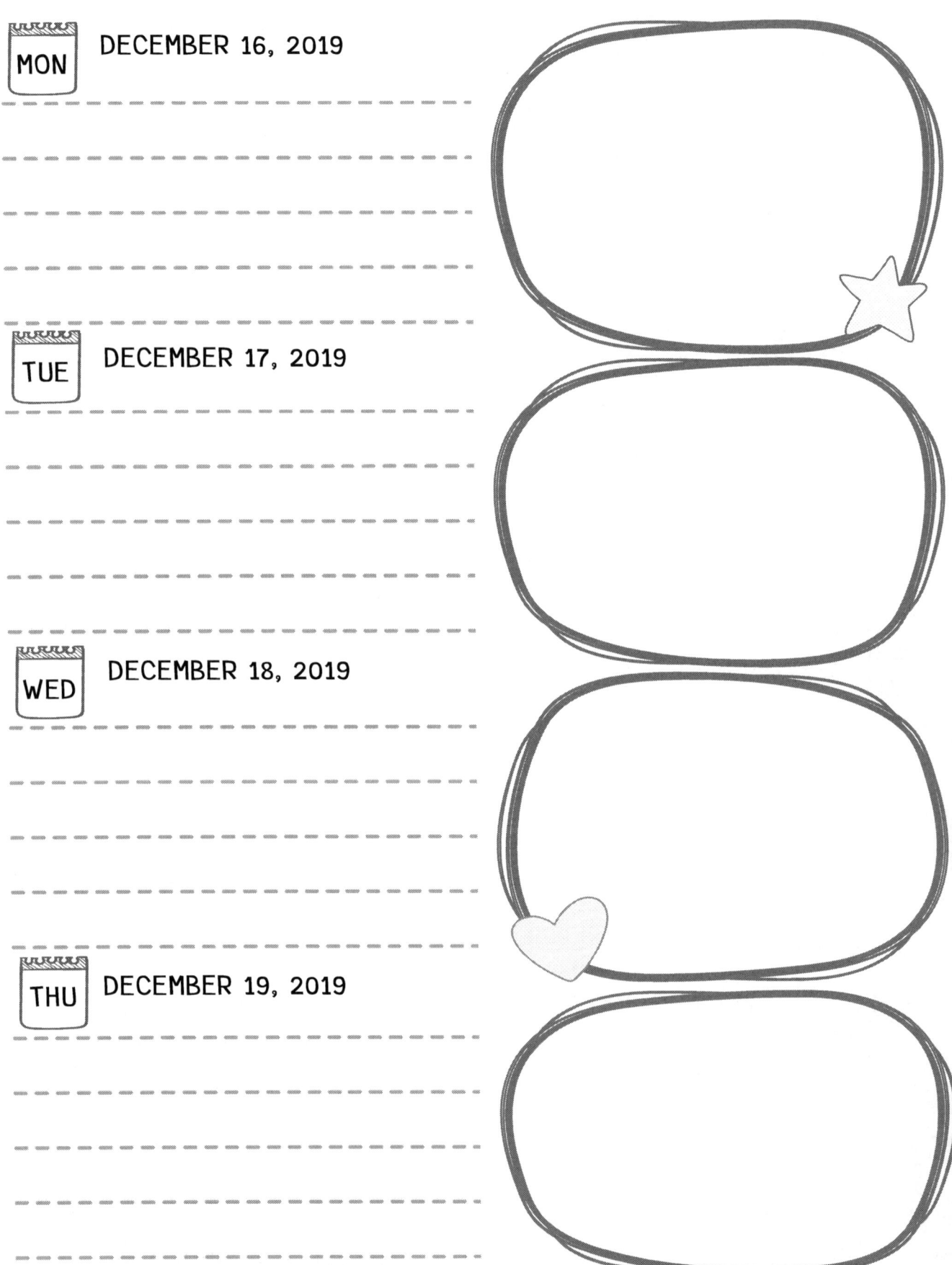

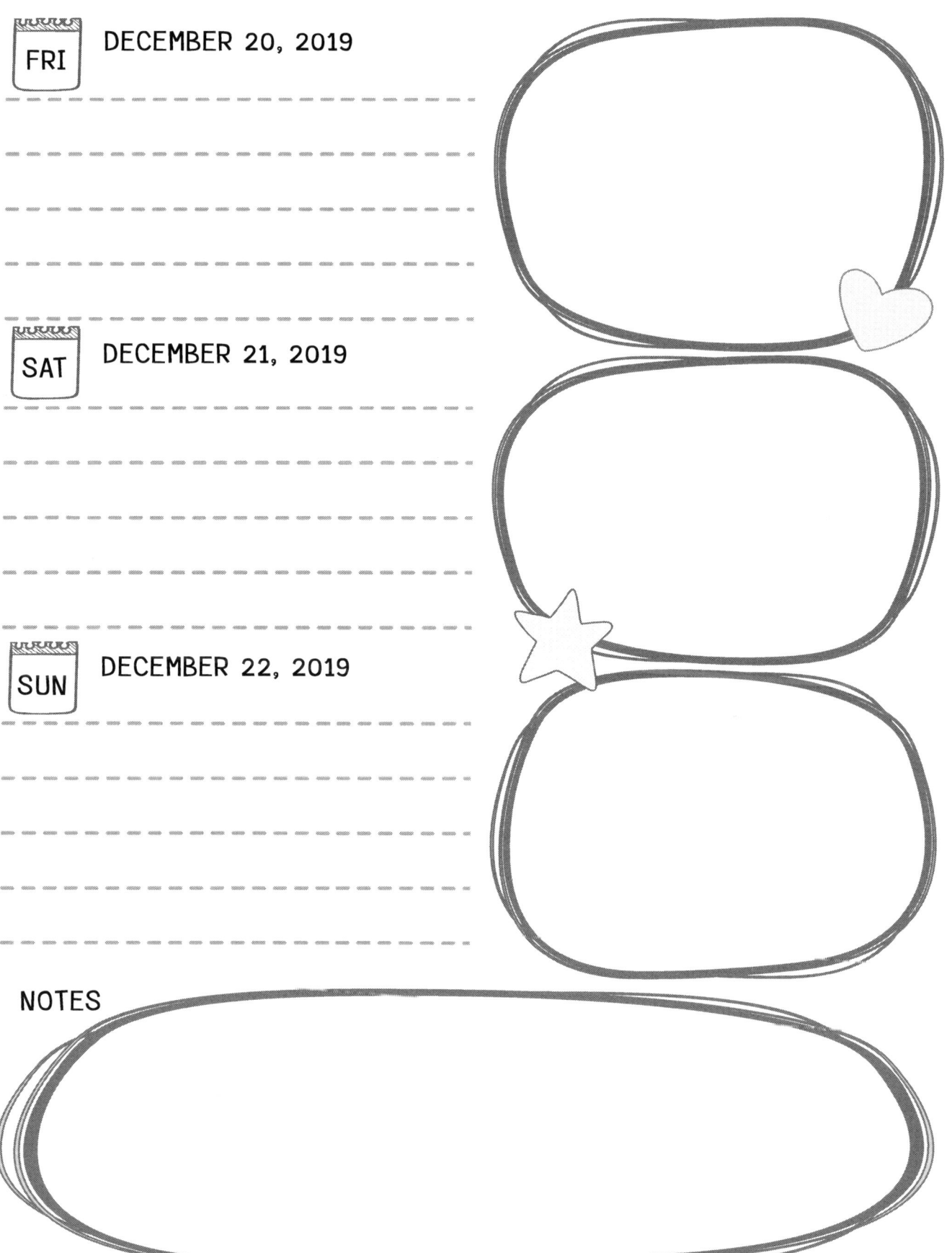

FRI DECEMBER 20, 2019

SAT DECEMBER 21, 2019

SUN DECEMBER 22, 2019

NOTES

MON DECEMBER 23, 2019

TUE DECEMBER 24, 2019

WED DECEMBER 25, 2019

THU DECEMBER 26, 2019

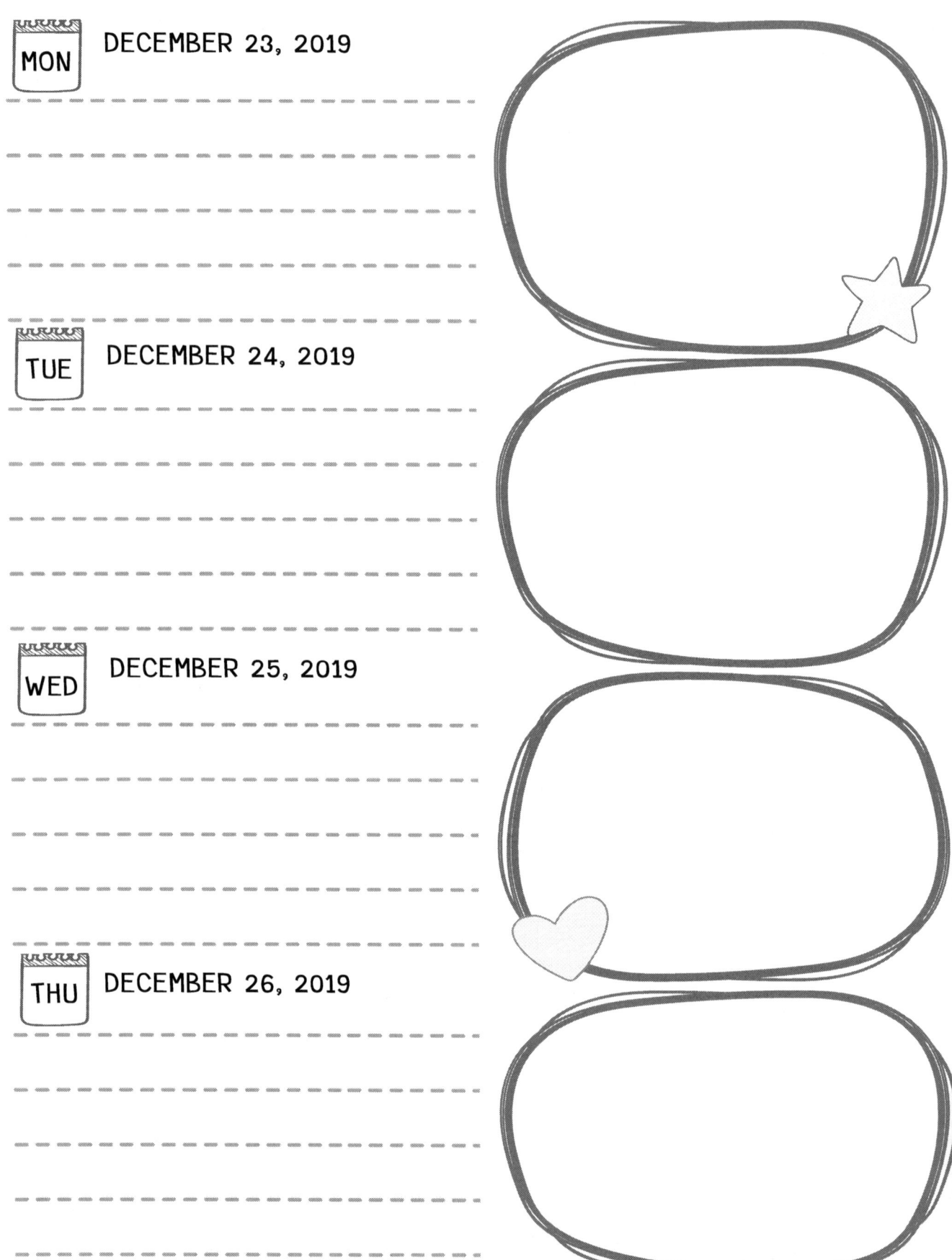

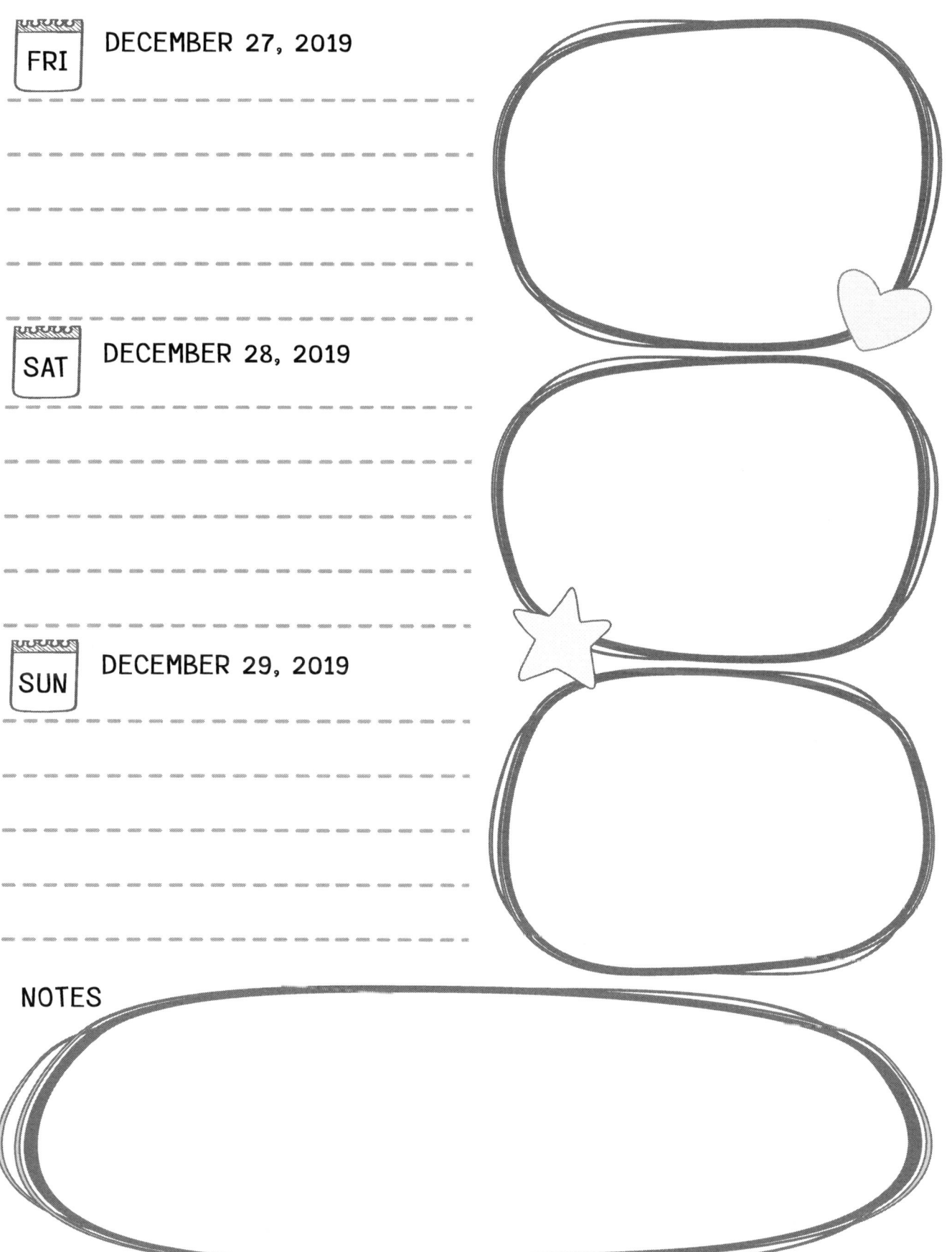

FRI DECEMBER 27, 2019

SAT DECEMBER 28, 2019

SUN DECEMBER 29, 2019

NOTES

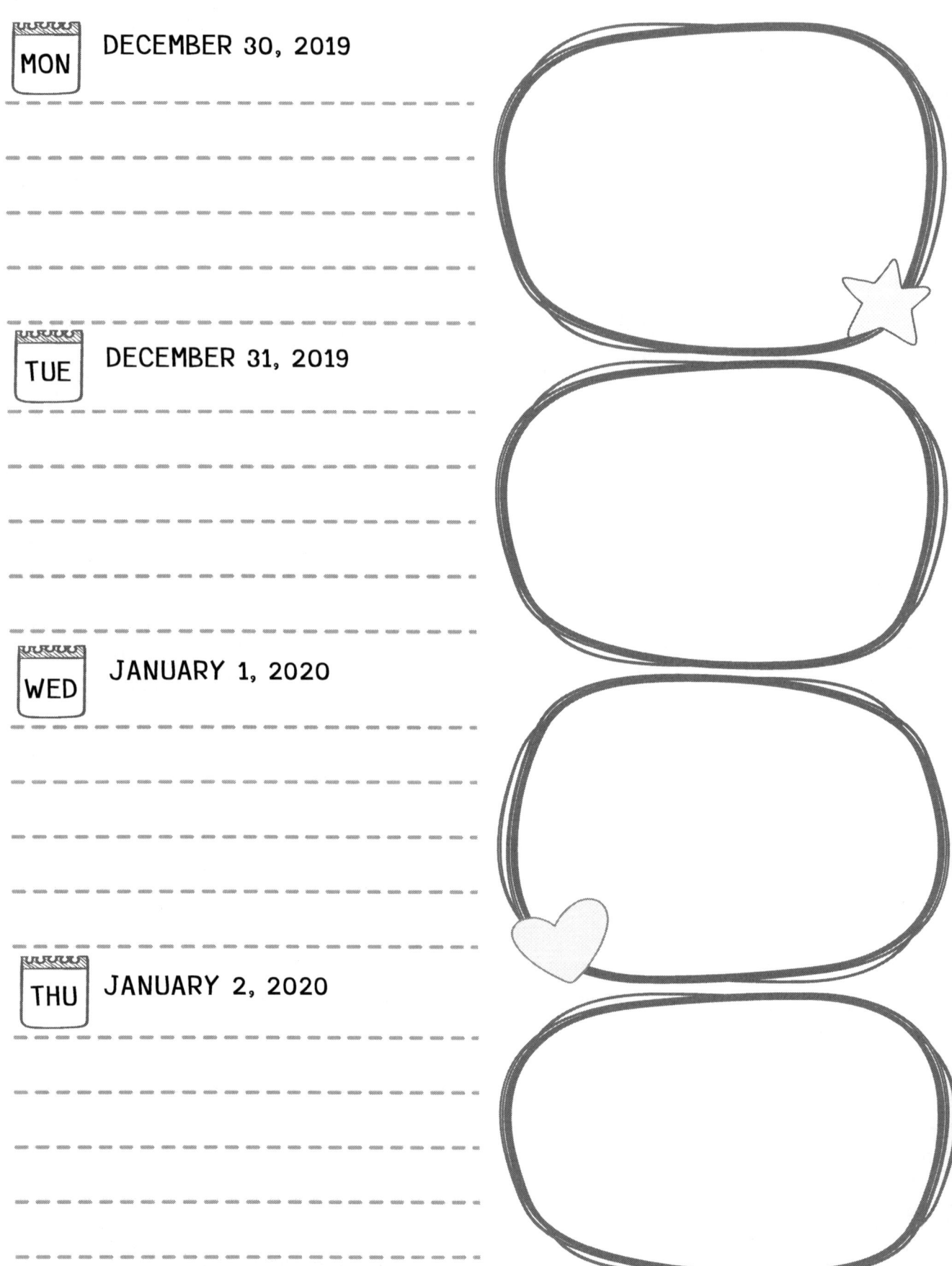

MON DECEMBER 30, 2019

TUE DECEMBER 31, 2019

WED JANUARY 1, 2020

THU JANUARY 2, 2020

FRI JANUARY 3, 2020

SAT JANUARY 4, 2020

SUN JANUARY 5, 2020

NOTES

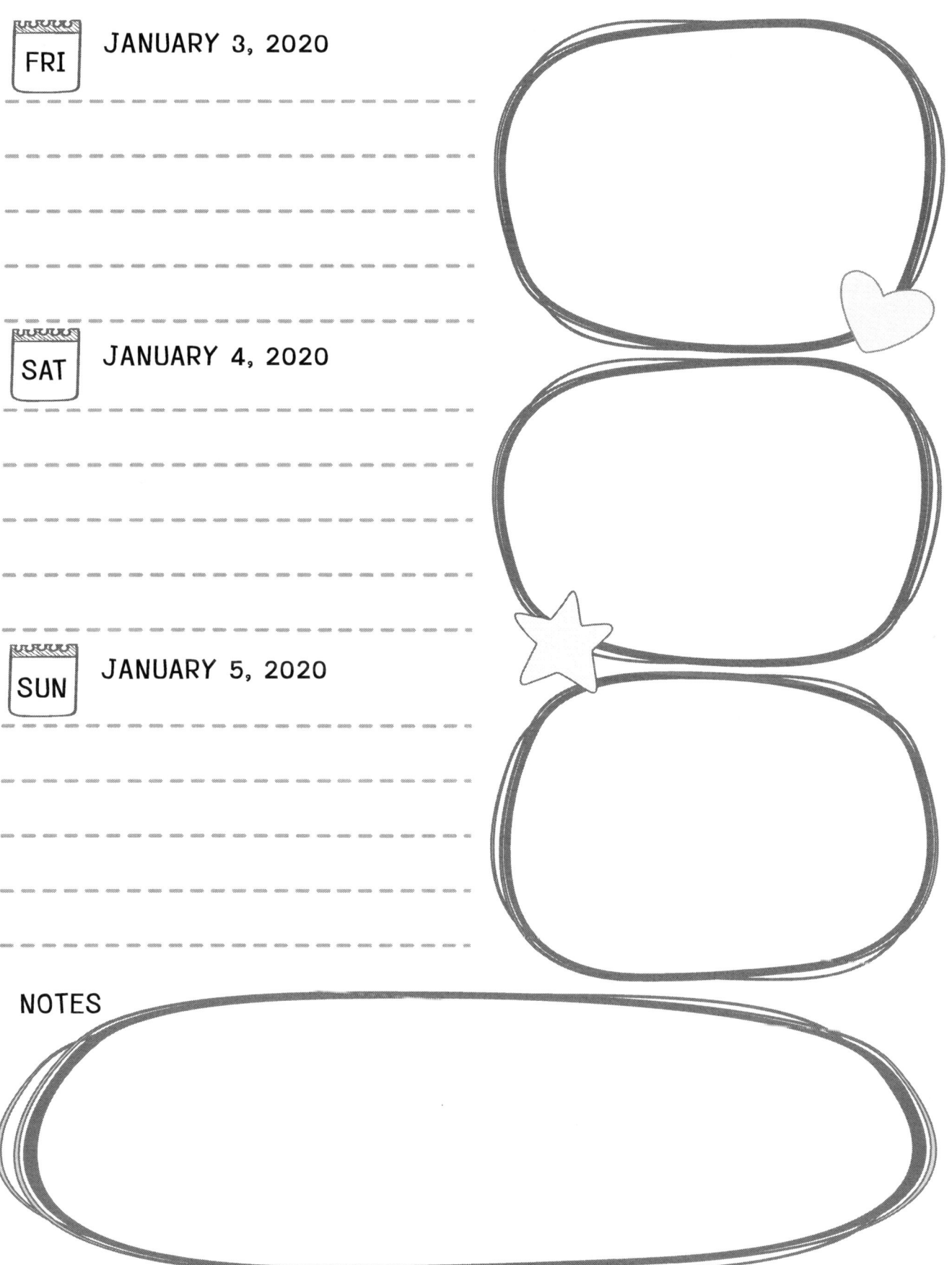

2020 Calendar

January

S	M	T	W	T	F	S
29	30	31	1	2	3	4
5	6	7	8	9	10	11
12	13	14	15	16	17	18
19	20	21	22	23	24	25
26	27	28	29	30	31	1
2	3	4	5	6	7	8

February

S	M	T	W	T	F	S
26	27	28	29	30	31	1
2	3	4	5	6	7	8
9	10	11	12	13	14	15
16	17	18	19	20	21	22
23	24	25	26	27	28	29
1	2	3	4	5	6	7

March

S	M	T	W	T	F	S
1	2	3	4	5	6	7
8	9	10	11	12	13	14
15	16	17	18	19	20	21
22	23	24	25	26	27	28
29	30	31	1	2	3	4
5	6	7	8	9	10	11

April

S	M	T	W	T	F	S
29	30	31	1	2	3	4
5	6	7	8	9	10	11
12	13	14	15	16	17	18
19	20	21	22	23	24	25
26	27	28	29	30	1	2
3	4	5	6	7	8	9

May

S	M	T	W	T	F	S
26	27	28	29	30	1	2
3	4	5	6	7	8	9
10	11	12	13	14	15	16
17	18	19	20	21	22	23
24	25	26	27	28	29	30
31	1	2	3	4	5	6

June

S	M	T	W	T	F	S
31	1	2	3	4	5	6
7	8	9	10	11	12	13
14	15	16	17	18	19	20
21	22	23	24	25	26	27
28	29	30	1	2	3	4
5	6	7	8	9	10	11

July

S	M	T	W	T	F	S
28	29	30	1	2	3	4
5	6	7	8	9	10	11
12	13	14	15	16	17	18
19	20	21	22	23	24	25
26	27	28	29	30	31	1
2	3	4	5	6	7	8

August

S	M	T	W	T	F	S
26	27	28	29	30	31	1
2	3	4	5	6	7	8
9	10	11	12	13	14	15
16	17	18	19	20	21	22
23	24	25	26	27	28	29
30	31	1	2	3	4	5

September

S	M	T	W	T	F	S
30	31	1	2	3	4	5
6	7	8	9	10	11	12
13	14	15	16	17	18	19
20	21	22	23	24	25	26
27	28	29	30	1	2	3
4	5	6	7	8	9	10

October

S	M	T	W	T	F	S
27	28	29	30	1	2	3
4	5	6	7	8	9	10
11	12	13	14	15	16	17
18	19	20	21	22	23	24
25	26	27	28	29	30	31
1	2	3	4	5	6	7

November

S	M	T	W	T	F	S
1	2	3	4	5	6	7
8	9	10	11	12	13	14
15	16	17	18	19	20	21
22	23	24	25	26	27	28
29	30	1	2	3	4	5
6	7	8	9	10	11	12

December

S	M	T	W	T	F	S
29	30	1	2	3	4	5
6	7	8	9	10	11	12
13	14	15	16	17	18	19
20	21	22	23	24	25	26
27	28	29	30	31	1	2
3	4	5	6	7	8	9

21522663R00078

Made in the USA
San Bernardino, CA
04 January 2019